P9-CEQ-476

Books by Roger Tennant

JOSEPH CONRAD   1981

CAST ON A CERTAIN ISLAND   1970

JOSEPH CONRAD

ROGER TENNANT

JOSEPH
CONRAD

Atheneum   *New York*   1981

Library of Congress Cataloging in Publication Data

Tennant, Roger.
    Joseph Conrad.

    Bibliography : p.
    Includes index.
    1. Conrad, Joseph, 1857–1924—Biography.
2. Novelists, English—20th century—Biography.
I. Title.
PR6005.O4Z882   1981   823′.912   [B]   80-69393
    ISBN 0-689-11152-5   AACR2

Copyright © 1981 by Roger Tennant
All rights reserved
Published simultaneously in Canada by McClelland and Stewart Ltd.
Manufactured by American Book–Stratford Press, Saddle Brook, New Jersey
Designed by Harry Ford
First Edition

Foreword

Even before he left the sea, Conrad had become a spinner of tales. John Galsworthy tells of passing tropical nights on the deck of the *Torrens* listening to the yarns of its Polish mate. When he settled on shore, he made his life into art, and having done so, regarded the artistic version as the only truth —"exact autobiography," as he said of *The Shadow Line* or *The Arrow of Gold*. Even *Heart of Darkness* was "experience pushed a little (and only very little) beyond the actual facts of the case." He wanted to be a legend, and did all that he could to conceal the facts. "Strange lapse of memory!" he would say, if one of them turned up to contradict him. When his young friend Richard Curle began to investigate the sources of "Youth," he was angry that these things should be "exposed for any fool to comment upon or even for average minds to be disappointed with."

His biographers, like his early listeners, have tended to succumb to his charm. G. Jean-Aubry spent twenty years in research before he published his "definitive biography" in 1957, but continually he uses Conrad's fiction as his prime source. Jocelyn Baines, in his "critical biography" of 1960, brings to the task a mind more academic but still insufficiently skeptical; for Conrad's life ashore, however, he does provide an accurate and fully-documented account, to which I am deeply indebted. Jerry Allen did much valuable research, but such was her love, she used it only to patch the fragile fabric of the legend. Indeed, it is only since the publication of Norman Sherry's two scholarly works, *Conrad's Eastern World* (1966) and *Conrad's Western World* (1971), that a reasonably accurate account of his life has been possible.

My own attempt has been inspired less by the obvious need than by a kind of obsessive compulsion. As a child in Hobart, I played on the beach just across the water from where the hulk of Conrad's *Otago* lay dissolving in the mud. In later years, while I had as yet no particular interest in his work, my duties took me to most of the places he had visited. It was in Korea, in the 1950s, living in a village almost as remote as Conrad's "Patusan," that I was sent a copy of *Lord Jim*, and reading it, discovered a lot about myself. In the 1960s I published a "Conradian" novel, now forgotten by the author as well as by the public. This was followed by a thesis on the relation of Conrad's art to his life, which I found so fascinating that I could not stop. I have lived with him so long that I like to think that I know just what he would do, or say, as he jerked his shoulders and threw away his newly lighted cigarette, in any imaginable situation.

I have tried to show how and why his books were written rather than to assess or expound them, but of course judgements cannot entirely be avoided. To discover which of his stories were truly written in his blood is, in a sense, to judge them. The biographer comes to feel that literary criticism is too important to be left to the literary critics.

I cannot claim to offer any new facts about Conrad: I have attempted, rather, to disentangle them from the fiction and to present a psychologically credible portrait of the man I regard as the greatest writer in the English language. For much assistance in the more literary aspects of my task, I am deeply grateful to Arnold Kettle, and to Werner Pelz for many insights into Conrad's philosophical views and his European background.

Contents

Contents

Illustrations

Conrad as a child
> (*Courtesy of The Beinecke Rare Book and Manuscript Library, Yale University*)

Conrad in Marienbad, 1883
> (*Courtesy of The Beinecke Rare Book and Manuscript Library, Yale University*)

Derebczynka Manor
> (*Courtesy of Humanities Research Center, the University of Texas at Austin*)

The *Tilkhurst*
> (*Courtesy of Humanities Research Center, the University of Texas at Austin*)

A street scene in Singapore
> (*Courtesy of the BBC Hulton Picture Library*)

Jessie George in 1896
> (*Courtesy of The Beinecke Rare Book and Manuscript Library, Yale University*)

Conrad in 1896
> (*Courtesy of Humanities Research Center, the University of Texas at Austin*)

Marguerite Poradowska
> (*Courtesy of Harvard University's Widener Library*)

A page from the manuscript of *The Nigger of the Narcissus*
> (*Courtesy of The Rosenbach Museum and Library, Philadelphia*)

R. B. Cunninghame Graham, circa 1890
> (*Courtesy of the BBC Hulton Picture Library*)

A motorcar outing to visit the Hopes, circa 1904
> (*Courtesy of the Humanities Research Center, the University of Texas at Austin*)

Illustrations

Conrad in 1904
(Courtesy of the BBC Hulton Picture Library)

The Conrads at the Someries
(Courtesy of Dodd, Mead & Company, Inc.)

Ford Madox Ford
(Courtesy of the BBC Hulton Picture Library)

A letter from Conrad to Pinker, January 18, 1909
*(Courtesy of the Trustees of the Joseph Conrad Estate and of the
Henry W. and Albert A. Berg Collection, The New York Public
Library, Astor, Lenox and Tilden Foundations)*

Conrad with Jessie and John in the study, Capel House, 1915
(Courtesy of the BBC Hulton Picture Library)

Conrad on his visit to America, 1923
(Courtesy of the BBC Hulton Picture Library)

x

PART ONE

ADVENTURE

1. *Pole, Catholic and Gentleman*

"A vast amount of red," says Marlow as he looks at the map, "good to see at any time, because one knows some real work is done there." The patches of pink that mark the Empire are linked by the dotted lines of its merchant routes: thousands of little ships, each with a red flag at its stern, lay their trails on the sleeping sea, or are swiped by its waking anger. Every year a few hundred go down, and a thousand seamen lose their lives, but hundreds more stream out to take their place. Where the dotted lines come together, as in the straits of Dover, "they emerge from the dull, colourless distances ahead as if the supply of rather roughly finished mechanical toys were inexhaustible in some mysterious cheap store away there, below the grey curve of the earth." Or they rest in the bright blue of Singapore, "dotted by garlanded islands, lighted by festal sunshine, with the eternal serenity of the Eastern sky overhead."

The year is 1888. Two figures, clad in white ducks, approach each other in the midday sun of Singapore. One of them is "an inch, perhaps two, under six feet, powerfully built," and he advances "with a slight stoop of the shoulders, head forward, and a fixed from under stare that made you think of a charging bull." His name is Augustine Podmore Williams, and he is a "water-clerk," the agent of a merchant selling ship's stores, on his way to seek the custom of an incoming ship. In his younger days he had once abandoned a leaking ship, loaded with Malayan pilgrims, which instead of sinking, had turned up to condemn him.

He probably does not notice the other figure in white, slight but heavy-shouldered, with a trim beard, gloves and cane, for he stays in the shade to protect dark eyes of a brilliance near to neurosis. The two men pass. They will never meet again, but the slight foreigner, fascinated by hearsay of Williams, will transfer his own sensitive soul into that bulky form and write a hundred and fifty thousand words about him—he will call him Lord Jim and send him to join Hamlet, Quixote, and Faust as another milestone along the path of Western man's self-understanding.

It is twelve years yet before that will begin, and it does not at the moment preoccupy the gentleman with the gloves and cane and the nervous twitch of the shoulders. He has just signed off after five months as mate on a tiny steamship tramping the Malay archipelago, and he is wondering whether he can afford the luxury of the harbor hotel—"there it was too, displaying its white pillared pavilions surrounded by trim grass plots." But he needs the money to pay his passage back to England, so he gives it "a hostile glance" and sets out to walk through the city to the Officer's Sailors Home.

Unable to obtain the command of a ship, to which his qualifications entitle him, doubtful even of his vocation as a seaman but still unaware of his possibilities as a writer, this is the moment at which he begins to feel some sense of his real task—and also, ironically, the moment at which the great ambition of his nautical career is about to be fulfilled. So perhaps it is an appropriate moment to see him pass by before turning to consider how it was that Józef Teodor Konrad Korzeniowski, son of gentlefolk from a coastless country in Eastern Europe, came to be an English master-mariner on his way to becoming one of the greatest novelists of the English language.

If the Allies had lost the First World War, and the Anglo-Irish gentry had found themselves having to deal with, or plot against, German overlords as well as to depend on Irish peasants, that would be something like the situation into which, on December 3, 1857, Conrad was born. His home was on a rented estate in a part of the Ukraine near Berdichev that

had been conquered by the Poles in the days when their kingdom stretched from the Crimea to the Baltic, but since the
partition of 1793 had been ruled by Russia. The Poles were
a minority who still owned much of the land and were now
providing doctors, lawyers and teachers, but for them a passion for Polish independence had to be tempered with the
thought that equally legitimate Ukrainian claims could destroy their substance.

In the attitudes of Conrad's father, Apollo, and his maternal uncle, Tadeusz Bobrowski (who would become, in effect, his guardian), one sees contrasting reactions to this
situation. In Apollo, who had no property of his own, it took
the form of a mystical, messianic pan-Slavism that believed
in the redeeming power of the peasants; for his uncle, established on a large estate, it encouraged a faith in Western
liberalism that would both free the serfs and conciliate the
Russians in "an orderly development towards democracy."
Conrad would come to regard these alternative hopes with a
more-or-less equal irony, but one can always sense in his
mind, and in his books, the residue of their conflicting claims
—an outward dislike for revolutionaries and inward sympathy, a willed conformity to bourgeois values ever-threatened
by an instinctive contempt, reflected in the subversive unease
of stories such as *The Secret Agent* or *Under Western Eyes.*

While still in the womb, Conrad was dedicated to a holy
cause: at his birth his father wrote a poem, "To My Son born
in the 85th year of the Muscovite oppression," and at his
baptism he wrote another:

> My child, my son, if the enemy calls you a nobleman
> and a Christian—tell yourself that you are a pagan and
> your nobility rubbish.
> My child, my son, tell yourself that you are without
> land or love, without Fatherland, without humanity—as
> long as Poland, our Mother, is enslaved (NP pp. 2,5).

Apollo had studied at St. Petersburg, where he "took up,
rather lazily, Oriental languages," but changed to the Faculty of Arts and developed a strong taste for French literature. He left without a degree (LL 1, p. 3). He was ostensibly
managing an estate but he wanted the world to be wholly
other than it was, and took refuge in the woods to write

while ever-increasing debts ate up the dowry that was his only security.

Conrad's mother, Ewa Bobrowska, came of a family better fitted to survive. Whereas the Korzeniowskis had lost their estates in repeated resistance, the Bobrowskis had more often lain low and prospered. They had strongly opposed the marriage, regarding Apollo as a most unsuitable son in law, and it was only after seven years' persistence, and five years after the death of her father, that Ewa overcame her scruples about disobeying his wishes (SD p. 20).

Less than two years after Conrad's birth in 1857, his father was forced to leave the estate, and he moved to Zhitomir, about thirty miles to the north, which was something of a Polish cultural center. Here he worked in a publishing house, putting out some of his own translations of French poetry, and was active in revolutionary causes. Fifty years later, provoked by a critic who accounted for *The Secret Agent* by saying that he was "the son of a revolutionist," Conrad would insist that his father was merely "a nationalist"—but his was a romantic and revolutionary nationalism, a "Polish messianic Slavism with its metaphysical dreamlands, its poetical grandiloquence, and its noble delusions," in which he was actively linked with the "Reds" and the anarchists (Fleishman, pp. 4–5).

Polish politics in the nineteenth century were of a tragic complexity that almost defies comprehension. The country was divided into Prussian, Russian, and Austrian sectors, each of which was involved in the differing ambitions of its rulers; it was inhabited by a mixture of races, with the Poles themselves often a minority, and this minority split into a ruling class (the *szlachta*) and peasants—in some areas, still serfs—providing a conflict of interests that foreign rulers could easily exploit. In the Russian zone there were families that had for generations cooperated with the Russians and shared their culture, and others who had through the generations resisted. Conrad admired an uncle who had fought with Napoleon against the Russians, but there were probably more of his relatives who had fought with them. And even those of the Polish gentry who actively opposed the occupation were divided into political extremes of left and right. The Russian policy of dispossessing rebellious landowners was creating a middle class that would eventually bring some moderation to the scene, but at this time it had merely sent to Paris a crowd of loud-voiced exiles who made their own contribution to the conflict and confusion. Thus, the distaste and the hopelessness with which Conrad would come to regard Polish politics, almost until the time of the First World War, were not without some justification.

Early in 1861, Apollo accepted an invitation to move to Warsaw to edit a new literary magazine, but within a few months rumors of a coming insurrection led to intense activity against Polish conspirators. On October 21, Apollo was arrested and taken to the Citadel, and on the evidence of Ewa's letters to him, she also was accused. After a lengthy investigation, they were condemned to exile. At his own request, Apollo was to be sent to Perm, in the Urals, where the governor was an old college friend, but perhaps because the Russian did not welcome the idea, their destination was changed —en route—to Vologda, a town about three hundred miles north of Moscow, where there was already a small company of Polish exiles. On the way, near Moscow, the Korzeniowskis' small child, now four, developed pneumonia but subsequently recovered after traditional treatment with "leeches and calomel." Vologda was built on a marsh, with a cold wet climate, and although the exiles were well treated, Ewa, already suffering from tuberculosis, became seriously ill (LL 1, p. 7; NP p. 7).

Then, in January 1863, came the last great Polish insurrection, instigated by the left, and opposed by much of the right and the center, as well as by a powerful Russian Army. Even so, it took months to suppress. The families of both of Conrad's parents suffered heavily, and from this time on there is a tone of despair in Apollo's letters to his friends and family. Many Poles escaped to the West, including one of Conrad's cousins, Aleksander Poradowski, who settled in Belgium, where he married a beautiful and talented Frenchwoman, Marguerite Gachet, who would become for many years Conrad's closest confidante.

Because of Ewa's illness, in July 1863 the Korzeniowskis were allowed to move south, to Chernigov, in the Ukraine; and from here, in August, Ewa took her son on a three-month visit to the estate of her brother Tadeusz at Nowafastów.

Conrad was now nearly six, and it is here that his first memories begin. In *A Personal Record*, a collection of memoirs originally written as magazine articles in 1908 and 1909, he describes the day of their return to exile, with "an elongated, bizarre, shabby travelling-carriage with four post-horses, standing before the long front of the house with its eight columns, four each side of the broad flight of stairs," while in the distance the police captain of the district sits in his troika to keep an eye on them. The crowd of relatives and servants on the steps includes the French governess who calls *"N'oublie pas ton français, mon chéri,"* and he says that "in three months, simply by playing with us, she had taught me not only to speak French but to read it as well."

Over the next two months his mother's health continued to decline, and she died on April 18, 1865, at the age of thirty-two (NP p. 8). The boy would now be left to share with his father a life of extraordinary loneliness and precocious literary education. Apollo was engaged on a "major work," a study of "Victor Hugo and his function as poet and citizen," and he was also translating Shakespeare. Conrad read his father's pages, so that very early his imagination must have been stretched by heights and depths and darkness, both in life and literature, not broken, but given a tragic temper that would make it impossible for him to deal in happy endings: Schopenhauer was to be his favorite among the philosophers.

He was sometimes sent to stay with his uncle, but on one such occasion, when he was nine, his father wrote, "He is pining for me, in spite of the fresh country air and in spite of being able to play with his cousin, just his age. He is pining under the doting wing of his grandmother and the indulgence of his uncle who has transferred to him all the love he bore his sister. . . . He is pining because he is foolish, and I am afraid he may stay that way all his life" (SD p. 39). In a sense Conrad would "stay that way all his life," sharing—perhaps as much by inheritance as example—his father's ascetic temperament and taste for isolation.

There is a story that once while staying with Tadeusz, Conrad interrupted a group of his elders to ask, "And what do you think of *me?*" (JB p. 22). It betrays a need, but both the question itself and the fact that it was remembered and handed on, are indications that despite the hardships of his youth, he was always made to feel cherished and important, and he never lost his self-confidence and his natural egoism. He had, from the age of five, an image of himself as "Pole, Catholic, and Gentleman" (SD p. 27), and although he would come to examine it with the irony of an extreme self-awareness, he never publicly abandoned it.

2. *A Squeeze of the Hand*

In the autumn of 1867, Apollo, increasingly ill with tuberculosis, was granted leave to travel. They moved to Lwów, in the Austrian sector of Poland, where Apollo again became politically active. He wanted to send Conrad to school, but on finding that the lessons were given in German, decided not to. The boy had occasional fits, which were thought to be epileptic, but he would grow out of them by the age of fourteen (NP p. 158).

Early in 1869 they moved west to Kraków, the ancient capital of Poland, which had now been incorporated into the Austrian province of Galicia. Here lay not only the tombs of Poland's ancient kings and bishops, but the best hopes for its future, for under the benevolent bureaucracy of the Austro-Hungarian Empire it was re-establishing itself as the main center of intellectual life and rational politics. It also shared something of Austrian cultural sophistication, the culture that produced such contemporaries of Conrad as Sigmund Freud and Robert Musil. Here, for the first time, Conrad went to school, and in later life he would always regard Kraków as essentially his "home town."

His father was now slowly dying, in a large apartment, attended by nuns, the air around him "all piety, resignation and silence. . . . I looked forward to what was coming with an incredulous terror. I turned my eyes from it sometimes with success, and yet all the time I had an awful sensation of

10

the inevitable. I had also moments of revolt which stripped me of some of my simple trust in the government of the Universe" (NLL p. 168). Nor would Conrad's later experience discourage this early mistrust: there has probably never been another writer with so profound a suspicion of everything that the rest of his world took for granted—in nature, society, or the human heart. His last major novel, *Victory*, ends with its hero, Heyst, saying, "Woe to the man whose heart has not learned while young to hope, to love—and to put its trust in life!" If in a sense Conrad was that man, at least he had a saving awareness of what he had lost.

Of the time of his father's last illness he goes on to say, "I don't know what would have become of me if I had not been a reading boy. There were many books about, lying on consoles, on tables, and even on the floor, for we had not had time to settle down. I read! What did I not read!" (NLL p. 168). If much of his reading was precocious, not all of it was: he read and loved the sea stories of Fenimore Cooper and Frederick Marryat, books that suited his age, stirred his spirit, and served to shape his destiny. Out of his love for these stories grew his dream of running away to sea, and in later years he said, "Perhaps no two authors of fiction influenced so many lives and gave to so many the initial impulse towards a glorious or a useful career" (NLL p. 58).

He shared also the adventures of the great British explorers. He mentions Sir L. McClintock's *The Voyage of the "Fox" in the Arctic Seas*, "translated, I believe, into every language of the white races," which first aroused his interest in studying the atlas; David Livingstone; Mungo Park in the Sudan and James Bruce in Abyssinia—"almost each day of my schoolboy life had its hour given up to their company," and "one day, putting my finger on a spot in the very middle of the then white heart of Africa, I declared that some day I would go there" (LE pp. 11ff.).

His father died on May 23, 1869, and the funeral was the occasion for a great, silent, patriotic demonstration. After revisiting Kraków in 1914, at the age of fifty-six, Conrad wrote, "I could see again the small boy of that day following a hearse; a space kept clear in which I walked alone, conscious of an enormous following, the clumsy swaying of the tall black machine, the chanting of the surpliced clergy at

11

the head, the flames of tapers passing under the low archway of the gate, the rows of bared heads on the pavements with fixed serious eyes" (NLL p. 169). In honor of his father's memory he was given the freedom of the city (LL 1, p. 23).

It had been his father's wish that Conrad should be educated here rather than in the Ukraine, so he stayed on in Kraków with his maternal grandmother, Teofila. A family council appointed her and a Count Wladyslaw Mlniszek as his guardians (NP p. 12), but it would be his uncle Tadeusz, with a great love for his sister's child and a desire to save him from what he regarded as the pernicious influence of the Korzeniowskis, who would really perform this role. He passed through Kraków in June 1870 and engaged a medical student, Adam Pulman, to be Conrad's private tutor (NP p. 12).

Accustomed to acquiring knowledge in rather a different way, Conrad never seems to have been very happy at school, and in 1872, at the age of fourteen, he began to express his desire to go to sea. He had trouble with his chest, and in May of the following year was sent to Switzerland, accompanied by Pulman, who had instructions to dissuade him from these dreams. Conrad tells of continued arguments that ended with his tutor calling him "an incorrigible, hopeless Don Quixote" (PR p. 44).

On his return from this trip in August 1873 he was sent back to Lwów, where a boardinghouse for orphans of the 1863 insurrection was managed by a distant cousin, Antoni Syroczyński. In *The Arrow of Gold*, which he claimed to be autobiography, there is a passage that he crossed out before publication in which he refers to an experience of his hero "in the last summer of his last school holiday." He falls in love with a flirtatious school girl who treats him cruelly:

> She amused himself again and again by tormenting him privately and publicly with great zest and method and finally "executed" him in circumstances of peculiar atrocity—which don't matter here.
>
> Perhaps he was unduly sensitive. At any rate he came out of it seamed, scarred, almost flayed and with a complete mistrust of himself, and an abiding fear . . . he said to himself: if that's it then never, never again. (SD *App.* pp. 287–288)

12

This girl was probably Tekla Syroczyńska, daughter of the cousin who kept the hostel, and we have also her view of Conrad, given many years later: "Intellectually well developed, he hated the rigors of school, which tired and bored him; he used to say that he had a great talent and would become a great writer. This coupled with a sarcastic smile on his face and frequent critical remarks on everything, provoked surprise in his teachers and ridicule among his colleagues" (NP p. 13).

This "abiding fear" of the opposite sex and "mistrust of himself" may help to explain the scarcity of women in both his books and his life, and his rather strange attitudes towards them when they do appear. The early loss of his mother, and perhaps also a certain inadequacy on her part, may have contributed to this. In his memoirs Tadeusz speaks of her, before her marriage, as having "a less easygoing nature" than her sister, "making far greater demands and, at that period, requiring more attention from others than she was ready or able to give them." Thus although he concludes that after her marriage "she always succeeded in fulfilling the role imposed by her duties" and "worthily representing the ideal of Polish womanhood," the picture is not one that suggests maternal warmth. Conrad also mentions that he had a Ukrainian peasant girl as his nursing mother, but as she belonged to their rented estate, there was no lasting relationship (LL 2, p. 194). The affection with which he speaks later of the French governess suggests that, all too briefly, she answered a need.

It appears that before his infatuation with the girl who can probably be identified as Tekla Syroczyńska, Conrad had been deeply influenced by another girl whom he had known in Kraków, and before he left Poland he would come to realize that she was the one that he truly loved. This girl was Janina Taube, who with her younger sister and four brothers was also under the guardianship of Conrad's Uncle Tadeusz. They lived with their widowed mother in the same building in which Conrad had stayed in Kraków in 1871 (NP pp. 218–219).

The older boys had been Conrad's best friends, but the realization that he loved their sister was something which, because of his unhappy first experience, he was reluctant to acknowledge. If we can trust another part of the cancelled

13

passage in *The Arrow of Gold,* because of this experience, he never revealed his love for Janina—"he rather affected to resist her influence. He even tried to cheat his own self in that respect." In *Nostromo,* Decoud loves Antonia Avellanos, and in the Author's Note Conrad says that she was modelled on this girl:

> How we, a band of tallish schoolboys, the chums of her two brothers, how we used to look up to that girl just out of the schoolroom herself, as the standard bearer of a faith to which we were all born but which she alone knew how to hold aloft with an unflinching hope. She had perhaps more glow and less serenity in her soul than Antonia. . . . I was not the only one in love with her; but it was I who had to bear the oftenest her scathing criticism of my levities—very much like poor Decoud—or stand the brunt of her austere, unanswerable invective. (p. xiv)

The character who seems to answer even more closely to this description, a girl with "more glow and less serenity," is Natalia in *Under Western Eyes.* And Razumov, the hero of that book, represents in a more extreme and fatal form, that very predicament in which Conrad found himself in relation to the girl, for the "faith to which we were all born" was, of course, Polish patriotism, to which Conrad was inwardly refusing to commit himself.

He persisted in his desire to go to sea, a struggle of which he wrote in 1904 that "echoes of it linger to this day. I catch myself in hours of solitude and retrospect meeting arguments and finding things to say that an assailed boy could not have found simply because of the mysteriousness of his impulses to himself" (PR p. 121). Though it may have seemed to Tadeusz an outlandish proposal, it had in its favor the fact that it would save Conrad from following in his father's path of reckless patriotism, and also from the danger of conscription into the Russian Army, where as the son of a "political convict" he could have been kept in the ranks for an indefinite term. His uncle's first hope had been the Austrian Navy, but he could not obtain for Conrad the necessary Austrian citizenship (SD p. 48).

14

For Conrad, familiar with the accounts of its great seamen and explorers, England seems already to have been his spiritual home, but his family had no connections there, and it was decided that he should go to Marseilles, where there were some distant relatives, the Chodzkos, who had their business with ships and would be able to find him a berth (Retinger, p. 21).

Sometime in October 1874, before beginning the long rail journey to the West, he went to say goodbye to the girl, and "that afternoon when I came in, shrinking yet defiant, to say the final goodbye I received a hand-squeeze that made my heart leap and saw a tear that took my breath away. She was softened at last as though she had suddenly perceived (we were such children still!) that I was really going away for good, going very far away" (*Nostromo* p. xiv). In the cancelled passage in *The Arrow of Gold* he says, "It was very little that she had done. A mere pressure of the hand. But he had remembered it for five and thirty years of separation and silence" (SD p. 288).

To the end of his life Conrad would record no other occasion on which his heart leaped or his breath was taken away, and indeed it may be that in a sense this was his deepest sexual experience. The girl would not be forgotten, but transmuted like Dante's Beatrice into higher spheres, become a heroine of Russian revolution, or in *Nostromo*, inspire Decoud to act out great things for his country and to die seeing a vision of her in the sky, "gigantic and lovely like an allegorical statue, looking on with scornful eyes at his weakness."

This may help to explain the way in which, in almost all of his stories the consummation of love is dreaded, evaded, or followed by immediate death and disaster. In *The Rescue*, his story of love between a seaman from the working class and a lady from high society, Lingard's hopes are more modest than those of Lady Chatterley's lover: "I shall shake hands. Yes, I shall take her hand—just before she goes. Why the devil not? I am the master here after all—in this brig—as good as anyone—by heavens, better than anyone—better than anyone on earth" (p. 178).

That squeeze of the hand was not forgotten, either, by Janina Taube. She stayed in Poland to become the Baroness de Brunnow, but in 1897, when Conrad's first works were published in England, she would write to him care of the publishers, and so initiate an occasional, courtly correspondence in French that would keep alive their romantic memories without ever trespassing upon the boundaries of propriety (NP pp. 218–222, 249–250).

3. *Le Petit Ami de Baptistin*

Conrad's relatives in Marseilles, the Chodzkos, were, according to Retinger, prosperous but "very Frenchified" (p. 21). They made their living in dealing with the French mercantile marine, and one member of the family, Victor, was an officer on a French ship. They may have regarded Conrad as a possible embarrassment, as they seem to have kept him at a distance: he never refers to them in any of his own writings, and records that on his first morning in Marseilles he woke up in a small hotel. They had arranged for a young Frenchman connected with the firm to look after him:

> This Solary (Baptistin), when I beheld him in the flesh, turned out a quite young man, very good-looking, with a fine black, short beard, a fresh complexion, and soft, merry black eyes. He was as jovial and good natured as any boy could desire. I was still asleep in my room in a modest hotel near the quays of the old port, after the fatigues of the journey *via* Vienna, Zurich, Lyons, when he burst in flinging the shutters open to the sun of Provence and chiding me boisterously for lying abed. How pleasantly he startled me by his noisy objurgations to be up and off instantly for a "three years campaign in the South Seas." (PR p. 122)

After the dark claustrophobic years as an orphan in Poland, Conrad blossomed in the sun of Provence, and welcomed

17

the wind and the salty spray in the little boats of the harbor pilots to which Solary introduced him. As *le petit ami de Baptistin*, he sailed with them regularly as they went out looking "for the sails of ships and the smoke of steamers rising out there, beyond the slim tall Plainier lighthouse cutting the line of the windswept horizon with a white perpendicular stroke" (PR p. 123).

As this preliminary test soon proved, he had the right kind of stomach for the sea, and the only recorded occasion on which he was sick was in crossing the Channel on his honeymoon. After two months he had absorbed enough of the pilots' knowledge to be able, later, to earn money himself by bringing in ships, but he was eager to sail beyond the pillar of Plainier, and by some arrangement with the firm of C. Delestang et Fils, engaged in the sugar trade with the French West Indies, he was taken on as a kind of working passenger on the *Mont Blanc*, a three-masted wooden barque of just under four hundred tons, for a voyage to the island of Martinique.

They sailed, just after his seventeenth birthday, on December 11, 1874.* The *Mont Blanc* was very much the smaller and the older of the two ships employed by Delestang, and in *The Mirror of the Sea* Conrad says that after a storm "she leaked fully, generously, overflowingly, and all over like a basket. I took an enthusiastic part in the excitement caused by that last infirmity of noble ships, without concerning myself much with the why or wherefore" (p. 155). The voyage to St. Pierre took more than two months, and the ship stayed there for six weeks before returning with its load of sugar. St. Pierre was a town of wealthy French planters, Negro servants, balconies, and bougainvilia. Occupied by the British during the French Revolution, it had largely escaped the turmoil—it was the France of the *ancien régime* running to seed in tropical splendor until, in 1902, it would be completely destroyed by volcanic eruption.

On the way back, the ship called at St. Thomas and Haiti, and reached Le Havre on May 23, 1875, just over five months after she had sailed. A month later Conrad set off again in

* Details of ships and their movements throughout this book are taken from the appendix to *The Sea Years of Joseph Conrad*, by Jerry Allen.

the same ship, but under a different captain, a man called Duteil, who would later tempt him to join in a smuggling venture. This time they spent nearly two months at St. Pierre, and in December reached Le Havre, where the ship was kept for repairs. In returning to Marseilles by train, Conrad apparently lost his trunk, and wrote to his uncle for more money.

Tadeusz was sending him, through the Chodzkos, a half-yearly allowance of four hundred roubles—equivalent then to a thousand francs, or just over $200 (NP p. 39)—which came out of his small inheritance, but Conrad exasperated his uncle with frequent requests for more, particularly when he was spending periods ashore. He now had six months to wait for another voyage, and became a regular visitor to the house of M. Delestang, whose wife seems to have been very kind to him. Delestang, whom Conrad describes as a "frozen-up, mummified Royalist," was a keen supporter of Don Carlos, a pretender to the throne of Spain who was supported by the Basques and by small reactionary groups in various capitals of Europe. They had engineered several successive uprisings in Spain, of which the last and least successful began early in 1876, so that Conrad must have heard much of this affair, though his own subsequent claims to have been involved in it do not seem to have any substance.

In July 1876, soon after the uprising had begun, he sailed again for the West Indies, this time on a larger and sounder ship, the *Saint-Antoine*. He was now listed as a "steward," which according to Aubry "placed him in rather a special position between officers and crew and which paid thirty-five francs a month" (SD p. 63). Put under the care of a Corsican seaman called Cesar Cervoni, who was told by the captain "to spare him too many contacts with the crew," he signed himself, aristocratically, as "Conrad de Korzeniowski" and was nicknamed "the Count," an ironic honor that he would later receive also from his fellow captains in the British service (WS p. 168; SD p. 67). It certainly indicates that he was not receiving any of the hard knocks and humiliations that would come to him as an ordinary seaman on British ships.

The mate of the *Saint-Antoine* was another Corsican, Dominic Cervoni, not related to Cesar. Dominic made a deep impression on Conrad as having the kind of animal perfection that he always envied, and Dominic will appear first, as himself, in *The Mirror of the Sea;* then as Nostromo; as Peyrol in *The Rover;* as himself again in *The Arrow of Gold;* and finally as Attilio in the unfinished *Suspense.* In *The Mirror of the Sea* he is described as a grave, broad-chested man of forty with bronzed face, thick black moustaches that "seemed to hide a perpetual smile" and eyes with "a look of perfectly remorseless irony."

The ship reached St. Pierre on August 18, 1876. Since from July to October the harbor is likely to be hit by hurricanes, French vessels were not allowed to stay there, but had to wait outside. There is thus no record of the ship's whereabouts for the next four weeks: it is possible that she went as far as Venezuela, as Conrad later claimed to have been there, and this is the only occasion on which he could have done so. There is no evidence, however, and it seems more likely that he invented his visit to support the "authenticity" of *Nostromo.* His tendency to mythologize these early voyages is well illustrated in *The Arrow of Gold,* in which he says, "I had just returned from my second West Indies voyage. My eyes were still full of tropical splendour, my memory of my experiences, lawful and lawless, which had their charm and their thrill; for they had startled me a little and amused me considerably" (p. 8).

In *Victory,* published forty years later, he transferred to the Malay archipelago one or two characters he had glimpsed at this time. He says of Heyst, the hero, who becomes very much the embodiment of Conrad's own sensibility, that he is based on "my visual impression of the man in 1876; a couple of hours in a hotel in St. Thomas (West Indies). There was some talk of him after we left our party; but all I heard of him might have been written down on a cigarette paper" (SY p. 37). The three villains of this story, Jones, Ricardo and Pedro, were also glimpsed here, and of Pedro he says that "this bestial apparition and a certain enormous buck nigger encountered in Haiti only a couple of months afterwards, have fixed my conception of blind, furious, unreasoning rage, as manifested in the human animal, to the end of my days. Of the nigger I used to dream for years afterwards. Of Pedro never. The impression was less vivid. I got away from him too quickly" (*Victory,* pp. xii–xv).

20

This "bestial apparition" from which he attempts to flee is symptomatic of Conrad's attitude towards violence. Rather than attempt to recognize and explore its echoes within himself, he tends to suppress them, and usually presents the violent as alien brutes beyond the limits of his empathy.

In arranging these voyages, the Chodzkos seem to have been concerned with indulging their cousin's whims rather than with having him trained as a seaman, and there is no evidence that he was working to qualify as a ship's officer. If this did not worry Conrad, it certainly worried his uncle, who was sending him frequent letters of instruction and rebuke: "What have you been working on during the voyage? You praise the present captain. So you have presumably profited from him? Did he give you lessons? If so, what? What did you work on yourself? Are you also working in English, or other languages?" (NP p. 44).

This is from a letter that Conrad found waiting for him when the *Saint-Antoine* returned to Marseilles in February 1877. He was expecting to sail again almost immediately, but he developed an anal abscess and had to be left behind (NP p. 176). He was now coming up to the age at which he would be liable for military service in Russia, and this disqualified him from serving in French ships. Indeed, it appears that it was only through some irregularity that he had been allowed to sail on the previous voyage (NP p. 45). He seems to have turned to the idea of some small trading enterprise, with the backing of Delestang, but in a letter about this, Delestang apparently used terms that Conrad regarded as insulting, and they quarrelled. All that we know of this is from his uncle's next letter in August:

> I do not deny that, if things happened the way you describe them, the honorable *épicier* treated you too loftily, unmindful of having before him a descendant of the excellent family of Nalecz[1]—that's agreed. I see from your account of the talk with him that you have *la repartie facile et suffisement acérée* in which I recognise your Nalecz blood—in this tendency to fly into a

[1] Korzeniowski was a name not uncommon in Poland, and "Nalecz" was used to distinguish Conrad's particular clan.

21

passion. . . . Unfortunately I do not perceive in this whole affair any trace of that prudent common sense of which on the distaff side you have the right to be proud, deriving it from the House of Jastrzembeczyk, to which I have the honour to belong. (NP p. 47)

How Conrad passed the next few months is not very clear. His claims to have been involved in the Carlist war in Spain cannot be taken very seriously, as by this time it was over, but he must have made the acquaintance of at least one of its participants, J. Y. M. K. Blunt, as Conrad's portraits of him, and his mother, in *The Arrow of Gold* are vivid, and in general accord with other sources. Blunt's mother, Mrs. Ellen Lloyd Key Blunt, was the daughter of the Washington lawyer Francis Scott Key, who wrote the "Star-Spangled Banner" and was the friend of presidents. She married a naval officer from Virginia, and after his early death, moved to Paris, where she let it be known that her husband had been "a President of the United States" and used her wit and beauty to keep herself afloat without much money. She wrote novels and poetry, was converted to Catholicism, and so captivated the French poet Théophile Gautier that he launched her as a Shakespearean actress, without success (SY pp. 72–74).

Her son John Young Mason Key Blunt had served in the French Army and the Papal Zouaves before becoming a cavalryman, and then a liaison officer with the forces of Don Carlos. "Eminently elegant," his style made a deep impression on Conrad. He had two "striking declarations," one of which was "I live by my sword" and the other, *"Je suis Américain, catholique et gentilhomme,"* and Conrad thought, "So such people did exist in the world yet! I had not been born too late" (*The Arrow of Gold*, pp. 13–17). Conrad, romantic, and liking to think of himself as "Pole, Catholic and gentleman," was no doubt ready to worship Blunt, who was nine years older, but he must have been disappointed, as it is the complete hollowness of the man that is emphasized in the book.

Left in Marseilles with nothing to do, Conrad was not immediately short of money, as his uncle had been persuaded to send him three thousand francs for a proposed long voyage. It appears that in these circumstances, towards the end of 1877, he met his former captain on the *Mont Blanc*, Duteil, and was drawn into some smuggling venture, possibly running guns to the Basques in Spain. According to a later letter from his uncle to a family friend, "he invested 1000 francs in it and made over 400, which pleased them greatly, so that on the second occasion he put in all he had—and lost the lot. This Mr. Duteil consoled him with a kiss and then went off to Buenos Aires. He, Konrad, was left behind, unable to sign on for a ship—poor as church mouse—and moreover heavily in debt" (NP pp. 176–177).

Of this "smuggling venture" Conrad wrote two allegedly autobiographical accounts, one in *The Mirror of the Sea*, and another ten years later, quite inconsistent with the first, in *The Arrow of Gold*. The latter would appear to be entirely fictional; the account in *The Mirror of the Sea* may have some factual base, but extensive research has failed to find any trace of either the ship or the incident, and Conrad's uncle, who subsequently "spent a fortnight in Marseilles investigating the whole affair" of the lost money, makes no reference to it. There is no evidence that Conrad was actively engaged in the venture into which he put his money, and it seems likely that the whole tale of the *Tremolino* was based on stories he had heard from Cervoni while on the *Saint-Antoine*. It is significant that Cesar Cervoni (whom Conrad describes as one of the participants), when speaking of Conrad to his children, mentioned nothing more than that he had known him as a well-mannered young man on the *Saint-Antoine* (WS p. 168).

However it may be, by March 1878 Conrad was stranded in Marseilles with no money, and unable to ask his uncle for more. According to the account given by Tadeusz, Conrad borrowed eight hundred francs from his best friend, Richard Fecht, a young German whom the uncle, when he met him, described as "a most prudent and worthy young man," and went to Villefranche, between Nice and Monaco, where a squadron of the American Navy was anchored, with the idea of enlisting. It is not known whether he made any contact with the Americans, but in any case they could not have accepted a foreigner. He then moved on to the casino, where he lost the money in an attempt to profit from "beginner's luck."

He returned to Marseilles, where he arranged his correspondence so that the addresses of his uncle and other nearest relatives were at the top, invited Fecht to tea, and just before the appointed time, shot himself in the chest, "not injuring any important organ" (NP p. 177). The wound did not prove to be very serious, but Fecht sent telegrams to Poland and in due course his uncle arrived:

> I spent a fortnight in Marseilles, at first investigating the whole affair and then the individual himself. Apart from the 3,000 francs which he had lost, I had to pay off as much again to settle his debts. Had he been my own son, I wouldn't have done it, but—I must avow— in the case of my beloved sister's son, I had the weakness to act against the principles I had hitherto held. (NP p. 177)

At the end of this letter to a friend, we find Conrad's charm beginning to work again—his uncle remarks that he seems to know his "trade" very well, that his manners are good, "as if he spends all his time in drawing-rooms," and he is liked by the French seamen, who call him "Monsieur Georges," and that he earns a little money by bringing ships into the harbor.

This self-inflicted wound, which for the sake of family honor his uncle described as received in a duel, may have been a calculated playing of Conrad's last card—his uncle's affection and concern—or it may have been a hesitant attempt at suicide in which, with his finger on the trigger, he found himself moving the muzzle away from the "vital organ." Whatever its motivation, the final result seems to have been satisfactory: his uncle was spared further trouble, and Conrad had crossed the "shadow line" to a new maturity. He was to abandon the role of "Monsieur Georges," gentleman adventurer living beyond his means, climb aboard an English cargo boat, and after one last quarrel, work his way up with a patient endurance that no one looking at his earlier life would have thought possible.

Bobrowski reported that though the French seemed to like

Conrad, he did not really like them. Certainly French bravado and concern for *l'honneur*, a little exaggerated no doubt in characters such as Delestang, Blunt, or Cervoni, seem to have brought out to his cost "the Nalecz blood—the quality of flying into a passion," and the desire to make a show. The cooler climate and the stolid democracy of England were to bring out that other side of his inheritance, the "prudent common sense" of the Bobrowskis.

He would not lose his sense of romance, but rather recover the boyhood context in which it first developed—Marryat's world of salt seas and hard continuing courage. Looking back in 1920, he would write of his "romantic feeling for reality" which "in itself may be a curse, but when disciplined by a sense of personal responsibility and a recognition of the hard facts of existence shared with the rest of mankind becomes but a point of view from which the very shadows of life appear endowed with an internal glow. . . . It is none the worse for the knowledge of the truth. It only tries to make the best of it, hard as it may be, and in this hardness discovers a certain aspect of beauty" (*Within the Tides*, pp. v–vi).

4. *To Sydney in Splendid Ships*

During his two weeks in Marseilles Bobrowski arranged with Fecht that Conrad should be put aboard a British ship as soon as possible, as France's close relations with Russia made the country dangerous for a Pole who had reached the age for military service. Tadeusz also agreed to increase Conrad's yearly allowance to twenty-four hundred francs (about $500), and gave twelve hundred francs of this to Fecht to look after (NP p. 197).

Thus, in April 1878, Conrad, now twenty, went on board what was presumably the first British ship that would take him—a small steamer called the *Mavis*, on its way to Constantinople with a cargo of coal. Fecht paid the captain four hundred francs as the first part of his premium as an "apprentice," which implied that he would receive some training (NP p. 52). It seems that in fact Conrad did not gain any privileges above those of an ordinary seaman, so that he came to feel that he was being exploited, and subsequently refused to have anything to do with the apprentice system on British ships.

He says that the first words that he heard in English were "Look out there!" as a rope was thrown at him from on high, which expresses very well the kind of reception he was likely to have had on the *Mavis*. Conditions on British ships were primitive and foreigners not common in the crew (NLL pp. 180–181). He soon became accustomed to being called "a

bloody foreigner" and the treatment of the Finnish sailor at
the beginning of *The Nigger of the Narcissus* probably conveys something of his own experience:

> "Get out of my road, Dutchy."
> The Finn did not move—did not hear.
> "Get out, blast ye!" shouted the other, shoving him
> aside with his elbow. "Get out, you blanked deaf and
> dumb fool. Get out."
> The man staggered, recovered himself, and gazed at
> the speaker in silence.
> "These damned furriners should be kept under. If you
> don't teach 'em their place they put on you like any-
> think." (p. 13)

Fecht wrote to Conrad's uncle that he had "got him off to
England," but in fact Conrad was sailing towards the very
danger that he was intended to escape. Russia and Turkey
were at war: the Russians had reached Constantinople and
were camped at San Stefano on the coast nearby. England,
unwilling to see Turkey fall to the Russians, was mobilizing
for war, and meanwhile the *Mavis* sailed on, with naval protection. Conrad later described the sight of the Russian tents
on the shore (LL 2, p. 124), and he must have known that
had he stayed in Poland he might well have been among their
occupants.

Under the British threat, the Russians agreed to meet at
Berlin and the *Mavis* safely unloaded her coal, went on across
the Black Sea to pick up a cargo of linseed oil and steamed
back past the Russian tents to reach the little port of Lowestoft on June 18, 1878. Conrad apparently regarded the captain's demands for more premium money as unreasonable,
quarrelled with him, and left the ship, losing the money he
had already paid (NP p. 54).

He then wrote to his uncle requesting his "advice" and
five hundred francs, which produced only a long and angry
refusal. He was now once more at the end of his tether, and
Lowestoft not the most promising of places at which to reach
it. It seems that he was soon befriended by an elderly business
man, Joseph Saul, who owned a pottery there. According to
Conrad's collaborator, Ford Madox Ford, Conrad and Saul
met in a pub and Saul took him home—"here he heard his

first English words to recognize them. They were: 'Eggs and bacon or marmalade?' " (Ford, 1924, p. 92). Saul owned a little schooner, the *Skimmer of the Sea*, which he used to fetch coal from Newcastle for his pottery, and Conrad was taken on as an ordinary seaman for wages of a shilling a month (SY p. 100).

In later years he could look back at this with satisfaction, but it must have been a time of testing for Monsieur Georges, Pole, Catholic and gentleman. He said that he learned his English from the crew of this vessel, which consisted of captain, mate, three other seamen and a cabin boy (SY p. 316). In his spare time he studied the newspaper as a means of learning English, and when he returned to Lowestoft on September 23, 1878, after his third round trip, he came across an advertisement that was appearing in several papers, including the *Times* of September 25:

> SEA.—WANTED, respectable youth YOUTHS, for voyage or term in two splendid ships for Australia, and others for India, etc.—W. Sutherland, 11 Fenchurch-buildings, Fenchurch-street, near rail. Established 1851.

Conrad wrote his first letter in English, perhaps with the help of Saul, and when he received no answer, decided to apply in person. He took with him a piece torn out of a map so that he could find his way without having to ask, and eventually he did, though it was "one of those courts hidden away' from the charted and navigable streets, lost among the thick growth of houses like a dark pool in the depths of a forest."

Mr. Sutherland was standing at a high desk, eating a mutton chop. "I produced elaborately a series of vocal sounds which must have borne sufficient resemblance to the phonetics of English speech, for his face broke into a smile of comprehension almost at once. 'Oh, it's you who wrote a letter to me the other day from Lowestoft about getting a ship.' " He explained that his job was to provide ships for young gentlemen who paid premiums, and that procuring berths for ordinary seamen was illegal. "There was an Act of Parliament which made it penal to procure ships for sailors. 'An Act—of—Parliament. A law,' he took pains to impress it again and again on my foreign understanding."

Nevertheless, the gentleman "managed to get round the

hard letter of it without damage to its fine spirit" and found Conrad a berth on one of the "splendid ships," the *Duke of Sutherland*, a wool clipper due to sail for Sydney on October 15. Conrad says that the nighttime roll-call scene in the opening pages of *The Nigger of the Narcissus* was based on his own embarkation on the *Duke of Sutherland* at Gravesend (LL 1, p. 77) :

> Before the cabin door Mr. Baker was mustering the crew. As they stumbled and lurched along past the mainmast, they could see aft his round broad face with a white paper before it, and beside his shoulder the sleepy head, with dropped eyelids, of the boy, who held, suspended at the end of his raised arm, the luminous globe of a lamp. . . . As the chief mate read out each name, one of the men would answer: "Yes, sir!" or "Here!" and, detaching himself from the shadowy mob of heads visible above the blackness of the starboard bulwarks, would step barefooted into the circle of light, and in two noiseless strides pass into the shadows on the port side of the quarter-deck. They answered in diverse tones: in thick mutters, in clear ringing voices; and some, as if the whole thing had been an outrage on their feelings used an injured intonation. . . . (pp. 16–17)

As a three-masted, full-rigged sailing vessel of more than a thousand tons, the *Duke of Sutherland* was no doubt a "splendid ship," but the splendor did not extend below decks, where conditions were primitive and the food meager and monotonous. In the novel, we see the crowded, sometimes flooded bunks in the nose of the ship, and the crew taking meals on deck, squatting barefoot round a communal pot. In a letter to a family friend, his uncle says that Conrad complained of "the uncomfortable conditions on English ships where no one is the least concerned with the crew's comfort, whereas he had counted on finding the same comfort he had had on French vessels" (NP p. 179). For this kind of life the twelve ordinary seamen on the *Duke of Sutherland* were paid a shilling a month, perhaps enough to buy two meals ashore.

It was a slow voyage, round the Cape and across the Indian Ocean, rough in places, becalmed in others, with no ports of call on the way. They reached Sydney on January 31, 1879, a voyage of three and a half months. No cargo could be found for the return, and the ship waited for five months, a period that must have seemed eternal in its boredom. One by one, the crew signed off, leaving Conrad to earn his keep as the ship's night watchman. The deep water of the harbor had allowed it to anchor at the end of the city's main street, and night after night he sat and watched as "the gas lamps began to twinkle in the streets," hearing the cries from the pubs, and the voice of a man calling "Hot saveloys!"—"I have listened for hours to this most pertinacious pedlar . . . fascinated by the monotony, the regularity, the abruptness of the recurring cry, and so exasperated at the absurd spell, that I wished the fellow would choke himself to death with a mouthful of his own infamous wares" (MS pp. 121–122).

In the mannered style of his memoirs he treats lightly this five-month imprisonment off the shores of nineteenth-century Australia, but perhaps it helps to explain his virtual avoidance of the continent in his fiction. No doubt he was still "a reading boy"—he mentions a one-volume edition of Shakespeare as part of his luggage, and he would have had time to finish it. At last the ship obtained a load of wool and wheat, and Conrad further employment: "I have carried bags of wheat on my back, bent almost double under a ship's deck beams, from six in the morning till six in the evening (with an hour and a half off for meals) " (PR p. 164). Then he was "about the rigging" until they reached London again in October 1879, more than a year after leaving.

He did not sign on again for an immediate repetition of this, but it did not turn him away from the sea. He asked his uncle to obtain a testimonial from Delestang with the idea of returning to the Mediterranean (SD p. 82), and in the meantime embarked on a steamship for a voyage to Greece. The ship left London on December 12, just after his twenty-second birthday, and called at a number of ports on the way to and from her destination. Conrad never liked the noise and dirt of steamships, and he did not get on with the captain whom, in a letter to his uncle, he described as "a madman." He also mentioned that he was coughing and feverish (NP p. 60) and he left the ship when she returned at the end of January.

In the shipping-agent's office he was introduced to a young business man called G. W. F. Hope, connected with a South

African mining company, who had once been an apprentice on the *Duke of Sutherland* but now preferred to indulge his love of the sea by sailing on the estuary of the Thames. They went for lunch together at the London Tavern, and despite what seemed to Hope to be Conrad's "very broken English," they began a life-long friendship.

At this time Conrad also met Adolf Krieger, who was to become the other close friend of his early days in England. American-born, of German parents, Krieger worked with the shipping agents Barr, Moering & Co., and became the agent through whom Conrad received payments from his uncle. Probably through Krieger, Conrad was offered the chance of becoming a "secretary" to a French-Canadian called Lascalle who had some project for making money in Canada, but his uncle advised him against it: "Ask yourself if it is sensible to stake your future on one man, whoever he may be, however great and noble, when that man is an American businessman and politician. It is nobler and more sensible to stake your future on a trade you have mastered by hard work" (NP p. 63). Conrad evidently decided to take the nobler and more sensible course, and sharing lodgings at Holloway with Krieger, he persevered with study for the examination that would qualify him as a second mate. In his letters he refers to two tutors, "Capt. Wyndham" and a "kind hearted Professor Newton" (SD p. 86) who were preparing him for an examination early in June.

As well as a written test with problems in navigation and the like, there was an oral examination on "seamanship," and it was this that Conrad most dreaded. He provides two accounts of the occasion, one in his memoirs, and the other through the lips of Mr. Powell, a character in *Chance*. In *A Personal Record* he says that the examiner must have been "unfavourably impressed by something in my appearance," which is not unlikely as it was hardly that of Lord Jim, "the kind that is not disturbed by the vagaries of intelligence and perversions of nerves, let us say," added to which his accent was, by all accounts, rather strange. In the end he was given a white slip of paper to confirm that he had passed. When he gave the doorkeeper a shilling tip on the way out, the latter said, "Well, I thought you were never coming out."

"How long have I been in there?"

31

"He kept you, sir, just under three hours. I don't think this ever happened with any of the gentlemen before" (PR p. 114).

In *Chance*, Mr. Powell receives a blue slip of paper, is kept one and a half hours, and gives the doorkeeper half a crown. Conrad had now crossed what was in those days the enormous gulf between seaman and officer—"The finest day in my life," Mr. Powell goes on to say, but what came after was not so pleasant—"the trying to get an officer's berth with nothing to show but a brand-new certificate." Mr. Powell describes endless trudging round the offices of shipowners and the filling in of forms of application, which "all properly addressed and stamped, he might just as well have dropped into the sewer grating" (pp. 5–6). This was no doubt Conrad's experience, for though he passed his examination at the beginning of June, it was late in August before he found a berth, as third mate on a wool clipper bound once more for Sydney. The *Loch Etive*, a fairly new full-rigged ship of 1287 tons, with a crew of twenty-eight, sailed from Tilbury on August 21, 1880. The captain, William Stuart, a Scot of forty-eight, was famed for keeping every sail to the wind and making record-breaking trips, and since the mate, William Purdu, had the same inclination and was too deaf to hear the warnings given by a change of wind, it was never dull:

> Night clouds racing overhead, wind howling, royals set, and the ship rushing on in the dark, an immense white sheet of foam level with the lee rail. Mr P——, in charge of the deck, hooked on to the windward mizzen rigging in a state of perfect serenity; myself, the third mate, also hooked on somewhere to windward of the slanting poop, in a state of utmost preparedness to jump at the very first hint of some sort of order. . . . Suddenly, out of the companion would appear a tall, dark figure, bareheaded, with a short white beard of a perpendicular cut, very visible in the dark—Captain S——, disturbed in his reading below by the frightful bounding and lurching of the ship.
>
> "By Heavens, Mr P——! I used to carry sail in my time, but——." (MS pp. 40–41)

Later in the voyage the second mate was taken ill, and Conrad became an "officer of the watch" with periods in charge of the deck, so that "the immense leverage of the ship's tall masts became a matter very near my own heart." One night, in a sudden shift of wind, he nearly lost them. Although there was enough noise on the deck "to wake the dead," Captain Stuart did not leave his cabin, but Conrad was called there when he came off duty and found him lying on his couch wrapped up in a rug with a pillow under his head:

"What was the matter with you up there just now?"

"Wind flew round on the lee quarter, sir."

"Couldn't you see the shift coming?"

"Yes, sir, I thought it wasn't very far off."

"Why didn't you have your courses hauled up at once, then?"

"Well, sir, she was doing eleven knots very nicely, and I thought she would do for another half-hour or so."

"Ah, yes, another half-hour. That's the way ships get dismasted." (MS pp. 43–44)

Whether or not, at this time, Conrad's English idiom had the perfection of these memoirs written in 1908, he must have had an amazingly retentive ear. Soon after leaving the sea he would be writing page after page of authentic dialogue for the seamen in the forecastle of the *Narcissus*, and few native English writers have captured so well certain forms of working-class humor. His pronunciation would always be stranger than he himself could realize, but he seems to have applied himself to becoming an Englishman with a kind of passion that made him lose all interest in Poland: not until late in life, captivated by the young Polish diplomat, Joseph Retinger, would he begin, reluctantly, to reconsider his roots.

With so much sail on the tall spars of the *Loch Etive*, Conrad's second voyage to Sydney took fifteen days less than the first. He passed his twenty-third birthday in Australia and left on January 11, 1881. There were seven new men in the crew, since five had left, and two were in a Sydney jail (SY p. 117).

Because of the prevailing winds it was the usual practice for ships to sail out round the bottom of South Africa and go home via the bottom of South America, stopping nowhere between London and Sydney, Sydney and London, traversing the whole earth and seeing nothing but the sea. On this journey, as they were crossing the Pacific they came upon an American whaler such as the one on which Herman Melville might have sailed some forty years before. The fur-capped crew had been two years at sea and caught three whales. The *Loch Etive* passed them a belated "Christmas present" of all her old newspapers and some figs (LE p. 33). Life on a whaler, lost for years like an albatross on the vast Pacific, evidently appealed to Conrad's imagination, and a little later, in his letters, he would begin to talk of a whaling venture.

He left the ship when she reached London on April 24, for he had had enough of Sydney, and longed for some more exotic part of the world. He was going to pay a great price to get there, and would make of it one of his best stories—"Youth." As Marlow says at the beginning of that story: "Bankok. I thrilled. I had been six years at sea, but had only seen Melbourne and Sydney, very good places, charming places in their way—but Bankok!" (p. 6).

5. Bound for Bangkok

Bangkok!—or thereabouts: but how to get there? After a month in London without success, Conrad was given the idea of going to Deal, where the roadstead was a favorite place for foreign ships to anchor on their way through the Channel. There, early in June 1881, he went on board the *Annie Frost*, a British-owned vessel that traded between Le Havre and that part of Vietnam then known as Cochin China. He was to be third mate on her next outward journey, after she had been to Le Havre and then London. However, in setting out for London, the ship collided with a lock in the basin at Le Havre. Conrad was thrown into the water, and had to be left behind for treatment. He presumably lost his luggage in the process, as he wrote to his uncle asking for ten pounds to replace it.*

Back in London, after a few more weeks he found work as second mate on the *Palestine*, a small and ancient ship, long laid up at Tilbury, which was to be brought out to carry a load of coal from Newcastle to Bangkok. In "Youth" he calls her the *Judea*, and he says, "You may imagine her state. She was all rust, dust and grime—soot aloft, dirt on the deck. She was about four hundred tons, had a primitive windlass, wooden latches to the doors, not a bit of brass about her, and a big square stern" (p. 5). For Captain Beard, aged fifty-seven, it

* The suggestion by Baines that Conrad invented the whole incident to get money from his uncle (JB p. 69) seems unlikely for the reasons given by Allen (SY pp. 151–153).

was his first command, while the only other officer, Mahon, was fifty (SY p. 318). In the story, to heighten the effect of "youth," Conrad uses their actual names, but makes them even older, and the narrator, Marlow, a little younger than himself, so that he is "like a small boy between two grand-fathers." Conrad was at this time twenty-three, but he would be twenty-five before the voyage was over.

The *Palestine* set off for Newcastle on September 21, 1881, but there were gales in the North Sea and it took three weeks to reach North Shields, where five of the ship's seven seamen walked off. Having missed her turn for loading, she was six weeks in Newcastle, and left with a new crew on November 29. After passing through the Channel she ran into rough weather, and leaked so badly that only perpetual pumping kept her afloat, but Conrad was young, and apparently enjoy-ing it—"I would not have given up the experience for worlds. I had moments of exultation. Whenever the old dismantled craft pitched heavily with her counter high in the air, she seemed to throw up, like an appeal, like a defiance, like a cry to the clouds without mercy, the words written on her stern '*Judea*, London. Do or Die' " (HD p. 12).

The men, less romantic, insisted on a return to Falmouth, where they walked out. A new crew was found, but extensive repairs were needed, which involved unloading the coal, and took nearly nine months. The men vanished again, but Conrad was determined to get to Bangkok. He had a few days leave in London—"I went to a music hall, I believe, lunched, dined, and supped in a swell place in Regent Street, and was back to time, with nothing but a complete set of Byron's works and a new railway rug to show for three months work" (HD p. 16).

According to the story, the ship was infested with rats, but on a moonlit night, after the repairs were completed and the coal reloaded from the hulk, "rat after rat appeared on the rail, took a last look over his shoulder, and leaped with a hol-low thud into the empty hulk. We tried to count them but soon lost the tale. Mahon said: 'Well, well! Don't talk to me about the intelligence of rats' " (HD p. 17).

In mid-September of 1882, a year after first leaving Lon-don, the *Palestine* set off again: "We had fair breezes, smooth water right into the tropics, and the old *Judea* lumbered along in the sunshine, mostly at the rate of three miles an hour."

She crept round the Cape and sweltered across the Indian Ocean until, after six months at sea, while sailing between Java and Sumatra, the six hundred tons of long-suffering coal in her hold began to show signs of spontaneous combustion. The smoke and heat increased, and on the following day water was poured into the hold, and four tons were thrown overboard. Smoke still poured out, and the next day the deck over the hold blew out.

The crew caught the attention of a passing steamer, which tried to tow the ship to the nearest beach on the coast of Sumatra, but the fire grew too rapidly, and they had to take to the boats and make for Muntok, a small harbor on an offshore island. These details come from the subsequent official investigation, and at this point diverge from Conrad's story, in which he makes the fire occur in the middle of the Indian Ocean, followed by some heroics on the part of the ship's commander and days of suffering in open boats. When, many years later, his youthful disciple Richard Curle started the fashion for ferreting out his sources and reported the facts, Conrad was rather angry that such things should be "exposed for any fool to comment upon or even for average minds to be disappointed with" (Curle, *Letters* p. 89).

A week later the steamship *Sissie* called in to take the crew on to Singapore, where the officers had their certificates taken away pending a court of enquiry. It provided Conrad with experience that he would use in *Lord Jim*, but in this case there was no drama: the report concluded "that the vessel was not prematurely abandoned and that no blame is attached to the master, officers, or crew. The officer's certificates are therefore returned" (SY pp. 157–159).

Conrad was stranded for a month in Singapore, the first of three long spells in that city. It is the only Asian port with which he became at all familiar, and provides the scene for several stories, including much of *Lord Jim* and most notably *The End of the Tether*, where Captain Whalley wanders through it, recalling its history, and incidentally following the path that Conrad often walked between the Harbour and the Officer's Sailors Home (ES p. 177). At this time the port was developing rapidly and filling up with the Chinese immigrants who would eventually form the bulk of the population. Near the docks were Emerson's Tiffin Rooms, where one could see such adventurers as William Lingard and John Dill Ross, on whose legends Conrad would base the "Tom Lingard" of his Malayan novels; the ship's chandlers, McAlister and Company, who employed Williams as a "water clerk"; and the Harbour Office ruled by Captain Henry Ellis, "the deputy Neptune of the circumambient seas," who appears as "Elliott" in *Lord Jim* and *The End of the Tether,* and under his real name in *The Shadow Line.*

A common sight was that of pilgrims boarding ships for Mecca, which for Conrad would be linked with his glimpse of Williams, once first officer on such a ship—"they streamed in with a continuous tramp and shuffle of bare feet, without a word, a murmur, or a look back; and when clear of the confining rails spread on all sides over the deck, flowed forward and aft, overflowed down the yawning hatchways, filled the inner recesses of the ship—like water flowing into crevices and crannies, like water rising silently even with the rim" (LJ p. 14).

We do not know how Conrad dealt with his loneliness in Singapore, except for one hint in *Victory,* in which Lena is imprisoned in a ladies' orchestra run by a German who calls himself "Zangiacomo." In the book Conrad puts them in Surabaya, a place he had never seen, but apparently there was such an establishment in Singapore—"the celebrated Tingel Tangel," run by an Austrian, in which the girls were Austrians and Poles. They "played in a string band and danced for the guests wearing white muslin frocks and blue sashes," and after each piece they were expected to mingle with the men and encourage them to order drinks (ES pp. 244–255). This is exactly the scene in which, in *Victory,* Heyst is overcome with compassion for Lena, and it is not difficult to imagine the lonely and romantic young exile being moved by the plight of some pale Polish girl trapped in the Tingel Tangel. Perhaps, like Heyst, Conrad rose from his bed to wrestle with "the obscure desires that move our conduct," and long after, let his imagination take the course that he had thought better of.

At the beginning of May 1883, Conrad returned to London as a passenger on a Spanish steamship, giving him his first glimpse of Aden and the Suez Canal. His friend Adolf Krieger had now married and moved to Stoke Newington, and this was where, over the next few years, Conrad would stay when in London (SD p. 83). Krieger corresponded with Conrad's uncle, and the allowance was paid through him. The two friends would subsequently quarrel over money lent to Conrad at the time of his marriage, and Sherry suggests, from hints of an external resemblance, that Conrad had the last word by making Krieger the model for his piglike Verloc in *The Secret Agent* (WS p. 328).

It was now five years since Tadeusz Bobrowski had seen his nephew, but he was naturally reluctant to invite him into the web of the Russian spider until he had become a British citizen. Conrad does not seem to have been in any hurry to apply for naturalization, but he volunteered to come to Kraków (SD p. 101). However, as Tadeusz' doctor had advised him to "take the waters" at the Bohemian spa of Marienbad, uncle and nephew arranged to meet there in July 1883.

Tadeusz must have been pleased with Conrad's perseverance, though he still regarded him as foolhardy, and had urged him to abandon the *Palestine* long before it reached Bangkok—"both Captain Beard and you strike me as desperate men who would go out of the way to see knocks and wounds, while your ship-owner is a rascal who risks the lives of ten brave men for the sake of a black-guardly profit" (NP p. 81). When they met, it seems that they got on together as never before. Conrad stayed a month, during which they moved on to Teplitz, where they met other Polish relatives. On his way home, Conrad wrote to his uncle from Dresden, and found a reply waiting in London : "Your letter from Dresden gave me real pleasure. . . . You were right in thinking that back in Teplitz I felt unhappy and depressed when I sat down to table, and lonely over my evening tea when I saw my Admiral's seat empty" (SD p. 102).

Soon after his return Conrad found employment with the *Riversdale*, a sailing ship of fifteen hundred tons with a crew of twenty-three. He would be second mate, at five guineas a month, contracted to wander the world for three years or more in search of profitable cargoes. The agreement read :

London to Algoa Bay & any ports and places in the Cape, Australian and New Zealand Colonies, India, China, Japanese & Red Seas and Straits and Persian

Gulf, North and South Pacific & Atlantic Oceans, United States of America between Portland and Galveston inclusive, West Coast of America and islands adjacent, West Indies and Mediterranean Sea to and fro for any period not exceeding three years and back to the port of final discharge in the United Kingdom or Continent of Europe between the Elbe & Brest (SY pp. 161–162).

In its odd combination of legal precision and geographical generalities the agreement conveys well enough the atmosphere of the merchant service, and its complete indifference to the claims of family life. Conrad was not destined to fulfil much of this great program of potential "to and fro," as he quarrelled with the captain. It seems that the latter had his family on board, as the crew-list includes his twelve-year-old son, who was paid a shilling a month as "second boy." The *Ferndale* in Conrad's novel *Chance* may reflect the *Riversdale*, and in this book a young officer refers to captains' wives—they "could work a lot of mischief on board ship if they happened to take a dislike to anyone. . . . They were like an extra chief mate of a particularly sharp and unfeeling sort who made his report in the evening" (p. 28).

When the ship reached Madras they took their quarrel to court, where the captain accused Conrad of being asleep on watch, and Conrad accused the captain of being drunk. It ended with an apology from Conrad, who agreed to pay sixty rupees as compensation for leaving the ship (Karl, p. 217*n*.). The captain then went on to run the *Riversdale* aground a little farther up the coast, and after eventual repairs, she was sold to a Hindhu (SY p. 163). In later years Conrad would entertain his friends with tales of her drunken captain.

Conrad crossed the subcontinent by rail to Bombay, and there, while he watched from the verandah of the Sailor's Home, there sailed into the harbor a ship "with all the graces of a yacht," the *Narcissus*, which was to provide the title and the frame for his first story of the sea. She had left England without a second mate, and Conrad was able to sign on at once for the homeward journey. He told Aubry that "the voyage of the *Narcissus* was performed from Bombay to London in the manner I have described," and that "most of the personages I have portrayed actually belonged to the crew of the real *Nar-*

cissus, including the admirable Singleton (whose real name was Sullivan), Archie, Belfast and Donkin" (SD p. 104). However the crew-list does not include a Sullivan, and as the story is told from the point of view of the men in the forecastle, it must have been based largely on Conrad's earlier experience, notably in the *Duke of Sutherland,* the only oceangoing ship in which he served as an ordinary seaman.

From the moment when he first comes aboard and involuntarily calls the whole ship's company to attention by crying out his name, the dark hero, Wait, dominates the fictional voyage of the *Narcissus.* It seems that here Conrad was heightening and interpreting rather than entirely inventing, for the *Narcissus* did have a black on board, who died on the voyage. He was Joseph Barron, aged thirty-five, who signed his agreement with a cross, and gave his place of origin as "Charlton." The only place of that name with a Negro population was Charlton County, Georgia, in the Okefenokee Swamp area near Jacksonville, Florida (SY p. 165). At the time of his birth in 1849, Barron would have been a slave. In the book he is given the more significant name of "Wait," after the West Indian who had been on the roll of the *Duke of Sutherland,* but his attitudes, as Conrad portrays them, are those of an American black rather than of a West Indian.

The *Narcissus* made the difficult westerly passage round the Cape of Good Hope in the autumn months, but nothing in the ship's log suggests disasters on the scale of Conrad's story. He told Aubry that the "Nigger" died just after the gale as described in the book (SD p. 104), but Barron's actual death is recorded as being on September 24, when the ship would have been much farther north.

The *Narcissus* did not, as in the book, or in Conrad's conversation with Aubry, sail into London, but ended her voyage at Dunkirk in October. The captain wrote on the back of Conrad's certificate of discharge: "I can recommend him to any Ship Master requiring his services as being a good and sober officer and should take him as Chief Officer if he should succeed in passing" (SY p. 170). To "succeed in passing" as a qualified chief officer would be Conrad's next task, and not an easy one.

In one attempt, in the written part of the test he accidentally put *W* for "West" instead of *E* at the end of a page of calculations, "but in consideration, I believe, of all my other answers being correct I was handed that azimuth paper back by the examiner's assistant, with the calm remark, 'You have fifteen minutes yet' " (LE p. 41). On the oral test, however, it seemed that as on a previous occasion the examiner had some deep distrust of this tense young man with his alien accent, and took him on a spectacular spiritual circumnavigation of the world, inventing ever-new hazards and disasters to be dealt with until Conrad finally gave the ship up as lost:

> "Nothing more to do, eh?"
> "No, sir. I could do no more."
> He gave a bitter laugh.
> "You could always say your prayers." (PR p. 116)

It was only at a second attempt, on December 3, 1884, that he passed, and even then it was some time before he found a berth, perhaps because he did not wish to go to Australia again, or "go into steam." On April 24, 1885, he signed on, still only as second mate, with the *Tilkhurst*, another full-rigged ship of about fifteen hundred tons, for a trip to the Far East. She sailed from Hull to pick up a load of coal at Penarth Docks, near Cardiff, and waited there for nearly a month.

This layover gave Conrad the chance to fulfil a promise he had made, on an earlier voyage, to a Polish sailor called Komorowski, who had stowed away on a German ship to escape service in the Russian Army and on arriving at Cardiff, had been helped by a Polish watchmaker called Klisewski. Conrad had been asked by Komorowski to repay a small sum of money (SD p. 105). Klisewski had fled to Britain after an earlier struggle for Polish independence, in 1830–1831. Conrad was given a warm welcome, and he made friends with one of Klisewski's sons, Spiridion, who was a little older than himself; they would correspond for some years.

Leaving Cardiff on June 10, the *Tilkhurst* made an apparently uneventful voyage, entirely on the open sea, to Singapore, and stayed there for nearly a month. One of her crew subsequently reported that Conrad, though a satisfactory seaman, was "a queer fellow for books" (SY p. 173). Conrad had written to Spiridion, beginning with "Dear Sir" and going on to say, "This globe accomplished almost half a revolution since I parted from you on the station at Cardiff: and old Father Time, always diligent in his business, has put his eraser over many men, things and memories: yet I defy him to obliterate ever from my mind and heart the recollection of the kindness you and yours have shown to a stranger, on the strength of a distant national connection" (LL 1, pp. 79–80). It was at about this time that, having seen his name misspelled in the registers of almost every British ship on which he had sailed, Józef Teodor Konrad Korzeniowski decided to use his third baptismal name, and wrote as "Mr J. Conrad, 2nd Mate, Ship Tilkhurst." He was not yet a British citizen, but to Klisewski he said, "I understand and readily accepted your reference to 'Home.' When speaking, writing or thinking in English, the word 'home' always means for me the hospitable shores of Great Britain" (LL 1, p. 81).

In another letter two weeks later he said, "Events are casting shadows, more or less distorted, shadows deep enough to suggest the lurid light of battlefields somewhere in the near future, but all these portents of great and decisive doings leave me in a state of despairing indifference: for whatever may be the changes of fortunes of living nations, for the dead there is no hope and no salvation" (LL 1, p. 81). He may have been embarrassed by the fervent patriotism of the elder Klisewski and evidently prefers to think of Polish hopes as something quite "dead."

These were probably his first extended letters in English— at least no earlier ones have survived. Coming seven years after his embarkation on the *Mavis* and four years before the beginning of his first novel, they show his taste for pessimistic philosophizing, and give hints of the style he would bring to his early books, with its long swell and overloaded syntax, as well as such favorite adjectives as "lurid" and "sombre." He was at this time very confident in his conservative opinions, and spoke of socialists as "disreputable ragamuffins" with "infernal doctrines born in continental back-slums" which must lead to "robbery, equality, anarchy and misery under the iron rule of a military despotism" (p. 84).

After a month at Singapore the *Tilkhurst* took on a cargo for Calcutta. One of the crew, who had been hit on the head in a brawl, became delirious, and on the night of the ninth day at sea he disappeared overboard (SY p. 172), but Conrad apparently never referred to this incident. The ship waited a further seven weeks at Calcutta, where Conrad passed his twenty-eighth birthday. Although he saw more of India than of some of the other places of which he wrote, he never used it as the background for any of his fiction, presumably because he feared to compete with writers such as Rudyard Kipling, who had lived there.

Conrad was now possessed with the idea of starting up in the whaling business and wrote to Klisewski that he was "brimful of exhaustive information on the subject. I have read, studied, pumped professional men and imbibed knowledge upon whale fishing and searching for the last four years." He had the promise of help from a man with experience, and the chance to buy a ship—all he needed was £1500, and he wondered whether he could borrow this on the security of taking out life insurance. Klisewski was not in favor of the idea, and Conrad seems soon to have forgotten it (LL 1, p. 79).

He came to have a great respect for the master of the *Tilkhurst*, Edwin John Blake—"short, stout, dignified, perhaps a little pompous, he was a man of singularly well-informed mind" (MS p. 9). In his younger days Blake had commanded a ship called the *Apse Family*, which was apparently the only choice of name left to the collective imagination of the firm of Apse and Sons after they had launched the *Lucy Apse*, the *Harold Apse*, the *Anne Apse* and the *John Apse*. This ship had the reputation of killing someone on every voyage, and what he heard of it from Blake, Conrad would later use for a potboiling story called "The Brute," collected in *A Set of Six*, in the Author's Note of which he refers to its source. When the *Tilkhurst* reached Dundee in June 1886, Blake asked Conrad of his plans. On being told by Conrad that as he now had just enough service, he was going to sit for his master's certificate, Blake "pronounced the memorable words: 'If you happen to be in want of employment, remember that as long as I have a ship you have a ship, too' " (MS p. 9). Conrad took the test at the end of July, but failed a paper on "The Day's Work," and possibly on arithmetic as well, so that he would have to sit again later in the year (Karl, p. 232).

He was also about to become a British citizen, and he completed the formalities on August 19, 1886. Tadeusz was greatly pleased—"I embrace wholeheartedly my Britisher and nephew" (NP p. 110). Conrad was an Englishman, and an Anglophile, with an amazing grasp of the language, but he had seen very little of England: most of his few months in the country had been spent lodging in the East End and tramping round shipping offices. The feeling of London, after coming off a ship, is conveyed in several of his early stories, notably the conclusion of "Karain," and always with something near to horror.

Sometime during this year there was another small event that was perhaps more significant than Conrad's becoming either an Englishman or a master mariner—he submitted his first piece of writing to an editor. The weekly paper *Tit-Bits* encouraged contributions from its readers, and in May 1886 it had announced a "Special Prize for Sailors." Although Conrad was still at sea at the time, he may have seen it on his return in June and it is probable that he did send something.

In 1908, when he was fifty and very hard up, he wrote a rather silly story for the *London Magazine* called "The Black Mate," about a ship's officer who dyed his hair to conceal his age, an idea suggested by his wife. Conrad obviously felt rather ashamed of it, and "on one of his naughty days," as his wife put it, he gave it out that it had been written for a *Tit-Bits* competition in 1886 (Mégroz p. 88). This is not convincing, as the story's easy and jocular style belongs very much to his later period, when he had become rather too much at home with the language. He repeated this claim in a letter to his agent as grounds for believing "that there will be nothing actually disgraceful in its inclusion in my collected editions" (LL 2, p. 264), but in the end he left it out. It can now be found in *Tales of Hearsay*, published after his death. As Conrad's "art" usually has some basis of fact at the bottom of it, it seems reasonable to presume that he did send something to *Tit-Bits* in 1886, but it was probably more primitive, and more serious, than "The Black Mate."

In November he tried again, this time successfully, for his master's certificate. His oral examiner was more relaxed than on previous occasions, and Conrad more assured. They talked about Poland, and he was advised to change to steam if he wanted to "get on"—"You will go into steam presently. Everybody goes into steam" (PR p. 117). Conrad never did, which further reduced his slim chance of obtaining a command. No doubt there was something about the silence and slow tempo of sailing ships that was essential to the maturing of his mind. Had he been tempted to "go into steam" in the interests of "getting on," it may be that, with his nautical ambitions satisfied, and his inner voices drowned by the clatter, he might have taken longer to recognize his true vocation.

6. *Into the Conrad Country*

At the end of 1886, Conrad, now twenty-nine, found a berth as a senior officer. He was to be first mate of the *Highland Forest*, an iron-hulled sailing ship of 1040 tons, built and owned by Scotsmen, but engaged in trade between Holland and the Dutch East Indies. That winter was one of record cold, and when he joined the ship at Amsterdam in January 1887 she was frozen in the harbor, with her cargo still frozen somewhere inland. The rest of the crew were on leave, and Conrad had orders to get things moving as quickly as possible.

He lived for a month in his little cabin, looking out on a frosty wasteland with only a Dutch caretaker to tend an inadequate stove. Each day he made a long tram-car journey into the city, the horses "painfully glistening with icicles," to sit in a warm cafe and write reports to the owners, or try to chivvy the ship's Dutch charterer, Hudig. "He was a big swarthy Netherlander, with black moustaches and a bold glance. He always began by shoving me into a chair before I had time to open my mouth, gave me cordially a large cigar, and in excellent English would start to talk everlastingly about the phenomenal severity of the weather. . . . His office was so warm, his fire so bright, his sides shook so heartily with laughter, that I experienced always a great difficulty in reaching for my hat" (MS pp. 48–51). It was not time wasted, for this is the character whom Conrad, in his first two novels, will transfer to a cool and lofty warehouse in the

47

tropics as the employer of both Almayer and the outcast Willems.

With a thaw in February, the cargo came in a flood, and Conrad had to supervise the loading of it. The distribution of the weight in a sailing ship critically affects its handling qualities: if the cargo is put too low the ship becomes excessively stable, rolling back violently every time the water rocks it sideways. When the captain arrived and saw how Conrad had done it, "a sort of smiling vexation was visible on his face," and he said, "Well, we shall have a lively time of it."

A lively time they had, as they ran into gales on the way south towards the Cape, and "neither before nor since have I felt a ship roll so abruptly, so violently, so heavily . . . she rolled and rolled with an awful dislodging jerk. . . . It was a wonder men sent aloft were not flung off the yards, the yards not flung off the masts, the masts not flung overboard." Conrad calls it "only poetic justice" when finally the rolling dislodged a spar which hit him in the back and "sent him sliding on his face for quite a considerable distance along the main deck." This spinal injury gave him "inexplicable periods of powerlessness, sudden acesses of mysterious pain" (MS pp. 53–55). In *Lord Jim*, the hero is made to suffer a similar injury, and there Conrad gives a more dramatic account of the demoralizing terror that a spinal injury can cause. Jim lies "dazed, battered, hopeless and tormented as if at the bottom of an abyss of unrest" and the "unintelligent brutality of an existence liable to the agony of such sensations filled him with a despairing desire to escape at any cost" (p. 11).

When the ship reached Samarang, in Java, on June 20, 1887, Conrad was examined by a Dutch doctor who said, "Ah, friend, you are young yet; it may be very serious for your whole life. You must leave your ship; you must quite silent be for three months—quite silent" (MS p. 55). Conrad was taken on to Singapore on the ship *Celestial*, whose chief mate, Brooksbank, would become one of his closest acquaintances in the East (SY p. 183).

At Singapore he went into the European Hospital, which was subsequently extended into what is now the city's General Hospital, and this experience also is described in *Lord Jim:* "The hospital stood on a hill, and a gentle breeze entering through the windows, always flung wide open, brought into the bare room the softness of the sky, the languor of the earth, the bewitching breath of Eastern waters. There were perfumes in it, suggestive of infinite repose, the gift of endless dreams." In the novel, these successive experiences of the malevolence of the open sea, the persuasive nihilism of spinal agony, and the perfumed languor of the tropics are presented as the preliminaries to that ultimate demoralization that overtakes Jim on the decks of the *Patna*. With Conrad the effect, though it may have been parallel and, as it were, emotionally equivalent to Jim's experience, seems to have been to bring nearer to the surface a less reposeful gift of dreams—his vocation as a writer.

After six weeks he moved to the Officer's Sailors Home (SY pp. 183), which he describes in *The Shadow Line* as "a large bungalow with a wide verandah and a curiously suburban-looking little garden of bushes and a few trees between it and the street" (p. 8). It was administered by the Harbour Office to provide inexpensive accommodation for stranded officers, under the charge of a "chief steward," an "unhappy wizened looking little man" whom Conrad seems to have found extremely unsympathetic.

In *Lord Jim*, as the hero's condition improves, he is able to walk into the city and associate with other seamen, whom he finds to be of two kinds: the few, who "led mysterious lives, had preserved an undefaced energy with the temper of buccaneers and the eyes of dreamers"; and the majority, who are too lazy for cooler climes, who loved "short passages, good deck-chairs, large native crews, and the distinction of being white" (p. 13). At first repelled by these men, Jim begins to envy "their appearance of doing so well on such a small allowance of danger and toil," and gives up the idea of going home. Conrad also gave up the idea, but probably more from a desire for romance and an interest in those other men "with undefaced energy and the temper of buccaneers" who "appeared to live in a crazy maze of plans, hopes, dangers, enterprises, ahead of civilization in the dark places of the sea." He would enlist on a ship that followed in the tracks of one of them, William Lingard, who had started trading from Singapore forty years before, and established his own small posts along the wild eastern coast of Borneo. Conrad's interest in the Lingard legend had probably been aroused by his friend Brooksbank of the *Celestial*, who had married Lingard's daughter (ES pp. 27–28, 317).

The ship, which, under "the eternal peace of the Eastern sea and sky," was to bring Conrad so much raw material for his writing as well as the benefits of "short passages, good deck chairs and large native crews" was not the *Patna*—though a ship of this name did frequent Singapore at the time (ES p. 45)—but the *Vidar*, a trim little schooner-rigged steamer of three hundred tons, built at Newcastle in 1871, and mainly owned by an elderly Arab. The captain, James Craig, then thirty-three, had also a share in the ownership. After his retirement to England in 1924, Craig told Aubry, "The first time I met Conrad was at the Shipping Office of Singapore about the middle of August 1887. He pleased me at once by his manners, which were distinguished and reserved. One of the first things that he told me was that he was a foreigner by birth, which I had already guessed from his accent. I replied that that did not matter in the least as he had his certificate. (It was quite difficult at that time to find officers in the East who were not over fond of the bottle.)" (SD p. 119).

In *The Shadow Line* Conrad uses the actual name, slightly misspelled, of the second engineer on the *Vidar*, John Nieven, so he is probably describing the actual man when he speaks of "a sturdy young Scot, with a smooth face and light eyes who was a fierce misogynist." The other white man on the ship, the chief engineer, was "young, too, but very thin, and with a mist of fluffy brown beard all round his haggard face. All day-long, at sea, or in harbour, he could be seen walking hastily up and down the after-deck, wearing an intense, spiritually rapt expression, which was caused by the consciousness of unpleasant physical sensations in his internal economy. For he was a confirmed dyspeptic" (p. 6). As well as the four white men, the little ship carried a Chinese engineer, a Malay *serang*, or boatswain, eleven Malays in the crew, and eighty-two Chinese for loading and unloading the cargo (SY p. 318).

Straddling the equator and filtering the vital passage between the Indian Ocean and the Pacific, the islands amongst

50

which the *Vidar* sailed had collected a varied flotsam of races and cultures, and because of their potential wealth and strategic position, were the object of rivalry between the British and the Dutch, both of them in conflict with more ancient Arab interests. In the fifth and sixth centuries, Indian traders and missionaries had brought Hinduism and courtly customs to the area, and had left a continuing concern with lineage and caste; but from the thirteenth century onwards, Islam had been the dominant influence, and was the religion of all but the more primitive tribes in the interior.

The great island of Borneo was the wildest and least developed area, the Dutch being securely settled only at the southern tip, while Brooke, the British "White Rajah," controlled the little state of Sarawak in the northwest. The eastern coast had been settled by Malayan nomads, many of them seagoing tribes that lived more by pillage and piracy than by cultivation. The Dutch patrolled this coast with occasional gunboats, but it has remained a haunt of pirates up till the present time. This is the area that Conrad would annex as his own particular literary province.

From Singapore, the *Vidar* sailed southeast into the Java Sea, where her first regular call was at Banjarmasin on the southern tip of Borneo. She then stopped at the coaling station of Kota Baru on an island off the southeast coast, which probably contributed to the picture of Heyst, on his island outpost of the Tropical Belt Coal Company in *Victory*. The ship then sailed across the Macassar Straits to Donggala on the Celebes, recrossed the straits to Samarinda, on the eastern side of Borneo, and continued northwards to trading stations at Berau and Bulungan, where her officers were probably the only white visitors.

The more important of the two stations was Berau (now called Tanjungredeb), a large settlement about forty miles up the river of the same name, where a Dutchman, Charles Olmeyer, was building his "folly," the big Malayan house that would be the first resting place of Conrad's literary imagination. This settlement also provides the scenery for "Patusan," where Jim would exercise his lordship. In his stories Conrad gave it the air of being more secret and uncharted than it really was, and he never disclosed its whereabouts. Its rediscovery by the explorers of his sources makes a story almost as strange and romantic as those he wrote about it.

Soon after Conrad's death in 1924, Aubry had an interview with Craig, the former captain of the *Vidar*, who through some slip of memory, or lack of familiarity with Conrad's books, identified the place with Bulungan (now renamed Tanjungselor), a smaller settlement further north that the *Vidar* had sometimes visited (LL 1, p. 94), and this put investigators off the trail for a generation or more.

There remained, however, hidden clues in Conrad's first two books, in which not only is the river called the "Pantai," which had been its name on the earliest charts, but also in the original manuscript of *Almayer's Folly*, Conrad had used an anglicized form of the name Berau. He changed it to "Sambir" before publication, but accidentally left "Brow" on what is now page 42 of the collected edition, where it still remains. The significance of this was realized, too late, by the American scholar John Dozier Gordan, who in research for a thesis on Conrad's early books, visited Tanjungselor in 1939 only to discover that it was not the place, and was unable to extend his trip to Tanjungredeb. He did, however, manage to interview a daughter and son-in-law of Olmeyer in Java, and so provide the first accurate information on the background of the books.

Before this, an English businessman and Conrad reader, F. Harold Gray, had accidentally come upon "Brow" in a trip from the Philippines, and made the identification in a journal published in Sarawak in 1937. This was pursued by J. G. Reed, a doctor working in Sarawak, but in 1941 the Japanese occupation served to protect Conrad's secrets for another four years. The Japanese imprisoned Reed, with a kind of poetic justice, at Muntok, where Richard Curle had provoked Conrad's first curse on those who exposed such things "for any fool to comment upon or even for average minds to be disappointed with" (MS p. 39). After the war Reed's health was ruined, but he spent the last years of his life collecting material on Tanjungredeb that was published by Jerry Allen in 1962.

In Conrad's day it was a large but comparatively recent settlement founded by seagoing Malayan nomads about thirty-five miles from the coast, at the point where two smaller rivers join to form the River Pantai or Berau, which goes on to become a great island-filled estuary. The settlement was divided into two sultanates with rival stockades, but the characters and politics with which Conrad filled it came from his reading of books about Malaya, for, as he said in a letter to Dent in 1917, "I knew very little of and about shore people. I was chief mate of the SS. *Vidar* and very busy whenever in harbour" (LL 2, p. 186). He particularly liked A. R. Wallace's *The Malay Archipelago*, which became his favorite bedside book. Wallace, who was there from 1854 to 1862, had shared with Darwin the discovery of natural selection, and probably contributed to Conrad's picture of Stein in *Lord Jim*.

William Lingard, the trader from Singapore, had given his name to a particular short-cut through the estuary, not suitable for steamships, but marked on Dutch maps of the time as *Baak van Lingard*, and this obviously supplied the inspiration for Conrad's plot in *An Outcast of the Islands*. Almayer, more correctly William Charles Olmeyer—Conrad probably never saw the name in writing—was related to Lingard by marriage, and acted as his agent in Berau until later Lingard established there his own nephew, Jim Lingard. In Conrad's time, Lingard had retired, but Jim had settled there, marrying the daughter of a Dyak chief, and was known as "Tuan Jim." Conrad translates this as "Lord," but it was a common term of respect such as might be bestowed upon any white man. None of the Europeans in Berau attempted any kind of "lordship" over the local population, and this aspect of Jim's career Conrad took from the exploits of Rajah Brooke in Sarawak.

The *Vidar* brought from Singapore manufactured goods such as pottery and returned with gutta percha, rattans, pearl shells, beeswax, dammar and Chinese delicacies such as bird's nests and sea-cucumbers (SY p. 185). In *A Personal Record* Conrad says that on his first trip they took on board at Donggala a donkey ordered by Almayer. Then recrossing the Straits of Macassar to Samarinda, they steamed north towards the entrance to Berau, of which he gives a picture in *Lord Jim*:

The coast of Patusan is straight and sombre, and faces a misty ocean. Red trails are seen like cataracts of rust streaming under the dark green foliage of bushes and creepers clothing the low cliffs. Swampy plains open out at the mouth of rivers, with a view of jagged blue peaks beyond the vast forests. In the offing a chain of islands, dark crumbling shapes, stand out in the everlasting sun-lit haze like the remnants of a wall breached by the sea. (p. 242)

In *An Outcast of the Islands* we see Lingard sailing up the river past populated clearings with reed dwellings built over the water, and "lonely stretches of sparkling brown water bordered by the dense and silent forest." There are "heavy scents of blossoms and black earth," creeks that are "black, smooth, tortuous—like byways of despair" and troops of monkeys that "profaned the quiet spots with capricious gam-bols and insane gestures of inhuman madness" (pp. 201–202). Lingard is described as loving it all with a great pos-sessive love, but Conrad's images rather suggest that he hated it, and it is Willems, in the same story, whose attitude seems nearer to that of the author—"baffled, repelled, almost frightened by the intensity of that tropical life which wants sunshine but works in gloom; which seems to be all grace of colour and form, all brilliance, all smiles, but is only the blossoming of the dead; whose mystery holds the promise of joy and beauty, yet contains nothing but poison and decay" (p. 70).

As one approached the settlement, an unusual hill forma-tion was visible behind it, fully described in *Lord Jim*—"two steep hills very close together, and separated by what looks like a deep fissure, the cleavage of some mighty stroke," and behind it the moon rises "as if escaping from a yawning grave." This may have symbolic reference to Jim's condition, and it also becomes the "historic hill" on which he defeats Sherif Ali, but it seems that, as so often with Conrad's sym-bolism, it is not pure invention, but the use of something branded on the memory, for behind Tanjungredeb there stands such a hill (SY p. 189).

On Conrad's first visit, it was early morning when the *Vidar* came alongside the landing stage, and he describes his first glimpse of Almayer, come to look for his donkey : "he was clad simply in flapping pyjamas of cretonne pattern (enormous flowers with yellow petals on a disagreeable blue ground) and a thin cotton singlet with short sleeves. His arms, bare to the elbow, were crossed on his chest. His black hair looked as if it had not been cut for a very long time, and a curly wisp of it strayed across his forehead" (PR p. 75). This was not the way for a white man to appear in public in the nineteenth century, and Conrad seems to take it as license to present him as a very much more disreputable character than he really was. He did not suffer the multiple misfortunes of his fictional counterpart: his wife was not a savage, but Johanna van Lieshout, an Eurasian of good family; his son became a well-to-do trader, and his daughters, educated in Surabaya, made good marriages. He retired to Surabaya and died there in 1900, six years after Conrad had killed him off with opium in the novel. The "folly," his large Malayan house, became the post office of Berau in 1910, and was destroyed in a raid by the U.S. Army Air Corps in January 1945 (SY p. 196).

The earlier house in which Almayer lived, pending the completion of the "folly," was probably very much as Conrad pictures it in his first book, with its traditional high roof where "a numerous and representative assembly of moths were holding high revels round the lamp to the spirited music of swarming mosquitoes," while "lizards raced on the beams, calling softly" and "a monkey, chained to one of the verandah supports—retired for the night under the eaves—peered and grinned at Almayer, as it swung to one of the bamboo roof sticks and caused a shower of dust and bits of dried leaves to settle on the shabby table" (pp. 15–16). Conrad had been invited there with the captain, James Craig, to taste what Almayer claimed to be "the only geese on the East Coast" (PR p. 86). It was Craig who had nicknamed the new house "Almayer's Folly" and, visiting Europe in 1896, he would be astonished to see his invention staring at him from a bookstall, but would not attempt to contact the author (LL 1, p. 102n).

Letters from his uncle at this time indicate that Conrad was continually worried about his own health, and his hostile attitude towards tropical jungles may well reflect a physical incompatibility. The "peace of Eastern skies" was proving less pleasing than the first prospect had promised: "the light and heat fell upon the settlement, the clearings and the river as if flung down by an angry hand. The land lay silent, still and brilliant under the avalanche of burning rays that had destroyed all sound and all motion, had buried all shadows, had choked every breath. No living thing dared to affront the serenity of this cloudless sky, dared to revolt against the oppression of this glorious and cruel sunshine." And if this, from *An Outcast of the Islands,* was what it was like on the land, the water could be even worse—"the sun-rays fell violently upon the calm sea—seemed to shatter themselves upon an adamantine surface into sparkling dust, into a dazzling vapour of light that blinded the eye and wearied the brain with its unsteady brightness." This is from the opening of *The End of the Tether,* the story of a man going blind, but the experience behind it is Conrad's own, for as Craig told Aubry, Conrad did at this time have fears of being blinded (SD p. 239).

Between August 22, 1887, when he joined the *Vidar,* and January 5, 1888, when he left her, Conrad made four trips to Berau, probably staying about three days each time (ES p. 139). Apart from his worries about his health, the voyage had by this time become something of "a monotonous huck-ster's round," and with the intention of returning to Europe, he signed off in the Shipping Office and walked through Singapore to settle once more in the Officer's Sailors Home.

7. The Gulf

In *The Shadow Line* Conrad describes in some detail his emotions during his next two weeks in Singapore, and as F. R. Leavis says, it shows us "a seaman by vocation, but such a seaman as could be at the same time a potential novelist by vocation too." He is, says Leavis, faced with the question "What for? Has life, has *my* life, no more meaning than is promised by a continual succession of days like those in which I have passed out of youth, beyond the shadow-line? Can I conceivably be fulfilled in a mere *career*—days passing as they pass now, with the prospect of professional advancement to make up for what is lost and gone?" (Leavis, 1967, pp. 99–102).

As if destiny wished to hasten his answer, the professional advancement that had seemed for ever beyond his grasp was suddenly to be thrust upon him. The *Otago*, sailing out of Adelaide under Captain John Snadden, had been on its way between Haiphong and Bangkok when the captain, who suffered from heart trouble, died at sea, and was buried off the island of Pulo Condore, by the southern tip of Vietnam. As the mate was not qualified as a master, when the ship reached Bangkok, the British consul requested one be sent from Singapore.

If the prelude to *The Shadow Line* is to be trusted, the steward of the Sailors Home was in a state of nervous exasperation over the inability of another officer, called Hamilton, to pay his bills, so that when the Harbour Office notified him of the opportunity, he tried to keep it secret until Hamilton had applied. However, another resident got wind of it, and persuaded the reluctant Conrad to apply, and he was apparently the man the Master Attendant preferred. Conrad kept among his papers the official memorandum issued by Ellis on January 19, 1888 :

> This is to inform you that you are required to proceed today in the S.S. *Melita* to Bangkok and you will report your arrival to the British Consul and produce this memorandum which will show that I have engaged you to be Master of the *Otago* in accordance with the Consul's telegram on a voyage from Bangkok to Melbourne, wages at fourteen pounds per month and to count from date of your arrival at Bangkok, your passage from Singapore to Bangkok to be borne by the ship. Further to receive a passage from Melbourne to Singapore if you are not kept on the ship. (LL 1, p. 103)

And so at last, Conrad came in sight of that mystical city that for eighteen months he had struggled to reach in the *Palestine*. The *Melita* steamed up the winding river "under the shadow of the great gilt pagoda" until :

> There it was, spread out on both banks, the oriental capital which had as yet suffered no white conqueror; an expanse of brown houses of bamboo, of mats, of leaves, of a vegetable-matter style of architecture, sprung out of the brown soil on the banks of the muddy river. It was amazing to think that in those miles of human habitations there was not probably half a dozen pounds of nails. Some of those houses of sticks and grass, like the nests of an aquatic race, clung to the low shores. Others seemed to grow out of the water; others again floated in long anchored rows in the very middle of the stream. Here and there in the distance, above the crowded mob of low, brown roof ridges, towered great piles of masonry, King's Palace, temples, gorgeous and dilapidated, crumbling under the vertical sunlight. (SL pp. 47–48)

As they approached the anchorage, the *Otago* came in sight, and "at the first glance I saw that she was a high-class vessel, a harmonious creature in the lines of her fine body, in the proportioned tallness of her spars." Going aboard—in the story—he seats himself in the captain's chair at the head of a mahogany table, and as he does so he finds himself looking into a mirror, and "I stared back at myself with the perfect detachment of distance, rather with curiosity than with any other feeling, except of some sympathy for this latest representative of what for all intents and purposes was a dynasty."

The mirror image has obvious connections with the theme of the story, which is very much—as Conrad put it in another tale that he based on this voyage, "The Secret Sharer"— the question of "how far I should turn out faithful to that ideal conception of one's own personality every man sets up for himself secretly." This question, which lies at the bottom of so much of his art, obviously was for Conrad, at this moment, the one great question. He would not altogether fail, but the ever-present fear of failure, and the consequences, and the reasons why, he would eventually pursue through the many pages of *Lord Jim*.

It appears that he had various difficulties in getting the ship to Singapore—confusion in her papers and delays with the cargo, navigational problems in the Gulf of Siam, and sickness among the crew. Out of each of these problems he would make a separate story, in which the actual events were merely the base for highly imaginative creations. The delay in Bangkok provided the background for *Falk*, the main idea of which came from a newspaper cutting (AK p. 118); the hazards of the passage through the Gulf would be the background for the saving of the fictional refugee Legatt in "The Secret Sharer," again inspired by reports of an actual event, while the sickness amongst the crew would be used in heightened form to provide the atmosphere of a "death-haunted ship" in *The Shadow Line*.

In *Falk*, Conrad suggests that the previous master had been cheating his employers and had left evidence of bribery and corruption in "a dusty old violin case," filled what should have been his account book with improper verses, and left a photograph of himself "taken lately in Saigon in the company of a female in strange draperies," together with a letter from his employers in which they complained that "they had not been favoured by a scratch of the pen for the past eighteen months." The phrase "favoured by a scratch of the pen" comes from an actual reply, which Conrad preserved, from Captain Snadden's partners in Adelaide, but refers to a period of six, not eighteen months (LL 1, p. 108).

Conrad's daily letters to the owners of the *Highland Forest* while ice-bound in Amsterdam are matched by two letters and a postscript written during his delay in Bangkok, and show the advantages of having a literary man in charge of a ship, but Captain Snadden's failings as a correspondent do not necessarily imply dishonesty. Thus while the building up of the late captain into a kind of romantic evil genius in *The Shadow Line* is obviously pure poetry, even the degree of distrust he receives in *Falk* may be largely for artistic reasons; his reputation in Australia suggests nothing of this, and he was himself part-owner of the ship. The clerk in the owner's office subsequently concluded that Conrad must have been misled by evil reports: "The account of Captain Snadden in *The Shadow Line* is absurd, but I do not blame Joseph Conrad for it. Captain Snadden was not an uncommunicative man; he was rather loquacious and never kept his ship loafing at sea" (ES App. H).

However it may be, there were difficulties. He says in *Falk* that "the crew were sickly, the cargo was coming very slow. . . . I would discover at odd times (generally about midnight) that I was totally inexperienced, greatly ignorant of business, and hopelessly unfit for any sort of command." And not only that, but the mate snored—"'shut himself up in his stuffy cabin punctually at eight, and made gross and revolting noises like a water-logged trombone. . . . Everything in this world, I reflected, even the command of a nice little barque, may be a delusion and a snare for the unwary spirit of pride in man" (pp. 155–156).

One of the crew had some gold coins stolen, an incident that in *Falk* he transfers to himself, while the search for the thief, aided by the British consul's constable, is apparently used in *Falk* as the search for Johnson, the British officer who has "gone native," and again in the search for Captain Brown in the back streets of Bangkok in *Lord Jim*—examples of how fully Conrad would exploit every moment of his Eastern experience.

The *Otago* was smaller, and her crew fewer in number, than Conrad implies in *The Shadow Line*. The mate, Born, was the only officer, and in addition there was a Dutch cook, a boatswain, and five seamen (SY p. 247). Their poor state of health is confirmed by a note given to Conrad by the Legation doctor :

> I think it is not out of place on my part that I should state, though not asked by you to do so, to prevent any misapprehension hereafter, that the crew of the sailing ship *Otago* has suffered severely whilst in Bangkok from tropical diseases, including fever, dysentery and cholera; and I can speak of my own knowledge that you have done all in your power in the trying and responsible position of Master of the ship to hasten the departure of your vessel from this unhealthy place and at the same time to save the lives of the men under your command.
> (LL 1, p. 109)

Born was probably an Australian of German origin. Since the *Otago* was the only seagoing ship that Conrad would ever command, Born was the only mate to serve under him, but it is typical of the air he would later adopt that in introducing him in *The Mirror of the Sea* Conrad says, "of all my chief officers, the one I trusted most was a man called B_____." He then goes on to say that "he had a red moustache, a lean face, also red, and an uneasy eye," and "on examining now, after many years, the residue of the feeling which was the outcome of the contact of our personalities, I discover, without much surprise, a certain flavour of dislike. . . . His eternally watchful demeanour, his jerky, nervous talk, even his, as it were determined silences, seemed to imply—and I believe did imply—that to his mind the ship was never safe in my hands." Born was older than Conrad, and he had a great devotion to the ship that "went so far as to make him go about flicking the dust off the varnished teak-wood rail of the little craft with a silk pocket-handkerchief," but it seems that the main root of the trouble was that "on first leaving port a bit of manoeuvring of mine amongst the islands of the Gulf of Siam had given him an unforgettable scare. Ever since then he had nursed in secret a bitter idea of my utter recklessness" (pp. 18–20).

The subsequent voyage down the Gulf as given in *The Shadow Line* may be largely fictional, but certainly its painful slowness was part of the original experience, for the ship took twenty-one days to reach Singapore (SY p. 322) :

> Mysterious currents drifted us here and there, with a stealthy power made manifest by the changing vistas of the islands fringing the east shore of the Gulf. And there were winds too, fitful and deceitful. They raised hopes only to dash them into the bitterest disappointment, promises of advance ending in lost ground, expiring in sighs, dying into dumb stillness in which the currents had it all their own way—their own inimical way.
>
> The island of Koh-ring, a great, black, upheaved ridge amongst a lot of tiny islets, lying upon the glassy water like a triton amongst minnows, seemed to be the centre of the fatal circle. It seemed to be impossible to get away from it. (SL p. 84)

This etching of the "black relief" of Koh-ring on Conrad's memory no doubt accounts for its appearance also in "The Secret Sharer," where it is chosen as the point where Legatt is to be put overboard. In that story the narrator almost wrecks the ship by running close in until "the black southern hill of Koh-ring seemed to hang right over the ship like a towering fragment of everlasting night" (p. 139), possibly reflecting some actual drift of the *Otago* that gave Mr. Born another "unforgettable scare."

They reached Singapore on March 2, 1888. In *The Shadow Line* the ship is met by a flotilla of naval vessels rushing to the rescue of the plague-stricken crew, but a cutting from the *Singapore Free Press* indicates that the reality was less spectacular :

> The British bark *Otago* bound from Bankok to Sydney with a cargo of rice, put into port here last evening for medical advice as several of the crew are suffering from fever and the Captain wished to get a further supply of medicine before he proceeded on his journey. Dr. Mugleston went on board and ordered three of the

crew to be sent to Hospital. The vessel is outside the harbour limits. (ES p. 322)

Even if it had not been quite so great and desperate an affair as Conrad would later make of it in what he called a piece of "exact autobiography," he had got the *Otago* safely out of the Gulf, and perhaps in the eyes of the mirror on the wall, if not in the uneasy eye of Mr. Born, he had not betrayed that "ideal conception of one's personality." And on a later occasion, as he tells us in *The Mirror of the Sea*, even Mr. Born had to admit, "but then, sir, you always do get out of a mess somehow."

8. *Island of Fair Illusion*

In addition to the three seamen taken to hospital, the boat-swain and the cook also chose to leave the *Otago* at Singapore, and as the crew had already been one man short, Conrad had to hold the ship back for a week while he found six new men. He left on March 9, 1888 (SY p. 253). His original mandate had been to take her to Melbourne, but the cargo obtained at Bangkok was for Sydney, so he went there without stopping on the way. Crossing the Great Australian Bight, famed for its rough seas, a following wind gave them "a famous shove":

> It was a hard, long gale, grey clouds and green sea, heavy weather undoubtedly, but still what a sailor would call manageable. Under two lower topsails and a reefed foresail the barque seemed to race with a long, steady sea that did not becalm her in the troughs. The solemn thundering combers caught her up from astern, passed her with a fierce boiling up of foam level with the bulwarks, swept on ahead with a swish and a roar; and the little vessel, dipping her jib-boom into the tumbling froth, would go running in a smooth glassy hollow, a deep valley between two ridges of the sea, hiding the horizon ahead and astern. (MS p. 75)

The arrival of the ship was recorded by the *Sydney Morning Herald* of May 8, with a report from the captain on the gale, which "continued with unabated fury for two days ere

64

it moderated. The barque behaved herself exceedingly well, and beyond plenty of water finding its way on board, no damage was done."

Henry Simpson and Sons of Adelaide, owners of the *Otago*, were evidently willing to confirm Conrad in command, so despite his lack of enthusiasm for Melbourne and Sydney, those "charming places," he had to be content with commuting between them for a few months until in August he was given the chance to sail to Mauritius. He asked the owners if he could take the ship there round the north of Australia, via the Torres Strait, since he had always been fascinated by the early attempts of Torres, Tasman and Cook to find this "North-West Passage of the Southern Hemisphere." This would be a much greater distance than the usual southerly route, but it would avoid the opposing westerly winds. The owners replied that they had "no objection to your taking the ship through the Torres Strait if you are certain that the season is not too far advanced to endanger the success of your passage by the calms which, as you know, prevail at times in the Arafura Sea" (LE p. 18).

Conrad commented that the season was "somewhat advanced," and anxious to leave at once, he set out from Sydney in "a heavy southeast gale. Both the pilot and the tug-master were scandalised by my obstinacy, and they hastened to leave me to my own devices while still inside Sydney Heads. The fierce south-easter caught me up in its wings, and no later than the ninth day I was outside the entrance of Torres Strait." He believed that he was commanding "very likely the first, and certainly the last, merchant ship that carried a cargo that way, from Sydney to Mauritius" (LE pp. 19–20). It arrived at Port Louis on September 30, 1888.

Originally an uninhabited speck in the Indian Ocean, Mauritius had been taken over by the French in the eighteenth century as a base on the route to India. Although subsequently captured by the British, it remained predominantly French in its culture, and was thus a place where Conrad could feel at home. Indeed it is possibly the only place, of all his ports of call, where he was invited into anyone's house, and apparently the only place where memories were preserved of his style and conversation. In Marseilles his uncle had spoken of his manners as giving the impression that he spent all his time in drawing-rooms, but it was now ten years since he had seen the inside of one.

At the office of the *Otago*'s agents, Blyth Bros. & Co., Conrad made friends with Henri Renouf, whose brother, Gabriel, an officer on a French ship, was already an acquaintance. In *A Smile of Fortune*, the short novel that he based on this voyage, he says that he had once lent Gabriel a small sum of money when he had been stranded in Bombay. These brothers belonged to an orphaned family, and with their two sisters lived with Louis Edward Schmidt, the treasurer of Blyth Brothers, who had married the elder of them, the younger sister being as yet unmarried. Called the "S———" family in Conrad's story, they are described as "one of the old French families, descendants of the old colonists; all noble, all impoverished, and living a narrow domestic life in a dull, dignified decay. . . . The girls are almost always pretty, ignorant of the world, kind and agreeable and generally bilingual: they prattle innocently in French and English. The emptiness of their existence passes belief" (pp. 34–35).

The phrases about dullness, decay and emptiness are probably the expression of a subsequent mood of resentment: to Conrad at that moment, a bachelor of thirty, courteous, cultured, and incredibly lonely, to be brought into such a household and to be confronted, for the first time since that pressure of the hand in Kraków fourteen years before, with a young woman, unmarried, "pretty, ignorant of the world, kind and agreeable and generally bilingual" was rather an overwhelming experience. It is hardly conceivable that he should not have fallen in love with her, and he did.

Paul Langlois, a director of the firm that chartered the ship, and with whom Conrad was in regular contact for several weeks, wrote down, forty years later, his impressions of him:

> Of slightly more than medium height, with forceful and highly mobile features, passing very quickly from gentleness to an irritability close to anger; with large black eyes, usually sad and dreamy, but gentle too, except for fairly frequent moments of annoyance; a determined chin, a kindly, well-shaped mouth, surmounted

by a dark brown moustache, thick and well trimmed—
such was his appearance, pleasant certainly, but with a
particularly strange expression that one finds difficult to
forget if one has seen it once or twice.

Langlois adds that in contrast to the other rough and sun-
burned captains who frequented the port, Conrad was always
"dressed like a dandy," and was referred to ironically as "the
Russian Count"—"I can see him still arriving almost daily
at my office dressed in a black or dark-colored jacket, a waistcoat usually light, and 'fancy' trousers, all well cut and of
great elegance; on his head a black or grey bowler set slightly
to one side, always wearing gloves and carrying a cane with
a gold knob." There were times when Conrad was nervy
and short-spoken, and on such days, "he had a twitch of the
shoulders and the eyes, and the slightest unexpected thing—
something falling on the floor, or the bang of a door—made
him jump. He was what one would now call neurasthenic; in
those days one said 'neurotic' " (JB pp. 96–97).

Langlois was evidently unaware of Conrad's acquaintance
with the Schmidt family, as he goes on to say that "during his
stay at Port Louis I do not believe that the taciturn Conrad
ever once took a walk, let alone mix with the society of the
place, to which his culture, his excellent education, his im-
peccable manners, and his personal elegance would certainly
have opened the doors." In fact, Conrad was a frequent visitor
to the Schmidt household, where he was fascinated by the
younger sister, Eugénie. She was doubtless ready enough for
a little flirtation with the elegant young captain, whom she
probably imagined as having a girl in every port, and she
would not have thought it necessary to tell him that a marriage had already been arranged for her with a local chemist.

The sisters came for tea on the *Otago*, and on another occasion he took them in carriages to the Jardin des Pample-
mousses, about six miles away. At the house, they sat on a
balcony overhanging the street, and in a family album he
answered twenty set questions on likes and dislikes, putting
down his answers in English in a suitably frivolous manner,
not committing himself as to "What name makes your heart
beat faster?" but expressing a preference for eyes of gray.

Perhaps there is a genuine Conradian touch in the answer to "What do you wish to be?"—"Should like not to be" (SD pp. 143–144).

He was fascinated, but he could not be unaware of the "emptiness" of that "narrow domestic life," and it evidently caused an inner conflict. He told them traveller's tales or had a lively argument with Eugénie, but "sometimes he would remain cold and preoccupied and seemed uninterested in the girls' talk of a forthcoming ball or the last race meeting and he would take his leave formally. They did not expect to see him again, but hardly had a few days gone by than the captain was back knocking at the door of the house on the corner of the Rue de la Bourdonnais and the Rue Saint-Georges" (SD p. 142).

Alone again on his ship he would wrestle with "the obscure desires that move our conduct" until a few days before he was due to sail, he went to Renouf's office to make a formal request for the hand of his sister. On being told of her engagement, he went back to his ship, and did not leave her for the two days that remained. In a letter to the other brother, Gabriel, he said that he would never return. When he came to write *A Smile of Fortune* twenty-two years later, he would transpose the temptation into quite other terms, though no doubt expressing what he felt to be the essence of it, by describing the narrator's infatuation with a sensuous, slovenly girl from a disreputable home (see Ch. 22).

9. *A Soft September Day*

The *Otago* left Port Louis on November 22 and sailing through the summer seas of the southerly route, reached Melbourne on January 5, 1889. If the ending of *A Smile of Fortune* is to be believed, in addition to her chartered cargo of sugar, the *Otago* had also a load of potatoes that Conrad had been persuaded to take as a private speculation, and on reaching Melbourne he had the good fortune to find a potato famine. This is typical of the kind of incident that he exploits rather than invents, so it may well be true.

That tic of the eyes and shoulders that Langlois had noticed would seem to suggest that the responsibilities of command, always under the critical eye of Mr. Born, did not suit Conrad's temperament. After a month in Melbourne he took the ship to Minlacowie in South Australia to wait another month for a harvest of wheat, to be transported no further than Adelaide. In a polite reply to an Australian correspondent, many years later, he recalled that "the farmers around were very nice to me and I gave their wives (on a never-to-be-forgotten day) a tea party on board the dear old *Otago* then lying alongside the God-forsaken jetty there" (SY p. 260). After failing to persuade his employers to send him to the South China Sea, and declining to sail again to Mauritius, he decided to give up. He resigned on March 26, and the owners wrote that they had "much pleasure in stating that this early severance from our employ is entirely at your own desire, with

69

a view to visiting Europe, and that we entertain a high opinion of your ability in the capacity you now vacate, of your attainments generally, and should be glad to learn of your future success" (LL 1, p. 116).

Conrad was abandoning the comparative wealth of $70 a month, but Europe was calling, and perhaps also his final vocation, to which there was added the voice of his uncle, in a letter that had awaited him at Melbourne—"I do not wish to influence you either to prolong or to shorten your stay . . . but for an old man who has not long to live, time is a matter of some interest" (NP p. 126).

He sailed from Adelaide as a passenger on the steamship *Nurnberg* and reached London in June. After a visit to Klisewski in Wales (SD p. 149) he took furnished rooms in Bessborough Gardens, by Vauxhall Bridge. His intention of seeing his uncle was delayed by the need to apply, through the Russian Embassy, for permission from the governor of the province in which he had been born (SD p. 149). During these summer months he was evidently meditating on that "outpost of progress" where Almayer had been threatened by the jungle. For Conrad, to reach such a place had been his dream, while for Almayer the dream was to escape from it, and for both of them the vision had been more powerful than "reality." "I was not at all certain that I wanted to write, or that I meant to write, or that I had anything to write about," but nevertheless one morning in September he called for the landlady's daughter to remove the breakfast pots and he "sat down to write."

"It was an autumn day," he tells us in *A Personal Record*, "with an opaline atmosphere, a veiled, semi-opaque, lustrous day, with fiery points and flashes of red sunlight on the roofs and windows opposite, while the trees of the square with all their leaves gone were like tracings of indian ink on a sheet of tissue paper." The leaves seem to have fallen rather early in the year, but as a symbolist poem on the theme of his future work the piece has its charm.

He goes on to say that "till I began to write that novel I had written nothing but letters, and not very many of these. I never made a note of a fact, of an impression or of an anecdote in my life. The conception of a planned book was entirely outside my mental range." This is doubtless true, and should be so, for the great writer deals with what experience has burned into his memory rather than with notes and anecdotes, while his transformation of this experience is so largely a subconscious process that a "plan" can be a crippling handicap. It is plain enough from the way that most of Conrad's novels grew from what were begun as short stories that a "plan" was the least of his necessities. The only recorded occasion on which he can be seen with one before beginning is in a letter to Galsworthy about *Under Western Eyes* (LL 2, pp. 64–65), and there the scheme was soon abandoned.

When, however, he adds that even "the ambition of being an author had never turned up amongst those gracious imaginary existences one creates fondly for oneself at times in the stillness and immobility of a day-dream" he is obviously overplaying his hand. He came of a literary father, and as a boy he had prophesied that he would "become a great writer." The loneliness and isolation not only of his childhood, but of all his subsequent life at sea, implies a balancing intensity of inner life that must have forced him to begin to write with something of that same compulsion with which, at certain seasons, birds begin to build nests. That at the age of thirty-one, having long felt an ill-defined dissatisfaction with life at sea, and some leisure to be used, he began to write, can hardly seem surprising.

At the same time, he was still far from any decision to abandon the sea. A book that satisfied his own standards would be a long, slow task, and its chances of publication, let alone financial success, must have seemed small. Nor had he abandoned his youthful dreams of adventure, so often concentrated on those spaces in the center of Africa, which were now the only blank spaces left on the map. In his writings he would manage to give an aura of "exploration" to his trips to Borneo or even his voyage round the north of Australia, but only in Africa did real mysteries remain, places where he might not merely retrace the steps of his early heroes, but add his name to their roll.

He renewed his friendship with Hope and Krieger, and the latter arranged for him to do some part-time work as supercargo with the London branch of the Antwerp shipowners Walford & Co., with the expectation that they would eventually offer him a ship (SY p. 264). Then in September

1889, again with Krieger's assistance, he began to negotiate with the Belgian authorities for the command of a steamboat on the river Zaire, then known as the Congo.

In the name of the "International Association for the Suppression of Slavery," formed as a result of the "Geographical Congress" he had summoned to Brussels in 1876, King Leopold of Belgium had obtained a virtual monopoly of trade in this area of Africa. In the past it had been left to the Arabs who, as great slave-traders, were now ripe for energetic suppression by the forces of "Progress" and "Free Trade." Behind these high aims, a vicious combination of greed, inefficiency, and lack of colonial experience were making it into what Conrad would call "the vilest scramble for loot that ever disfigured the history of human conscience and geographical exploration," but before he went there it had all the qualities of romance aroused by his boyhood reading, of which he offers an incident in the life of Mungo Park as an epitome: ". . . the vision of a young, emaciated, fair-haired man, clad simply in a tattered shirt and worn-out breeches, gasping painfully for breath and lying on the ground in the shade of an enormous African tree (species unknown), while from a neighbouring village of grass huts a charitable black-skinned woman is approaching him with a calabash full of pure cold water, a simple draught which, according to himself, seems to have effected a miraculous cure" (LE p. 15).

This vision of a fair, tattered and emaciated young man filled with the pure spirit of adventure will find its place, with suitable irony, in *Heart of Darkness*, where he becomes the "harlequin." The incident of the charitable African woman he will appropriate for himself, recounting it to both Ford Madox Ford and Edward Garnett as part of his Congo experience, and telling them that "she saved my life" (EG p. 14).

As a result of Krieger's efforts, Conrad was called to Brussels early in November for an interview with Albert Thys, aide-de-camp to Leopold and acting manager of the Congo enterprise. Thys was a heavy, powerful man, said to convey a sense of physical oppression on those he met, but briefly dismissed in *Heart of Darkness* as "an impression of pale plumpness in a frock coat." Conrad was evidently promised work, and severed his connection with Walford & Co., but when after two months he had heard nothing more, he was prompted by his uncle to write to a relative in Brussels, Aleksander Poradowski, who had contacts with the heads of the company.

Conrad was now due to visit his uncle, and hoped to have his permit from the Russians sometime in January. He therefore wrote to Poradowski suggesting that he might call on him on his way back from the Ukraine. Poradowski replied that as he was in poor health, and about to have a serious operation, it might be better to make an early visit (SD p. 149). Conrad therefore arranged to go to Brussels on his way out, but was further delayed—"those scoundrels in the Russian Consulate refuse to visa my passport"—and did not arrive until February 5, to be told that his cousin was now critically ill. He died two days later (GS p. xv).

Poradowski's wife, Marguerite, then forty-two, was the daughter of Emile Gachet, a well-respected French scholar who had worked for the Belgian government. A noted beauty, she had won a reputation as a writer, and was just beginning a period of considerable success. In May, one of her short novels would be awarded a French Academy prize, and over the next decade her work would regularly be serialized in the *Revue des Deux Mondes*, while her shorter stories found outlets such as the literary supplement of *Le Figaro*. It is obvious that she and Conrad felt an immediate affinity. He had arrived at an awkward moment, and went on to Poland without waiting for the funeral, but he took with him a copy of her first novel, *Yaga*, about Polish life in Galicia, where she had once lived with her husband (SD pp. 155–156; GS pp. 6, 15, 96).

Conrad and Marguerite began at once a frequent and increasingly affectionate correspondence, and would exchange many philosophical thoughts on illusions, dreams and the tragedy of existence, though it would still be some years before Conrad came to reveal to her his own literary ambitions. She was the elder, by ten years, and he always called her his "aunt," a form that permitted playful affection but emphasized the difference in their ages. It may well be that Marguerite was, for a while, in some sense "in love" with Conrad, but it is unlikely that marriage was ever considered seriously by either side. They were both mature enough to be realistic: she was unfamiliar with English, and though not wealthy, she moved in the highest circles of French society and culture. It would have been as impossible for Conrad to live under her patronage in Paris as it would have been for her to face the isolation and poverty of his life in England. She never remarried, and died in Paris in 1937 at the age of eighty-nine (GS p. xv).

Conrad's luggage included also his own manuscript, now "advanced to the first words of the ninth chapter," which he nearly lost in Berlin—"on an early, sleepy morning, changing trains in a hurry, I left my Gladstone bag in a refreshment room. A worthy and intelligent *koffertrager* rescued it" (PR p. 19). In Warsaw he stayed with Poradowski's sister, whose husband, Charles Zagórski, he had met when with his uncle at Teplitz (SD p. 102). They became his best-loved Polish relatives. Mrs. Zagórska, then widowed, would provide him with a refuge when he came to be trapped in Poland in 1914, and their daughter Aniela would be entrusted with the Polish translation of his books.

He wrote to Marguerite from Warsaw, and again from the inn at Lipovets while waiting for the horse-drawn sleigh that would take him for an eight-hour drive through snow-covered fields and villages to his uncle's estate at Kazimierówka (SD p. 156). The servant who met him said that Bobrowski had hardly slept since the arrival of the telegram saying that Conrad was on his way (GS p. 5).

He stayed for two months, and his uncle presented him with a volume of elaborate and well-annotated accounts of the money that had been spent on him since the death of his father. With its combination of affectionate messages and fussy financial reckoning it conveys very well the pathos of their relationship, and it ends: "Thus the upbringing of Master Conrad to man's estate has cost (apart from the capital sum of 3600 roubles given him) 17,454 roubles" (NP p. 201). At that time the sum would have been equivalent to about $8750.

10. *A Merry Dance of Death and Trade*

In Brussels, Marguerite Poradowska was now using her influence on Conrad's behalf, with some effect, but as a woman of beauty moving in the "highest circles" she was able to extract verbal promises that those at lower levels and in more distant places would not, as it turned out, feel obliged to fulfil. By April 11, before he left the Ukraine, Conrad had received assurance that Thys had written to him at his London address, and after returning there he crossed to Brussels and signed a three-year contract. At this time an expedition was being prepared to search for minerals in Katanga, the as-yet unexplored area of the Congo's southern tributaries. It would proceed by steamboat as far as navigation was possible, and it seems quite clear that Conrad was promised the command of this boat, but this was not written into his contract, under the plea of "secrecy." Back in London, Conrad wrote to Zagórski, "As far as I can make out from my 'service letter' I am destined to the command of a steamboat, belonging to M. Delcommune's exploring party, which is being got ready; but I know nothing for certain as everything is supposed to be kept secret" (LL 1, p. 126).

After crossing again to Brussels, he travelled by train to Bordeaux to catch a French steamship, the *Ville de Maceio*, which sailed on May 12, 1890. "We left Bordeaux on a rainy day," he wrote to Marguerite. "A dreary day, a not very merry sailing : haunting memories, vague regrets; still vaguer hopes" (GS p. 10). He had often been down the west side of Africa, but now he was seeing it at closer quarters—"the edge of a colossal jungle, so dark green as to be almost black, fringed with white surf." The ship called at Tenerife, Dakar, Conakry, Freetown and Grand Bassam on the Ivory Coast : "We pounded along, stopped, landed soldiers, went on, landed custom-house clerks to levy toll in what looked like a God-forsaken wilderness, with a tin shed and a flag-pole lost in it; landed more soldiers—to take care of the custom-house clerks, presumably" (HD p. 60).

Passing Dahomey, which the French were just in the process of annexing, they saw a warship "shelling the bush" : "Her ensign dropped limp like a rag; the muzzles of the long six-inch guns stuck out all over the low hull; the greasy, slimy swell swung her up lazily and let her down, swaying her thin masts. In the empty immensity of earth, sky and water, there she was, incomprehensible, firing into a continent" (HD p. 61).

In *Heart of Darkness* Marlow speaks of growing apprehension as the ports of call become increasingly hot and fever-haunted. Here, "the merry dance of death and trade goes on in a still and earthy atmosphere as of an overheated catacomb" —it was the area that before the development of modern medicine was known as the "White Man's Grave." In a letter to Zagórski, Conrad wrote, "What makes me uneasy is the information that 60 per cent of our company's employees return to Europe before they have completed even six months' service. Fever and dysentery! There are others who are sent home in a hurry at the end of the year, so that they shouldn't die in the Congo. God forbid! It would spoil the statistics which are excellent, you see! In a word, it seems that there are only 7 per cent who can do their three years service" (LL 1, p. 126). Conrad, always pessimistic about his chances, seems by now to have been thoroughly discouraged, and on reaching Libreville on June 10 he wrote to Marguerite to ask her to arrange for his transfer to one of the ocean-going ships that the company was, incorrectly, rumored to be building (GS p. 13).

After further stops at Loango and Banana, at the mouth of the river, the *Ville de Maceio* reached its destination at Boma on June 12. About sixty miles up the river, Boma had been the main port for the slave trade in earlier times, and the Belgians had developed it as their administrative center. In the first draft of *Heart of Darkness* Conrad gave a full ironical account of the place, with its hotels, trams, civil servants and general "advanced state of civilisation," but omitted this from the published version, presumably because it would weaken the atmosphere of primitive exploration. By 1890 the river was busy with steamboats and dotted with trading settlements and mission stations, but in his novel Conrad pictures it as it might have been ten years before. As in Malaya, he came a little too late for the era of high romance, and he would make up for it by writing what were, in a sense, "historical novels."

From Boma the river was still wide and navigable as far as Matadi, thirty miles away, after which falls and rapids required an overland trek of two hundred miles to Stanley Pool. From there, small steamboats could go up the river for another thousand miles to Stanley Falls, beyond which the great tributaries that run south for a further thousand miles were still unexplored. Marlow, and presumably Conrad also, travelled to Matadi on a "little sea-going steamer," and his impressions of the arrival as given in the novel are probably fairly close to actuality: "At last we opened a reach. A rocky cliff appeared, mounds of turned-up earth by the shore, houses on a hill, or hanging to the declivity. A continuous noise of the rapids above hovered over this scene of inhabited devastation. A lot of people, mostly black and naked, moved about like ants. A jetty projected into the river. A blinding sunlight drowned all this at times in a sudden recrudesence of glare" (pp. 67–68). As in Singapore, the "sparkling dust" of a tropical sun did not suit his optic nerves.

Making his way ashore, Marlow comes upon "a boiler wallowing in the grass" and "an undersized railway truck lying there on its back with its wheels in the air. One was off. The thing looked as dead as the carcass of some animal." Then, "a slight clinking behind me made me turn my head. Six black men advanced in a file, toiling up the path. They walked erect and slow, balancing small baskets full of earth on their heads, and the clink kept time with their footsteps. Black rags were wound round their loins, and the short ends behind waggled to and fro like tails. I could see every rib, the joints of their limbs were like knots in a rope; each had an iron collar on his neck, and all were connected together with a chain whose bights swung between them rhythmically clinking" (p. 68).

Conrad had about two weeks at Matadi, and began to keep a diary, though he would put very little in it except complaints. The first entry reads: "Feel considerably in doubt about the future. Think just now that my life amongst the people (white) around here cannot be very comfortable. Intend avoid acquaintances as much as possible." He was not treated as a member of the forthcoming expedition, but simply as another employee, and while waiting at Matadi was expected to fill his time with the "idiotic employment" of packing ivory into cases (CD, p. 7).

At Matadi, Conrad met Roger Casement, who would later become British consul, and play a leading part in exposing the scandals of the Congo. Conrad wrote in his diary, "A positive piece of luck. Thinks, speaks well, most intelligent and very sympathetic" (CD, p. 7). He would later speak highly of Casement to R. B. Cunninghame Graham (LL 1, p. 325), but this admiration would not survive the revelation of Casement's treasonable activities in the First World War. Joseph Retinger recalls that when asked to join other writers in an appeal for Casement's pardon, Conrad "refused it with vehemence, telling me at the time that he once shared a hut on the Congo with Casement, and that he ended up by utterly disliking the man" (p. 40). This must no doubt be seen in relation to Conrad's complex and precarious balance of feeling about revolutionaries, and his own insecurity in a wartime atmosphere of xenophobia (see Ch. 27).

On June 28 Conrad set out with a Belgian, two Danes and a large band of porters for the overland trek to Stanley Pool. It was grassland and scrub rather than jungle, "a stamped in network of paths spreading over the empty land, through long grass, through burnt grass, through thickets, down and up chilly ravines, up and down stony hills ablaze with the heat" (HD p. 70). His diary records finding the dead body of a native at a camping place on July 3, and on the next day, "saw another dead body lying by the path in an attitude of meditative repose." The other entries are more personal and less profound: "Today fell into a muddy puddle—Beastly! The fault of the men that carried me." Each day they started early, at five or six, so as to complete the day's march before the sun reached its midday heat. At night it was chilly, and he mentions a "heavy cold in the head." "No sleep" and "mosquitoes" are also frequent entries.

At Manjanga, half way, the party stayed for seventeen days, since the Belgian was sick and the station, managed by an Englishman, "most comfortable and pleasant." They reached their destination, Kinshasa, on Stanley Pool, on August 1. Now a city, Kinshasa was even then a large settlement with "twenty-eight European establishments" (SY p. 272). The Belgian operations were managed by Camille Delcommune, the younger brother of the man who was to lead the expedition, and there seems to have been an instant antipathy between Camille and Conrad that resulted in Camille being portrayed as the repulsive "Manager" in *Heart of Darkness*. Conrad found that the *Florida*, the steamboat he was to have taken over, had been wrecked, so he was sent off as supernumerary on another boat, the *Roi des Belges*, to gain some experience. Photographs show these steamers as looking rather like open-sided double-decker buses, with a paddle wheel at the stern and an upright boiler fed with logs. They were carried overland in pieces by porters and put together at Kinshasa.

The *Roi des Belges* set off on August 4, with Delcommune also on board, and the second little book of Conrad's diary, which begins at this point, is full of notes and sketches on the navigation of the river. In the novel Marlow says, "Going up that river was like travelling back to the earliest beginnings of the world, when vegetation rioted on the earth and the big trees were kings. An empty stream, a great silence, an impenetrable forest." They passed sandbanks where "hippos and alligators sunned themselves side by side," wooded islands, and occasional clearings with a village of peaked grass roofs (HD pp. 92–96).

The alternation of hot days and chilly nights that gave Conrad his colds also produced a thick white fog on the river, which he uses in the novel to surround the evil shrine of Mr. Kurtz, and with rather less restraint in his earlier story "An Outpost of Progress," where it is the "mist penetrating, enveloping and silent; the morning mist of tropical lands; the mist that clings and kills; the mist white and deadly, immaculate and poisonous," out of which is heard the approach of the steamboat with "shrieks, rapid and piercing, like the yells of some exasperated and ruthless creature."

Moving on at about thirty-five miles a day, the boat reached Stanley Falls a thousand miles and twenty-eight days later, on September 1. This was also a considerable settlement, with plantations, warehouses and barracks, but Conrad still had hopes of going on into the unknown with Delcommune's expedition. The captain of the boat was taken ill at Stanley Falls, and Conrad was in charge for the return to Kinshasa, though he also had been suffering from fever and an attack of dysentery (GS p. 17).

They had with them one of the company's agents, called Klein, who was seriously ill and who died on board on September 21. As Conrad used "Klein" instead of "Kurtz" in the original manuscript of *Heart of Darkness*, Klein came to be regarded as the source of the novel's demonic hero. Subsequent investigation, however, has revealed no trace of any such remarkable qualities (WS p. 75). In so far as Conrad had any external source, it would seem to be an adventurous Belgian agent called Hodister, whom he never met, but of whom he may well have heard envious gossip such as Marlow hears of Kurtz. Like Conrad and Kurtz, Hodister had influential connections in Brussels, and one of his patrons, Wauters, was also a friend of Marguerite Poradowska's. An eloquent opponent of the slave trade, and a highly successful collector of ivory, he was eventually killed in a tribal war in Katanga incited by rival Belgian and Arab interests, and had his own head put on a post in the manner that Kurtz, in the story, treats his victims (WS pp. 95–118). It seems clear, however, that he was simply a brave, intelligent adventurer, with none of the Nietzschean complexities of Conrad's creation.

Conrad brought the *Roi des Belges* back safely to Kinshasa by September 24, a downstream journey of eighteen days, but Delcommune was evidently not convinced of Conrad's competence, and their mutual antipathy seems now to have been extreme (GS p. 15). Even so, Conrad was evidently still expecting to go on the expedition, as on the day of his return he wrote to his cousin Maria Tyszkowa, "I am very busy with all the preparations for a new expedition to the River Kasai. In a few days time I shall probably be leaving Kinchassa again for a few months, possibly even for a year or longer" (NP p. 212).

In the next two days, however, his hopes were completely killed. The Delcommune brothers did not want him. Not only was he left out of the expedition, but his original command, the *Florida*, when repaired, was to be given to a Belgian captain called Carlier, and Conrad was told that he would have to wait until a new boat was assembled, "in June of next year perhaps." In the meantime he had the humiliation of doing odd jobs while the expedition assembled, and could only avenge himself, eventually, by satirizing it in *Heart of Darkness:*

> It came in sections during the next three weeks, each section headed by a donkey carrying a white man in new clothes and tan shoes, bowing from that elevation right and left to the impressed pilgrims. A quarrelsome band of footsore niggers trod on the heels of the donkey; a lot of tents, camp-stools, tin boxes, white cases, brown bales would be shot down in the courtyard, and the air of mystery would deepen a little over the muddle of the station. . . . Who paid the expense of the noble enterprise I don't know; but the uncle of our manager was the leader of that lot.
>
> In exterior he resembled a butcher in a poor neighbourhood, and his eyes had a look of sleepy cunning. He carried his fat paunch with ostentation on his short legs, and during the time the gang infested the station spoke to no one but his nephew. (pp. 87–88)

All this was reported to Marguerite, then on a visit to Poland, and she wrote to Thys from Lublin telling him that Delcommune had said "that any promises made in Europe do not bind him as long as they are not in the contract, and the promises that you were so good as to make him, Sir, are not in the contract. . . . It is sad to think that a man of Captain Korzeniowski's abilities, accustomed to commanding ships, should be reduced to this inferior post and exposed to such deadly diseases" (LL 1, pp. 139–140).

In a letter to Marguerite, Conrad said that he was not likely to serve his full three years, since either the manager would find an excuse to get rid of him, or "another attack of dysen-

tery will send me back to Europe, if not into another world."
He added that he was about to leave by canoe for a wood-cutting
expedition, camping in the forest for two or three weeks, and
he might have "a shot or two at a buffalo or elephant" (GS p.
18). There is no record of his shooting an elephant, but he
was soon ill enough to be sent home, and three weeks later he
was being carried down the river with dysentery and malaria.

The journey, which when going upstream required an overland trek, could be made in part downstream by canoe. Conrad
set off at night, on October 19, 1890, "in a big canoe with
only half the proper number of paddlers," and on one bend
of the river he "failed in being the second white man on record
drowned at that interesting spot through the upsetting of the
canoe. I got round the turn more or less alive, though I was
too sick to care whether I did or not" (PR p. 14). A Captain
Duhst who accompanied him on the last part of the journey,
overland, mentioned Conrad in his diary as a man "continually sick with dysentery and fever" (WS p. 62). He carried
away from this short adventure symptoms of malaria that
would periodically plague him, but out of it would come one
of the richest and most resonant of his works of art.

11. *The Shade of Old Flaubert*

Back in London in January 1891, Conrad had malaria, and badly swollen joints, first sign of the gout that would turn its screw with every passing year, and some of his hair was falling out (NP pp. 136–137). He went across to Brussels to see the widowed Marguerite Poradowska, which doubtless inspired the highly effective final scene in *Heart of Darkness* in which Marlow goes to the city to visit Kurtz's "intended": "She came forward, all in black, with a pale head, floating towards me in the dusk. She was in mourning . . . I noticed she was not very young—I mean not girlish. She had a mature capacity for fidelity, for belief, for suffering" (HD p. 157). His uncle feared that he might be tempted to marry Marguerite and gave him lengthy warnings, calling her "a worn out female" who would be "a stone round your neck for you—and for her as well." She was using her influence to find Conrad a ship, but could only produce another offer from Africa, which he declined (NP pp. 143–148).

On his return from Brussels, Conrad was taken by Krieger to a Dr. Ludwig, who ordered him to bed, and eventually had him removed to the German Hospital at Dalston, on the north side of London (SY p. 285). Six weeks later, out again, but still not well, he went, on Ludwig's advice, to a spa at Champel, just outside Geneva. He stayed at the Hotel-Pension de la Roseraie, and Aubry, who visited it in 1925, describes it as "a square white house of three stories standing in a shady garden close to the River Arve, where the road runs along beside the river . . . half an hour's walk along the Roseraie would take him to the center of Geneva" (LL 1, p. 145). This was the scenery Conrad would use for *Under Western Eyes*, made familiar by further visits in 1894 and 1895, when he would hear of the incident that inspired the plot, and finally with his family in 1907, just before he began the story.

Marguerite had now moved to Paris, and Conrad called there on his way back to London in June (GS p. 29). In letters to his uncle he refers to a possible job "in business" to be found through his old friend Hope, with whom he went yachting in the estuary of the Thames. Sitting on the deck of Hope's cruising yawl in the evening, he probably told tales of the Congo in very much the way that he describes in the opening pages of *Heart of Darkness*, where the narrator "sat cross-legged right aft, leaning against the mizzen mast. He had sunken cheeks, a yellow complexion, a straight back, an ascetic aspect, and, with his arms dropped, the palms of the hands outwards, resembled an idol" (p. 46).

He had attacks of malaria all through the summer, but in August, Krieger found him a temporary post in charge of a warehouse belonging to his firm. He now had rooms at 17 Gillingham Street, not far from his former lodgings (LL 1, p. 157). He found the warehouse work "displeasing," and with ill health and uncertainty about the future, was in a state of depression that he could share only with Marguerite. He wrote to her, in French:

> I have nothing at all to say. I vegetate. I do not even think—therefore I do not exist (so, Descartes). But someone else (a scientist) has said "Without phosphorus no thought." From which it seems that it is the phosphorus that is absent, and I—I am always there. But in that case I exist without thinking which (according to Descartes) is impossible—Great God! Am I Punch? The Punch of my childhood, you know—the back broken in two, the nose on the ground between the toes; the legs and arms splayed stiff, that attitude of profound despair, so pathetically funny, of toys thrown in a corner. (GS p. 38)

This letter was written in October, and later in the same month he received an unexpected offer of work that would

Conrad as a child

Conrad in Marienbad, 1883

Derebczynka Manor, near Berdichev, where Conrad was born

The *Tilkhurst*, on which Conrad sailed to Singapore in 1885.
At 1500 tons, it was typical of the full-rigged cargo-carrying
ships on which Conrad spent most of his years at sea.

A street scene in Singapore, in the latter part of the nineteenth century

Jessie George in 1896
Conrad in 1896

Marguerite Poradowska, the French wife of
Conrad's exiled cousin, Aleksander. She became,
in the 1890s, Conrad's closest confidante.

The N of the "N"

Donkin writhed a little on the box. He looked unwillingly. Jimmy was mute. His two long bony hands smoothed the flannel upward as though he had wished to gather in all up under his chin. A tear, a big solitary tear escaped from the corner of his eye and without touching the hollow cheek fell on the pillow. His throat rattled faintly.

And Donkin watching the end of that hateful nigger felt a great sorrow on his heart at the thought that he himself some day would have to go through it all — just like this — perhaps. His eyes became moist. "Poor beggar" he murmured. The night seemed to go by in a flash; it seemed to him he could hear the irremediable rush of precious minutes How long would this blooming affair last? Too long surely. No luck He could not contain himself. He got up and approached the bunk. Wait did not stir. Only his eyes appeared alive and his hands continued their smoothing movement with a horrible and tireless industry. Donkin bent over.

— "Jimmy" he called low. There was no answer but the rattle stopped. Jimmy's chest heaved. Donkin

— "D'yer see me?" he asked trembling. looking away bent his ear to Jimmy's lips, and heard like the rustle of a single dry leaf driven along the smooth sand of a beach. It shaped itself. Jimmy was speaking.

— "Light ... the lamp ... and ... go" he said.

A page from the manuscript of *The Nigger of the Narcissus* describing the death of Wait, which shows how Conrad strove for perfection.

A motorcar outing to visit the Hopes, circa 1904. *From left to right:* Conrad, Jessie (partially hidden), Conrad Hope and Borys

. B. Cunninghame-Graham, rca 1890

Conrad in 1904

Ford Madox Ford

The Conrads at the Someries, Luton, Bedfordshire, in 1908

18 Jan '09

Dear Pinker.

I send you some ppp of which please have only one copy made. There is no hurry as I am too busy writing to bother about revising just now.

The enclosed bills pray settle directly — as done before. I hate having to send them — as always.

From the received acc I see that B. wood and Heinemann have not sent them Statements. I can't forbear a groan at the miserable result of royalties from US. Have you Harper's Statement of S A[merican] sales? One would like to have some idea — but after all as the publishers are not controlled their Statements aren't worth much. All the same I haven't any doubt that my time will come yet. It will.

Yours ever J. Conrad

PS. In order that you may not think the last statement of the letter above a meaningless boastful cry I will say that I base my conviction on the axiom that "force never fails" — and force (not brutality) is the only attribute which no reviewer or critic has ever denied to my work. Not one. On the contrary every critic has felt its presence itself. It is there. I count on it. Charm, subtlety sentiment do go to waste sometimes. Force (not the parade of force but the genuine power of it) never fails.

Conrad was working on *Under Western Eyes* when he sent this letter to Pinker on January 18, 1909. With its plea for further financial aid and reiterated faith in his own talent, it is typical of Conrad's letters to his agent throughout the period from 1904 to 1912.

Conrad with Jessie and John in the study, Capel House, 1915

Conrad on his visit to America, 1923

lead to what were to be the last, and perhaps the happiest, of his days at sea. He had at some time made the acquaintance of a Captain Cope, who had just been given the command of one of the few remaining sailing ships, the *Torrens*. Cope liked to have men of some distinction on his ship, and it was a considerable compliment to Conrad to be asked to be his chief officer (LE p. 40).

The *Torrens* was a clipper of 1334 tons, built in 1875 at a cost of £27,000, the last such ship to be launched, and probably the fastest and the finest. She had a crew of forty, and in addition to her cargo could carry up to sixty passengers in comfortable cabins. In 1880 she had made the run between Plymouth and Adelaide in sixty-four days, an unbeaten record (SY pp. 286–287). The crew-list included, as well as two cooks and two pantrymen, two butchers, and they took on board a collection of birds and animals to provide fresh meat and eggs, as well as a milch cow (LE p. 45).

Conrad's duties included the supervision of five apprentices, and Marlow is doubtless echoing this experience when he speaks of being greeted by one of them in later life—"I would remember a bewildered little shaver, no higher than the back of this chair, with a mother and perhaps a big sister on the quay, very quiet but too upset to wave their handkerchiefs at the ship that glides out gently between the pierheads; or perhaps some decent middle-aged father who had come early with his boy to see him off, and stays all morning because he is interested in the windlass apparently, and stays too long, and has got to scramble ashore at last with no time at all to say goodbye" (LJ p. 44).

It appears that Conrad was well liked by his apprentices, and in later years some of them wrote to him, including one who said in 1923, "I have loved you more than any man I ever knew except my own father and I revere the memory that was made upon the most irresponsible of human beings, the schoolboy, because I had only just left school when I had the honour of being your boy. I remember so distinctly the trouble you took in the silent watches of a tropical night to teach me the different ropes" (LL 1, p. 156*n*). John Galsworthy, who would travel on the *Torrens* as a passenger, also commented on Conrad's sympathetic handling of the boys.

They reached Adelaide at the end of February 1892, and

set off again five weeks later. The voyage had evidently been good for Conrad, and his uncle was able to write in October that a letter from his nephew "gave me much pleasure by its gaiety and the news of your good health." It is in this letter that Tadeusz makes the first reference to the fate of Conrad's cousin Stanislaw, whose arrest as a student for alleged subversive activities would provide a major source for *Under Western Eyes* (see Ch. 21).

Conrad now had hopes of eventually commanding the *Torrens*, and this probably influenced him to stay on, for otherwise this life, though pleasant, did nothing to fulfil his two deepest desires—for strange places and for leisure in which to write. He was kept very busy, and there is no record of anything being added to the history of Almayer at this time, though on the outward leg of the next journey he did, for the first time, show to someone else what he had written. This privileged man was W. H. Jacques, who had just left Cambridge, and suffering from tuberculosis, was making the round voyage in the hope of a cure. Conrad gave the pale young man the manuscript, and so we come to what is the emotional climax of *A Personal Record:*

> Next day, but this time in the first dog-watch, Jacques entered my cabin. He had a thick woollen muffler round his throat, and the MS. was in his hand. He tendered it to me with a steady look, but without a word. I took it in silence. He sat down on the couch and still said nothing. . . . "Well, what do you say?" I asked at last. "Is it worth finishing?"
>
> "Distinctly."
>
> "Were you interested?"
>
> "Very much!"
>
> "Now let me ask you one more thing: is the story quite clear to you as it stands?"
>
> "Yes, perfectly." (pp. 16–18)

They say no more, and after this, in *A Personal Record,* Jacques dies. It appears, however, that his actual death was not quite so artistically well-timed, since he sailed back to England with the *Torrens* and died in London four months later. When this was subsequently taken up with Conrad, he could only say, "Strange lapse of memory!" (SY p. 290).

They reached Adelaide on January 30, 1893, Conrad having attained the age of thirty-five on the way, and waited there seven weeks, in oppressive summer heat. Conrad spent some of the time in the hills behind the city, and may at last have added something to *Almayer's Folly*. For reading material he had a long letter from Marguerite, and copies of the *Revue des Deux Mondes* containing the two instalments of her latest story "Popes et Popadias" (SD p. 190).

Just before they sailed again on March 23 there came on board the *Torrens* two talented young men who would become for Conrad lifelong friends. Edward Sanderson and John Galsworthy were both twenty-five, and had been close since their days at Harrow School. Sanderson was one of the elder of the thirteen survivors of the sixteen children of Lancelot Sanderson, headmaster of a large preparatory school at Elstree. They were a lively intellectual family who would not only nurture Conrad in his early days ashore, but would also, chiefly through Edward's sister Monica, be instrumental in bringing Galsworthy to an awareness of his possibilities as a writer.

At this time Galsworthy was simply killing time in travel rather than face a legal career for which he had no inclination. His father, model for "Old Jolyon" in the Saga, was a solicitor who had acquired a vast amount of property. The son, after an undistinguished career at Cambridge, had been sent to Canada to cure him of his love for a poverty-stricken young teacher of music, but as this affection still persisted, he had been persuaded by his father to sail around the world, ostensibly to gain knowledge of maritime affairs. Sanderson had offered to go with him, and they had set off with the prime intention of visiting Robert Louis Stevenson in Samoa.

From Sydney they had gone to a remote part of Fiji where Galsworthy had a cousin who was a planter, and while returning on an adventurous overland trek, Sanderson had gone down with dysentery and nearly died. He was nursed by Galsworthy in a native hut, and finally carried out on a bamboo litter. This was more the kind of thing that should have happened to Conrad in Africa, and later, talking to Edward Garnett, he would more or less imagine that it had (EG p. 14). Because of Sanderson's illness, the two friends returned to Australia without meeting Stevenson, and were now bound for Capetown, the *Torrens*'s only port of call on the way home.

In one of his first letters from the ship, Galsworthy wrote, "The first mate is a Pole called Conrad and is a capital chap, though queer to look at; he is a man of travel and experience in many parts of the world, and has a fund of yarns on which I draw freely." Recalling these impressions after Conrad's death in 1924, he wrote, "Very dark he looked in the burning sunlight—tanned, with a peaked brown beard, almost black hair, and dark brown eyes, over which the lids were deeply folded. He was thin, not tall, his arms very long, his shoulders broad, his head set rather forward. He spoke to me with a strong foreign accent. He seemed strange on an English ship" (*Castles in Spain*, p. 101).

Sanderson recalled that they both sat up through the night watches with Conrad, and "Jack availed himself of this to the utmost . . . he had missed Stevenson but he had found Conrad" (Barker, p. 40). Conrad told tales "of ships and storms, of Polish revolution, of his youthful Carlist gun-running adventure, of the Malay seas, and the Congo." Thus although Conrad said nothing to these young men of his literary ambitions, perhaps fearing ridicule, he would seem to have already, in the form of "oral tradition," the full repertoire of his subsequent fiction.

Cope had expressed his intention of returning to steam, and of recommending Conrad to succeed him, but back in London he changed his mind (SD p. 194), so it was Conrad who resigned. His uncle was anxious to see him for what he rightly guessed would be the last time, and Conrad went to Kazimierówka late in August, staying for about a month. Towards the end of the visit Conrad was taken ill again, and had to be nursed for five days by his uncle (GS p. 53).

He continued to write to Marguerite, who evidently felt very close to him, and jealous, since the news that a niece of hers in Poland was about to marry, at the time of Conrad's visit, led her to jump to the conclusion that she was marrying Conrad (GS p. 53). She was "beseiging" Tadeusz with "voluminous letters so illegible that I had to read them with a magnifying glass" (NP p. 165).

Back at his rooms in Gillingham Street, Conrad began again to look for work, but without success. It had been said of his father that he wrote best when he was in a bad mood, and this seems to be true also of the son—the most memorable patches in his letters are the expressions of despair. He wrote to Marguerite, "I am now unemployed and, since my return from Poland have spent my days in disheartening idleness . . . there are times when the mind is numb, when months slip by, and when hope itself seems dead. . . . It seems to me I have seen nothing, see nothing, and never will see anything. I could swear that there is nothing but the void outside the walls of the room where I write these lines. Surely this is like the beginning of hopeless imbecility" (GS p. 54).

In his search for a berth he was calling regularly at the offices of the London Shipmaster's Society, whose secretary, Captain Froud, was a congenial acquaintance, to whom he had written from Africa (CD p. 7). He was also seeing Krieger and Hope, and at some time during this period they had introduced him to a twenty-one-year-old girl, Jessie George, who worked as a typist for an American firm called Calligraph. He was the first "foreigner" she had met, and his manner seemed to her strange and extravagant, but he aroused in her a "lively interest," so that she would continue to ask his two friends for news of him (CC p. 9).

At the end of November, Froud found him work as second mate on the *Adowa*, a two-thousand-ton British steamer chartered by a newly-formed agency that was to ferry French emigrants to Canada. He joined her in London on December 4, 1893, and she sailed across to Rouen to wait. Jessie George, who thought that by this time he had forgotten her, received at her home address a large bouquet with a card that expressed the intention of calling next time he was in London. It was signed "Konrad Korzeniowski," and was at first a mystery, as he had been introduced as "Joseph Conrad" (CC p. 10).*

The *Adowa* sat for a month or more at Rouen, in the middle of the winter, like a repetition, in lower key, of Conrad's experience on the *Highland Forest* just seven years before. Then he had been first mate, bound for the Far East in a sailing ship: now he was second mate, shuttling immigrants, in steam. His only consolations were the growing manuscript of *Al-*

* This is assuming with Aubry and Jessie Conrad in *Joseph Conrad and His Circle*, that they first met in 1893. Conrad, in a letter to Poland, and Jessie in her earlier book, *Joseph Conrad as I Knew Him*, suggest 1894. The story of their courtship, as told by Jessie, seems to be more consistent with the earlier date.

mayer's Folly and the thought that it was, as he told Marguerite, "convenient to have a job near Europe." And he was at least in the birthplace of Gustave Flaubert, out of which Ford Madox Ford would make one of the best of his apocryphal anecdotes: "Conrad published his first novel—*Almayer's Folly*—in England in 1895. But the book was begun—and the coincidence is one of the most curious in literary history—on the margins and endpapers of *Madame Bovary* whilst his ship was moored to the dockside in Rouen harbor, and the portholes of his cabin there gave a view of the house which Flaubert described as being the meeting place of Emma Bovary and Rodolphe. That would be in 1893" (Ford, 1938, p. 766).

Conrad's version is more restrained: "I indulge in the pleasant fantasy that the shade of old Flaubert, who imagined himself to be (amongst other things) a descendant of the Vikings, might have hovered with interest over the decks of a 2,000 ton steamer called the *Adowa*, on board of which, gripped by the inclement weather alongside a quay in Rouen, the tenth chapter of *Almayer's Folly* was begun" (PR p. 2)—while in Flaubert's version it was Leon rather than Rodolphe whom Emma met at Rouen.

The idea that Conrad was a fervent disciple of Flaubert was strongly pressed by Ford, but has little support from either the text of Conrad's work or his own declarations. Indeed, he once said that he had not even read *Madame Bovary* when he wrote *Almayer's Folly* (LL 2, p. 206), which was a slight exaggeration, as in a letter to Marguerite in 1891 he mentions re-reading it with "respectful admiration" (GS p. 44), but that was two years after his own book had been begun. It appears that the warmer-hearted Alphonse Daudet was the writer that he most admired at this time, and to Marguerite he would wonder whether he dare offer Daudet a copy of his own first book (GS p. 91).

On the *Adowa*, the view from his porthole was not so much Flaubert's Hotel de Boulogne as "a wide stretch of paved quay brown with frozen mud. The colouring was sombre, and the most conspicuous feature was a little cafe with curtained windows and a shabby front of white woodwork." He had no particular duties, and was able to carry on writing, but he had to share his cabin with the third mate, so that there hovered over his shoulder not only the shade of old Flaubert, but the shadow of young Cole, carrying a banjo:

> "What are you scribbling there, if it's fair to ask?"
> It was a fair enough question, but I did not answer him, and simply turned the pad over with a movement of instinctive secrecy. (PR p. 5)

The crew were bored and short of money, and no emigrants appeared, only some directors from Paris who "went from end to end of the ship, knocking their silk hats cruelly against the deck beams." When he was not working on his book, Conrad kept warm in the little cafe, where he sometimes got slightly drunk, as on the evening when he had collected an advance copy of Marguerite's latest novel from the station in Rouen, and wrote to her on a piece of paper borrowed from the proprietor, with "a delicate scent of inebriety":

> Last evening I escaped from the ship for the pilgrimage to the station. I have my package numbered four thousand and something. Consider for a moment a work of art entitled "Package No. 4000, etc, etc"!! I said to the person at the window: "Sir, your notice of receipt is an outrage." "Beg Pardon?" "An outrage; you are bourgeois rascals. Do you understand?" "No," he replied, "but you're an anarchist, you are! Where is your bomb?" Upon which, while he is crying for "Help!" I flee and throw myself into a cab. "Driver," say I, "I'm in a hurry. Unhitch your horse—the cab will go faster." "Splendid idea!" cried he. And that is how I escaped from the police, thirsting for my blood. (GS pp. 59–60)

A few days later the ship returned to London, as her top-hatted charterers, the Franco-Canadian Transport Company, had given up, and Conrad left her on January 18. He had written to Marguerite asking her if she could help him to get work as a pilot on the Suez Canal, then under French control, but nothing came of this. He was also interested in a job in the pearl fisheries off the Australian coast (GS pp. 56–57), but all that he did in the end was to settle again at Gillingham Street and get on with *Almayer's Folly*: without consciously willing it, or as yet realizing it, he had become a full-time author.

There is no record of Tadeusz writing to Conrad again after they had parted in September 1893, and then suddenly in February, Conrad received news of his death (NP p. 20). This was the man who had in effect been his father for twenty-five years, and written to him with a regularity and a frequency that few fathers could match, "extending over me a paternal care and affection, a moral support which I seemed to feel near me in the most distant parts of the earth" (PR p. 31). This was the disappearance of Conrad's one fixed point in the world: he no longer had a home. "It seems as though everything is dead within me," he wrote to Marguerite, "as if he had carried away my soul with his" (GS p. 63). When *Almayer's Folly* was completed, Conrad would dedicate it to "the memory of T.B."

It appears that he visited Marguerite again in Paris sometime in February, and it may have been on this occasion that he first told her about his book, since he had never mentioned it in previous letters, but from now on would refer to it continually. Early in April he told her that he was struggling with the penultimate chapter, "a struggle to the death you know! If I let up I am lost! . . . . I begrudge each minute I spend away from the paper. I don't say 'from pen' for I write very little, but inspiration comes to me in staring at the paper" (GS pp. 64–65). A lifelong conviction that inspiration came to him from "staring at the paper" seems to have been a costly mistake. He needed fresh air and exercise, and the sea always gave him good health, but after he left it he never acquired the habit of walking. He would sit and sit, in front of blank paper, until his joints froze, and over and over again in his letters he refers to the agony of days, and even weeks, passed in this posture. Flaubert had said, "One can think and write only when sitting down," and apparently Conrad had never heard Nietzsche's reply: 'There I have caught you, nihilist! The sedentary life is the very sin against the Holy Ghost." Later Conrad's friend Perceval Gibbon would occasionally "ventilate" him in the sidecar of his motorcycle, and in his last years he loved to be driven by his son, too fast, in an open car.

Taking advantage of warm invitations he had received on the *Torrens*, he wrote to Edward Sanderson, and was asked to stay at Elstree. Later, he would dedicate *The Mirror of the Sea* to Sanderson's mother, Katherine, "whose warm welcome and gracious hospitality cheered the first dark days of my parting with the sea." Galsworthy's sister, a frequent visitor, wrote that "Ted and his mother took a hand, and considerable trouble in editing the already amazingly excellent English of their Polish friend's 'Almayer' manuscript, and in generally screwing up Conrad's courage to the point of publication" (JB p. 134).

The book was completed on April 24, and Conrad wrote to Marguerite to inform her of the death of "M. Kaspar Almayer, which took place this morning at 3 a.m." Following closely the actual death of his guardian, it marked also the end of his life as a sailor. He had written a book. He would never return to the sea.

He brought ashore, on the one hand, a great wealth of experience, and on the other an enormous ignorance, of England, of ordinary social life. The slow silence of sailing ships, with the isolation of long passages at sea, and lengthy stays in foreign ports, where "I would not have cared to form social connections, even if I had had the time and opportunity" had allowed him a great deal of contemplation, recollection, and introspection. The depths and subversive insights, the fruitful self-awareness of his art can be seen as its reward. But in the details of day-to-day living, outside the confines of a ship, in the flicker of psychological shadows between sensitive men and women, in love, or family life, he would be unsure of himself. Yet even these limitations could be a source of strength. They encouraged him, on the one hand, to depths of introspection and self-analysis, as a source for the inner life of his characters, and on the other hand, like a skillful landscape gardener with a small garden, to create illusions of space and knowledge, to invent new forms and techniques. He would never be, like Henry James, apparently omniscient in his world: his characters would be met and dealt with very much as people coming on to a ship, people who offer only anecdotes from their past, inviting one to seize on the symbolic incident or the significant gesture, to guess and to analyze. He had to guess, and perhaps more than any other writer of his age, he has made us all more aware of the fact that we all have to guess, even about ourselves.

PART TWO

CREATION

12. *Obscure Desires*

On September 9, 1894, the publishing firm of T. Fisher Unwin received a letter that began:

Gentlemen,

On the 4th July 1894 there was delivered in your Pub⁹ offices of Paternoster Row a typewritten work.

Title: *Almayer's Folly:* it was enclosed in brown paper wrapper addressed to J. Conrad, 17 Gillingham St., S.W. and franked, for return by parcel post, by twelve 1ᵈ stamps. The brown paper package was put between two detached sheets of cardboard secured together by a string. One of the cardboard sheets bore your address. The boy mess. produced the usual receipt slip, duly signed, but I do not remember the name or initials of the signature. (JB p. 137)

After some ironic apologies the letter concludes that the book, "however worthless for the purpose of publication" is "very dear to me. A ridiculous feeling—no doubt—but not unprecedented I believe. In this instance it is intensified by the accident that I do not possess another copy, either written or typed." The letter reflects the condition of Conrad's nerves after more than two months of waiting. He had hesitated for some time about seeking a publisher, and then hesitated between two of them, until from the office of his friend Froud

97

at the Shipmaster's Society, he had called a messenger boy to take it to Unwin (LL 1, p. 159).

Unaware of the leisurely habits of publishers, he had lived ever since "in the shadow of the sword," sharing his "torments" with Marguerite, and even going to the spa at Champel again to cool his nerves. By then he had given up hope, and he told Marguerite that he would reclaim it from the publisher and let her rewrite it in French, under her name, while he, as "K," would be referred to as collaborator (GS pp. 75–77). On his return from Switzerland he wrote the letter quoted above, and was told that the book was "under consideration." After waiting a further month, he was at the beginning of October about to insist on its "unconditional return" (GS p. 80).

Though it may not have seemed so to the waiting author, his intuitive impulse to choose Unwin had been infallible: his book had been given to the one man in England most likely to respond to his alien genius, Edward Garnett, who would help to establish many other unorthodox writers, including W. H. Hudson and D. H. Lawrence. On October 4, in "the first type written letter I have ever received," Conrad was told of the book's acceptance. The terms were not generous —a once-for-all payment of £20. When he saw Unwin a few days later he was told, "We are paying you very little, but consider my dear Sir, that you are unknown and your book will appeal to a very limited public" (GS p. 81).

Garnett, then only twenty-six, but already established as a force in the literary world, was invited by Unwin to meet Conrad in November, and he later wrote, "My memory is of seeing a dark-haired man, short but extremely graceful in his nervous gestures, with brilliant eyes, now narrowed and penetrating, now soft and warm, with a manner alert yet caressing, whose speech was ingratiating, guarded, and brusque by turn." When Unwin made a reference to his next book, Conrad said coolly, "I don't expect to write again. It is likely that I shall soon be going to sea" (EG pp. vi–vii).

He had in fact already begun a story, "Two Vagabonds," that would grow into his next book, but he was probably hoping to elicit some strong assurance of his talent, an assurance that as yet could hardly be given; but according to the Author's Note to Conrad's next book, Garnett did say, "You have the style, you have the temperament; why not write another?" This was enough—"on getting home I sat down and wrote about half a page of *An Outcast of the Islands* before I slept."

It would be simply "another," a kind of sequel to *Almayer's Folly*, though in point of time it is set in an earlier period of Almayer's life. It is filled with the same exotic scenery, but written with much less inner compulsion. It took Conrad a year of hard work and headaches, and his mood was often that expressed in a letter to Marguerite early in 1895—"Ah, My God. How everything is black, black, black. This is one of my bad days" (GS p. 91). In April he decided to go to Champel again "to try what mountain air combined with an active fire-hose (twice a day) will do for divine inspiration" (EG p. 23).

Conrad stayed there for a month, and told Garnett he was "working every day—tolerably bad work." He made friends with Emilie Briquel, a twenty-year-old girl who was staying at the pension with her family. They rowed on the lake; he listened to her playing the piano, and gave her a copy of *Almayer's Folly*, which she began to translate into French (Karl, pp. 351–354). For her, as she noted in her diary, it was no more than "friendship," and there is no reason to think that it was any more for Conrad, but it could have seemed more to Marguerite, if Conrad had made some references to Emilie, her charm, her music, and her translation. It provides a possible explanation for an apparent break in Conrad and Marguerite's correspondence at this time—after a letter of Conrad's of June 11, 1895, Marguerite would preserve no more letters until the time of her visit to England in 1900.

Meanwhile, *Almayer's Folly* had been published, and acclaimed as few first novels have ever been, before or since. There was praise at every level, from the *Daily Mail* to the intellectual *Saturday Review*, whose new editor, Frank Harris, had enlisted Bernard Shaw to write on the theatre and H. G. Wells to deal with novels. Wells described it as "a very powerful story indeed, with effects that will certainly capture the imagination and haunt the memory of the reader." The *Spectator* prophesied that Conrad would become "the Kipling of the Malay Archipelago," and above all others, the *Sun* gave it lengthy treatment as the "Book of the Week," in which the *Sun*'s founder and editor T. P. O'Connor said, "This is a book a few people have already read with rapture; bye and bye everybody will read it, and then the world will know that a great new writer and a new and splendid region of romance have entered our literature" (June 9, 1895). If there was a dissident note, it came from those who found outlandish places "tiresome": "Borneo is a fine field for the study of monkeys, not of men" (Gordan, p. 272). In America, where the book was published at the same time, there was similar praise, and later the powerful H. L. Mencken would write, "If it is not a work of absolute genius then no work of absolute genius exists on this earth" (SY p. 14).

Conrad must have been dazzled; he was probably also given a false sense of security. The prophecy that "everybody will read it" was not immediately to be fulfilled. The philosophical pessimism, the psychological realism, and the Gallic sophistication that had so powerfully attracted the critics would just as powerfully repel the British public. As a result of its reception by the press most of the small first edition was sold to the shops, but they "rested for years on the bookseller's shelves" and "the title *Almayer's Folly* long remained a jest in the trade" (EG p. 66).

Garnett tried to assure him of "the necessity for a writer to follow his own path and disregard the public's taste," but Conrad strongly disagreed. "But I won't live in an attic. I'm past that, do you understand? I *won't* live in an attic!" (EG p. 9). He wanted to write good books, and sell them, as Dickens and Hardy had done, but they had been closer to the people, and combined their genius with a common touch that Conrad lacked.

In the meantime, he had not entirely forgotten the young typist to whom he had sent a bouquet before going to Rouen. Jessie George was the second of nine siblings, of whom the younger were still children. Her father, who had died about a year before her first meeting with Conrad, is a hazy figure, described on her birth certificate as a "warehouseman," and on her marriage certificate as a "bookseller." Although Jessie later expressed indignation at Ford Madox Ford's poetic reference to her as "the daughter of a Folkestone boatman" (CC p. 69), she does not provide any alternative information.

After the bouquet, weeks, and then months had passed, until one afternoon while she was sewing by the window of her mother's terraced house in Lyden Grove, in the South London district of Peckham, there was the unusual sight of a hansom cab, and "a faultlessly dressed figure leapt swiftly to the ground almost before the vehicle had ceased to move. The swing of the square shoulders became instantly familiar to me. . . . I remember thinking to myself as I watched that there appeared a very definite purpose in his quick movements—something fixed and final" (CC pp. 10–11). He took her out to dinner, with her mother, who was puzzled and silent, and said afterwards, "Oh, dear: one could never take him for an Englishman, and he doesn't look French, either. . . ." The courtship continued with walks, chaperoned by Jessie's younger sister, Ethel, then thirteen, of whom Conrad became very fond.

In the summer of 1895 he became involved in helping Hope's brother-in-law, Rorke, who was being swindled out of some claims on a gold-reef near Johannesburg by a syndicate of Germans operating from Paris. Conrad went to Paris, where through the influence of Marguerite, the syndicate was reformed and $40,000 was sent out to Rorke. In writing to Edward Sanderson, Conrad did not think it necessary to mention his cousin, and told him that "I enlisted many influential and sympathetic people for my cause. Pascalis of the *Figaro*—Guesde (a deputy) and the bankers Jullien and Epstein. All acquaintances of my young days" (LL 1, p. 179). He also professed to know Rorke, and would later add the operation of a South African gold mine to his legendary past. He was given some shares as a reward for his services, and as he was also due to receive fifteen thousand rubles from his uncle's estate (NP p. 21) and £50 from Unwin as an advance on *An Outcast of the Islands*, he must have had some feeling of security, which took the pressure off his job-seeking, and even allowed him to think of marriage.

Towards the end of 1895, Hugh Clifford, a young colonial officer in Malaya, later knighted, was passing through Singapore on his way to England when he came upon *Almayer's Folly* in a bookshop, and bought a copy to read on the boat. It soon became obvious to him that the author "didn't know anything about Malays," but nevertheless he found it so

101

fascinating that he read it three times, wrote to Conrad, and went to see him at his "dismal lodgings." This was the beginning of a lifelong friendship, and later, as colonial secretary of Ceylon, Clifford would "sell" Conrad to his guests, notably the editor of *Harper's*, and Gordon Bennett of the *New York Herald*, who would thus come to serialize *Chance*.

On a rainy morning early in February 1896, Conrad met Jessie at Victoria Station and took her to the National Gallery. She noted his nervous excitement, and a look of "gloomy determination" on his face. He sat her down, "and without any preamble began: 'Look here, my dear, we had better get married at once and get over to France. How soon can you be ready? In a week—a fortnight?'" One of the points he put in favor of haste was the English weather, another was that he did not have long to live, and he also said that he had no intention of having children, causing Jessie's mother to say afterwards that in that case, "she didn't quite see why he wished to get married" (CC p. 12; AK p. 105).

In speaking of his first meeting with Conrad, Garnett had said that "I had never seen before a man so masculinely keen yet so femininely sensitive" and it seems that this bisexual quality was associated with a lack of sexual desire that is equally plain both in his books and in his life. He shows no trace of puritanism, but his view of sexual attraction is cool and rather close to that of Schopenhauer—it is a cruel trap by which Nature secures the continuation of the species, regardless of the interests of the individual, an attitude most obvious in *A Smile of Fortune*, but never far below the surface in his more conventional stories.

At the same time, he had also an incurable romanticism, which he would examine with irony, but never entirely lose. Both Heyst in *Victory* and Roderick Anthony in *Chance* have the feeling that they are rescuing damsels in distress, as also Lord Jim, and this was probably not absent from Conrad's feelings towards Jessie. His insistence that there could be no children, in an age before contraceptives had been introduced, suggests fears of impotence, for which a case has been made, based on repeated symbolic evidence in the stories that he was writing at this time (Moser, pp. 50ff).

In his psychoanalytic biography of Conrad, Meyer notes that the theme of "exogamy"—marriage outside one's own tribe—is conspicuous in Conrad's novels, and that only in such cases can he convey "a credible expression of erotic feeling." In stories such as *Chance, Victory* or *The Rescue* in which both lovers are white, they "expend most of their sexual energies by backing and filling in a morass of inhibition." Thus, although it might seem that in any case Conrad's circumstances gave him no option but to marry outside his tribe, and at a lower social level, it is also consistent with the attitudes revealed by his writing.

After his proposal, Conrad disappeared for a few days, and then invited Jessie and her mother to dinner and repeated his ultimatum. Despite her mother's disapproval, Jessie accepted. When she got home again, Mrs. George announced to the other eight children, "Jessie has engaged herself to Captain Conrad, the foreign sailor—and—will be married in six weeks time. Let me get to bed"—leaving them all to burst into tears (CC p. 15). Before the wedding Conrad made Jessie burn all his letters to her, which fits the general pattern of his distraught behavior, but might also have been inspired by a more rational concern for his literary reputation (AK p. 105).

An Outcast of the Islands was published in March 1896 and received with respect, but with less enthusiasm than its predecessor. Its central character, the brutish Willems, is less interesting than Almayer, and as Conrad says in an Author's Note added much later, "the mere scenery got a great hold on me as I went on, perhaps because (I may just as well confess that) the story itself was never very near my heart." In the *Saturday Review* Wells was again sympathetic, calling it "perhaps the finest piece of fiction that has been published this year," but, "one fault it has, and a glaring fault. . . . Mr. Conrad is wordy; his story is not so much told as seen intermittently through a haze of sentences. He has still to learn the great half of his art, the art of leaving things unwritten. . . . he writes so as to mask and dishonour the greatness that is in him."

Evidently this bit deep, for Conrad went so far as to write to the article's anonymous author, and was greatly surprised to find that it was Wells, who "descended from his 'Time-Machine' to be as kind as he knew how." The rebuke was heeded, and later he wrote to Wells, "For the last two years

103

I have lived on terms of close intimacy with you, referring to you many a page of my work, scrutinising many sentences by the light of your criticism" (LL 1, p. 248).

After grinding out *An Outcast of the Islands* Conrad evidently wanted to write something into which he could put more of his own emotions, and he began *The Sisters*, a story about a young man from Eastern Europe who moves to France, but it expresses Conrad's ideas rather than his experience, and it is not easy to read. A week before the wedding he took both Jessie and the manuscript to stay with the Garnetts at their cottage near Limpsfield in Surrey, and Garnett does not seem to have approved of either. He advised Conrad to drop *The Sisters* in favor of something more saleable, such as a sea story about Lingard, the sea captain who appears in both his first novels, "a sort of glorified story for boys." This was disastrous advice, but at that time, as Garnett later admitted, "the depth of his creative vision eluded us." The inconsistency with Garnett's earlier advice to Conrad to "follow his own path" was presumably due to concern about his finances.

Writing after his return, Conrad calls Garnett a "Gentle and Murderous Spirit," but reluctantly agreed to "surrender to the infamous spirit which you have awakened within me, and as I want my abasement to be very complete, I am looking for a sensational title" (EG p. 45). This was the beginning of *The Rescue*, which would hang round Conrad's neck, unfinished, for the next twenty-five years.

Jessie could not have had much in common with Garnett, or with his wife, Constance, equally high-powered, who was translating all the nineteenth-century Russian novelists, and on Conrad's future visits to Limpsfield Jessie would stay at home. Garnett was against the marriage, and just before it was due to take place sent a final warning, but in this respect Conrad was not willing to submit to the "Gentle and Murderous Spirit." He was not exactly "in love"—this, in a story he was soon to write, he would call a "sacred and poetic fiction," nor did Jessie share any of his intellectual interests, but there was a kind of instinctive affinity and mutual need that time would confirm and justify. In his reply to Garnett he says, "If one looks at life in its true aspect then everything loses much of its unpleasant importance and the atmosphere becomes cleared of what are only unimportant mists that drift past in imposing shapes. When once the truth is grasped that one's own personality is only a ridiculous and aimless masquerade of something hopelessly unknown the attainment of serenity is not very far off" (EG p. 46).

This belief that one's conscious personality is "only a ridiculous and aimless masquerade of something hopelessly unknown" is an attitude to the left of Freud,* and very near to that of Nietzsche, who was proud of having Polish ancestors. It is more readily acceptable, perhaps, to the Slavonic temperament than to the Anglo-Saxon. It is obviously close to Dostoevsky's vision, and it is fundamental to an understanding of Conrad—the theme that will be endlessly annotated in *Lord Jim*. It is also relevant to Heyst in *Victory*, who before he runs away with Lena, paces up and down at night, "accustoming his mind to the contemplation of his purpose . . . for the use of reason is to justify the obscure desires that move our conduct" (p. 83).

Contemporary photographs show Jessie as a plump but very attractive young woman, though apparently not to Conrad— he describes her in a letter to Zagórski as "an inconspicuous little person (if the truth must be told, she is, unfortunately plain) " (NP p. 45). He was quite sure that she worshipped him. The desires that moved Jessie, obscure or not, we shall never know, but one can guess that that "very definite purpose . . . something fixed and final" that she saw in him when he first visited her belonged more to her mind than to his. Her plight was rather less extreme than that of Winnie in *The Secret Agent* or Lena in *Victory*, but it had something of the same nature, and perhaps for her, as for them, the appearance of a courteous and enigmatic gentleman from another world seemed the providential answer to the problem of an "obscure and painful existence."

The wedding took place on March 24, 1896, at the Registry Office in Hanover Square, near Oxford Circus. The day was bright and sunny. Conrad, supported by Hope and Krieger, was half an hour late. Jessie was accompanied only by her mother, the stark simplicity no doubt conforming to the dictates of Joseph rather than the dreams of Jessie. He

* Conrad did not read Freud until late in life, and thought him a bigot, an example of "the decline of men who have arrived at certitude" (Hervouet, p. 326).

105

was thirty-eight and she was just twenty-three. The ceremony was followed by lunch at a hotel, and a visit to Jessie's home, where a wedding cake was cut, and Conrad was upset by the wailing of her younger brothers and sisters.

Then the couple went back to Conrad's lodgings, where his bride was put to work sending off announcements of the marriage to his acquaintances, which he went out to post at 2:00 A.M. As he closed the door on coming in again, "the curtain pole fell to the ground and our brilliantly lighted windows faced the street uncovered. An unkind stroke of fate—with the dawn yet some few hours distant." That is all that Jessie says of their wedding night, but perhaps she had acquired something of her husband's art in the use of symbols to convey her message. The dawn, when it came, found them busy with preparations for a move to France. Mrs. George got up early to see them off at Waterloo, and Jessie, having had strict instructions not to display any emotion, had to wait until his back was turned before, for the benefit of her mother, she could quickly raise her handkerchief to her eyes (CC pp. 19–20).

13. *A Dark Knot of Seamen*

Conrad had arranged to spend a few months in Brittany, a plan that combined the notion of a honeymoon with the intention of getting down to work. The crossing must have been rough, as Jessie refers to other passengers crawling on all fours, and even her husband was sick. They travelled to Lannion and put up at the Hotel de France, where he "started writing at once." The Frenchman who sat next to Jessie at the dining table was treated to high courtesy by Conrad until one evening it changed to sudden fury, and he made Jessie get up and sit on the other side of him. The Frenchman, taking her for Conrad's daughter, had asked permission to pay her his addresses. On the other hand, when an English traveller referred to her as "Mrs. Conrad," Conrad was quite mystified : "Mrs. Conrad? To whom are you referring?" (CC pp. 20–25). Although she might almost have been his daughter, his real need was for a mother, and her relationship to him would become increasingly maternal, but under a form of wifely obedience that in their early years was not much Victorian as Oriental.

They spent the first few days driving round the countryside looking for somewhere to live, and finally rented a newly built fisherman's cottage just off the coast on the Ile Grande, "all kitchen downstairs and all bedroom upstairs on as rocky and barren an island as the heart of (right thinking) man would wish to have." Conrad was able to reassure Garnett that his wife was "a very good comrade and no bother at all. As a matter of fact I like to have her with me" (EG p. 50). It was only *The Rescue* that was causing bother. The whole idea of it was at odds with his real needs and interests, and every few days he wrote to Garnett asking for advice or approval, and always expressing exasperation.

One of the first letters that he received in France was from the Zagórskis, acknowledging the arrival of a copy of *An Outcast of the Islands*. As he held the book in his hand, unable to read it, Charles Zagórski "regretted that as a result of the exceptional conditions of your life your talent should be lost to our literature and become the fortune and heritage of foreigners" (SD p. 216). This was a note that would soon be sounded, in less friendly style, by others in his native land. A wandering Polish philosopher, Wincenty Lutoslawski, would visit them briefly after their return to England, and publish an article in a Polish newspaper on "The Emigration of the Talents." It began a long controversy, in the course of which Conrad was even attacked as a "traitor," and it seems to have escaped their notice that he had emigrated not as a "talent," but as a schoolboy who wanted to be a sailor. He had politely told Lutoslawski that "I should never have dared to foist my attempts upon the beautiful literature of Poland," but nevertheless he was hurt, and in *A Personal Record* he would attempt to justify conduct that he saw as "quixotic" rather than shameful (pp. 53–57).

Although the view that the whole of Conrad's subsequent literary output was an obsessive attempt to expiate this primal sin is hardly tenable, it may well have influenced his choice of themes, and in particular, *Lord Jim*. In a book written in 1930, Gustav Morf pointed out the parallels between what Conrad himself called his "jump" out of Poland and Jim's jump from the *Patna*, which happens before he has realized what he is doing—"I had jumped, it seemed." And when Jim says that he can never again face his father, he was no doubt expressing very much what Conrad must have felt with regard to the shade of Apollo.

After three weeks in Brittany Conrad sent Garnett the first instalment of what was then called "The Rescuer": "Is the thing tolerable? Is the thing readable? Is the damned thing altogether insupportable? Am I mindful enough of your teaching—of your expoundings of the ways of readers?" (EG p. 54). He took Jessie for drives in the country, and was impressed by the "concentrated and purposeful vigor of the landscape." He used it at once as the background for his first short story, "The Idiots," about a family of idiot children who, as Jessie's memoir confirms, they saw along the verge of the road. It reads almost like a parody of French "realism," in which brutal peasants and unsympathetic priests and officials drive the mother to kill her husband and then herself. In the Author's Note to the volume in which it is collected, Conrad calls it "an obviously derivative piece of work." Jessie typed it, and it was accepted by a magazine called *The Savoy*, which paid him £42, more than twice the sum he had received for *Almayer's Folly* (Watt, 1980, p. 74).

Early in May, after his first trip with Jessie in a little boat they had hired, Conrad had an attack of malaria, accompanied by gout which crippled his left wrist. The gout was of an hereditary kind, caused by an inability of the body to get rid of uric acid, and commonly appears at around the age of forty. It can be precipitated by emotional disturbance, and with Conrad the psychological and the physical seem to have alternated as "cause" and "effect." Gout was then a medical mystery, and he would try all kinds of bizarre remedies, such as carrying raw potatoes in his pocket to collect the poisonous humors.

Jessie says that "for a whole long week the fever ran high, and for most of the time Conrad was delirious. To see him lying in the white-canopied bed, dark-faced with gleaming teeth and shining eyes was sufficiently alarming, but to hear him muttering to himself in a strange tongue, to be unable to penetrate the clouded mind or catch one intelligible word, was for a young, inexperienced girl truly awful" (AK p. 35). This experience of his wife Conrad will use, with great effect, in his story "Amy Foster," in which the girl comes to fear, and finally to hate her foreign husband.

Garnett had expressed satisfaction with the first instalment of "The Rescuer," which being about a ship in Malayan waters, is convincingly done, but at the end of Part 1, his improbable plot requires the appearance off the coast of Borneo of a yacht carrying three members of high society, for one of whom, Mrs. Travers, Lingard is to conceive a fatal passion.

This was something quite outside Conrad's experience, and he just could not tackle it. After seventeen days he wrote again to Garnett saying that "I have written one page. Just one page. I went about thinking and forgetting—sitting down before the blank page to find that I could not put one sentence together" (EG p. 59).

Into this sterility came a fortunate interruption in the form of an unwanted tin trunk from England. It was the trunk Conrad had used on his trip to Africa: it had been filled with litter and left at his lodging to be collected on return, but the landlady, presumably fearing that he never would, had sent it on (CC p. 32). It contained some rolls of paper, which Conrad threw into the grate; his sea boots, which he threw "into the furthest corner of the kitchen"; and two little black notebooks that contained his Congo diary, and this was what he needed. He began to write "An Outpost of Progress."

It does not have the depth and artistry of his later and longer *Heart of Darkness*—it was "the lightest part of the loot I carried off from Central Africa," but it was a readable, saleable story that went with the grain of his talent perhaps more than anything he had yet written. It describes the gradual demoralization of two agents taken straight from Brussels and left too long in the wilderness, and in its strong emphasis on social conditioning one can see again the influence of French literature.

At about the same time he wrote another stranger, shorter and more poetic story called "The Lagoon." He described it to Garnett as a "tricky thing with the usual forests—river—stars—wind—sunrise, and so on—and lots of secondhand Conradese" (EG p. 75). This is so, and in Max Beerbohm's *Christmas Garland* one can find a parody of it in third-hand Conradese, but it contains haunting passages and is probably the nearest that Conrad ever came to an expression of religious emotion. Its two protagonists are "the white man" and "the Malay," involved in the death of the Malay's wife. For the white man, "in that fleeting and powerful disturbance of his being the earth enfolded in the starlight peace became a shadowy country of inhuman strife, a battlefield of phantoms terrible and charming, august and ignoble, struggling ardently for the possession of helpless hearts. An unquiet and

mysterious country of inextinguishable desires and fears"
(p. 194).

Conrad was an atheist, but without a trace of that optimistic rationalism that often accompanied nineteenth-century
"unbelief," so that rather like Hardy, he would dwell always
in this "shadowy country" of struggling phantoms and "inextinguishable desires and fears." It may not have been comforting, but it allowed him a combination of intellectual integrity and poetic depth.

The rolls of paper that he had thrown into the grate were
the mixed-up manuscripts of his first two books. Jessie secretly carried them up to the loft, and began to sort them out,
starting guiltily if her husband's footsteps approached, after
which she hid them at the bottom of her suitcase (CC p. 34).
A few years later she would bring them out and sell them for
about ten times as much as the publisher had originally paid
for them, and about one tenth of what they would be worth
to the American collector who purchased them.

Towards the end of this six-month stay in Brittany, Conrad
began something nearer to his heart, and his experience,
than anything he had done before—*The Nigger of the
Narcissus*, the distillation of his years as a seaman. He started
enthusiastically, and very seriously, re-enacting with Jessie in
the cottage kitchen the roll-call scene on the *Duke of Sutherland* (see Ch. 4). He was also giving Jessie a taste of the
perils of the sea. Sailing out, rather recklessly, in the little
boat they had hired, they were once lost in a fog, they were
stuck on a mudbank and rescued by a passing fisherman, they
were becalmed at sea and given a risky tow by a passing
steamer, and they were caught by a squall and almost sunk by
a buoy that had broken adrift. Jessie seems to have enjoyed it
all, apart from occasional seasickness or cruel rebukes from
the master mariner. With small boats, as with horses, and
later cars, Conrad seems to have conformed to Balzac's view
of the Polish race as having "the mentality of a cavalry
regiment."

Conrad was thinking of moving on to the Basque country,
but a chance visit from an unknown Englishman changed his
course. The Englishman's forthright advice to Conrad to
stop risking his health in out-of-the-way places and settle

down to write in England, instead of producing the angry reaction Jessie had expected, resulted in compliance (CC pp. 27–39). The couple went home and stayed with the Hopes while they looked for a house in the same Essex village of Stanford-le-Hope.

The only one they could find was newly built and semi-detached, near the station. After giving Jessie £50 with which to furnish it, Conrad went off to stay with friends, leaving "minute instructions" for the day of his return : "I was to be ready dressed for the evening and taking my ease in the drawing-room three days after the arrival of the furniture; the new maid was to be instructed to answer his ring and show him into the room; the meal was now to appear; he was to be shown his study, complete with bookshelves and all the necessary paraphernalia, etc. . . ." When the moment came, she was unable to resist running to the door, and was rebuked for spoiling the whole effect by her "childish impetuosity." This was followed by "sweeping condemnations" of all she had done, and she was, she says, "too shy and diffident to stand up for myself—as I should have done later." In a letter to Sanderson at this time Conrad mentions her regular "fainting fits," which were presumably her only form of defense. He called the house "a damned jerry-built rabbit hutch," and felt too ashamed to ask any visitors there (CC pp. 43–44).

All this time he was working away at what he calls in a letter to Garnett "my beloved Nigger." It poured out of him with nervous vitality into a manuscript that is buried under corrections, cancellations and changes, but by November it was almost complete (Gordan, pp. 130–131). Garnett showed some of it to Sidney Pawling of Heinemann, who accepted it, and passed it on to W. E. Henley, editor of the *New Review*, as suitable for serialization. Henley was an influential figure who had backed James M. Barrie, Kipling and Wells, and was also highly regarded as a poet. Conrad thus had good reasons to rejoice when he approved of the *Nigger*—"Now I have conquered Henley I ain't 'fraid of the divvle himself" (LL 1, p. 198).

For Christmas 1896 Conrad and Jessie went to stay with the Klisewskis at Cardiff. Spiridion had married early and his sons were already nearly as old as Jessie. She had been dressed up in a matronly manner in long black gown, cloak and black bonnet, but she soon went off with them to their "den" at the top of the house to play cards, and "it was almost morning when our elders appeared and ordered us off to bed." Although her husband "began to lament my over-developed sense of humour," his "stern disapproval could not damp my spirits" and "that Christmas was one of the happiest I remember since my childhood days" (CC pp. 47–48). They never went there again.

By the middle of January 1897 the book was finished: the *Narcissus* sailed into London and was "shorn of the glory of her white wings" as "the shadows of soulless walls" fell upon her. In the darkness of the shipping office the noble Singleton makes his mark and the clerk calls him "a disgusting old brute," but as "the dark knot of seamen" drift past the Tower the sun comes out and "the stained front of the Mint, cleansed by the flood of light, stood out for a moment dazzling and white like a marble palace in a fairy tale. The crew of the *Narcissus* drifted out of sight."

All of Conrad's experience of the sea went into this book, so much so that he will have little more to say on the subject. In the authenticity of its detail it preserves for eternity the feeling of life on a nineteenth-century sailing ship, but it is of course much more than a documentary novel: it is the Nigger who dominates it, and it seems as though he represents, by reason of his violent background, his fatal illness, and his powerful will, a kind of symbol and summation of the human condition, and enables Conrad to convey, perhaps more powerfully than in any other book, the heights and depths of his tragic vision.

14. *Friendships and a Birth*

Garnett had sent *The Nigger of the Narcissus* to Heinemann because, although Garnett worked for Unwin, he felt
that he did not sufficiently appreciate Conrad's talent. However, Conrad had already accepted from Unwin a £50 advance
for a book of short stories, and to this end, early in 1897, he
wrote "Karain," another Malayan story. Its length of eighteen
thousand words, divided into six short chapters, is about
halfway towards the novella form that would suit him so well,
and it also moves towards the narrative style that would later
be used by "Marlow." It is told in the first person by a seaman who represents "we out there," exactly the manner Conrad would still be using for his last major work, *Victory*, in
1914. By imagining himself as a seaman talking to a circle
of friends, he reduces the weight of his earlier "Conradese"
and gives it more of a spoken rhythm.

"Karain" is, at one level, a straightforward story of adventure, but with philosophical depths for those with ears to
hear. This is how Conrad would solve the problem of winning
a public without sacrificing his own artistic integrity—he
was learning to weave like a seamless robe a story that could
be read at different levels.

It was sent, at Garnett's suggestion, to David Meldrum at
the London office of *Blackwood's Magazine*, who strongly
recommended it (BM p. 4). This Scottish publication had
published many great authors, including George Eliot, and

114

earlier in the nineteenth century had been a vehicle of the "Gothic" school, serializing writers such as Mary Shelley and James Hogg, and providing a major source of inspiration for the young Brontës. Now, under William Blackwood, it tended to prefer well-written stories of colonial adventure, so that Conrad's association with the magazine over the next five years would encourage him to stress the elements of straightforward adventure in his stories and in this way win a wider public than he might otherwise have done. Indeed, it is one of the seeming paradoxes of his career that it was while he was under the constraint of satisfying the somewhat schoolboyish tastes of *Blackwood's* readers that he wrote his best books.

Becoming a contributor to *Blackwood's* was rather like joining a club, or a regiment: one was expected to read the magazine, know, and like, the other contributors, be contented with one's wages, and wholly loyal to the King and "the Firm." The final arbiter of whether or not a story was "too strong food" for its readers was "Aunt Bee," who kept house for her bachelor brother William and was noted for her "austere and presbyterian way of life" (BM p. 202). Conrad's *Falk* and Stephen Crane's "The Blue Hotel" are examples of what would not pass. Conrad would get on well with Meldrum at the London office, who had a better appreciation of his talents than did William Blackwood in Edinburgh. Blackwood's nephew George, who never cared much for Conrad, would be the main cause of his eventual break with the firm.

In an appreciation of Henry James, written in 1905, Conrad said that he had "some twenty years of attentive acquaintance" with his work. This would go back to his days on the *Tilkhurst* and helps to explain why, early in 1897, he sent James a copy of *An Outcast of the Islands*, with a lengthy inscription telling of how James's "Exquisite Shades, with live hearts and clothed in the wonderful garment of your prose" had stood "consoling by my side under many skies . . . with the bright serenity of Immortals." A few weeks later James responded with a copy of *The Spoils of Poynton* and an invitation to lunch. Conrad was then thirty-nine and James fifty-three, and in his biography of James, Leon Edel reconstructs the scene:

We can imagine the two face to face. Both were short men. James was all repose and assurance. Conrad, with his head tucked between his shoulders, his strong Polish accent, looked at James with eyes which seemed to live in a wild dream and which somehow, for all their penetration, sought the very "heart of darkness." The man who would write the tale of such a search faced the man who would write "The Beast in the Jungle." The two stories speak for the two temperaments. Conrad, making the descent into the irrational jungle of himself, James fearing the irrationality, walking anxiously and warily through the dense growth of human consciousness. . . . (p. 49)

Sadly, but perhaps not surprisingly, the two temperaments failed to establish any fruitful exchange. Their acquaintance, further distanced by being conducted mainly in French, never progressed beyond occasional ambassadorial exchanges. Conrad would be generous in his praise of James, but James would never admit Conrad to be more than a talented writer of the sea, and if Ottoline Morrell's memoirs are to be trusted, regarded him socially as less than civilized (see Ch. 24).

Conrad gave Jessie *The Spoils of Poynton* to read, though he thought her quite incapable of understanding it; but she would try most sincerely, even pretend to enjoy it, "for the purpose of giving me pleasure. And she will read every line! 'Pon my word it's most touching and only women are capable of such delicately penetrating sacrifices" (EG p. 90). That Conrad later became aware of the insensitivity of his early treatment of Jessie is evidenced by *The Secret Agent*, in which the relationship between Verloc and Winnie can be seen as a comic-strip version of his own domestic life (WS pp. 363–371).

Jessie was also occupied in looking for a better house, limited by Conrad's insistence that it should be within walking distance of their only firm friends, the Hopes. Eventually she found Ivy Walls, an Elizabethan farmhouse on the land of a local farmer who used one wing of it to house one of his workers. He was willing to rent the rest of it for £28 a year, which was hardly more than they were paying for the "jerry-built rabbit hutch," and they moved there in March 1897.

In a letter to Sanderson in July, Conrad refers to his difficulties with "The Return," the last and least successful of the stories for Unwin's volume, *Tales of Unrest*. It is a humorless psychological drama about the limitations of the bourgeoisie who ignore "the hidden stream, the stream restless and dark; the stream of life profound and unfrozen," a theme perhaps better suited to the talents of Lawrence. At the end of the letter he adds, "there is no other news—unless the information that there is a prospect of some kind of descendant may be looked upon in the light of something new. I am not unduly elated." This seems to be, if anything, an understatement of his attitude towards this aspect of the unfrozen stream of life. Jessie was made to feel quite guilty—had he not emphasized that there were to be no children? "It seemed to me that I had played him false, as it were—although my common sense showed me that I was not alone to blame" (CC p. 51).

"An Outpost of Progress" was published in *Cosmopolis* in two parts in June and July of 1897. Its radical critique of "civilisation," which it calls a "rubbish heap," and the implied condemnation of colonialism, attracted the attention of R. B. Cunninghame Graham, a Scottish aristocrat, writer and explorer with some Spanish blood, who was a courageous supporter of all the more radical causes. He saw Conrad as a kindred spirit, and wrote to congratulate him. Conrad, suffering an extreme of intellectual isolation, responded with enthusiasm. Over the next few years they would meet occasionally and correspond frequently, but Graham, despite his social concerns, and his talent as a writer, seems to have lacked the kind of maturity and self-awareness that would have been needed for full communion with Conrad. One finds Conrad largely playing the role that the other's attitudes seem to demand—that of the man of action, at home in all the world's peculiar places and tight corners, but never exposing one's heart—or admitting to a mistake.

Graham was famed in Parliament for saying "I never withdraw" and Conrad seems to have found it necessary to adopt a similar attitude. When Graham pointed out a spelling mistake in a Spanish term in "Tomorrow" Conrad attributed it to a printer's error, but never changed it (LL 1, p. 314), and when the problem arose of whether, as a South

American, Nostromo would have ridden a mare, Conrad could face Graham out magnificently by saying that this might apply in other parts, but not in Chile (LL 1, p. 338)—trivial points, but they illuminate the relationship.

Conrad was now in the position of having both his intellectual friends, Garnett and Graham, united in an enthusiasm for the Left that he could hardly share, but at least one never again hears him talking about socialists as the scum of the earth. For his new friends, Kipling was the great enemy—as Garnett literally underlined it in a letter to Graham, "the *genius* of *all we detest*." Conrad had, understandably, a considerable admiration for Kipling's work, and when in Graham's first letter Conrad is invited to approve Kipling's consignment to Hell, he suggests that "he shall sojourn in Hell only a very short while," in view of the quality of his writing. Graham was not satisfied with this, so Conrad gave up—"I wouldn't in his defence spoil the small amount of steel that goes to the making of a needle" (LL 1, pp. 208–209).

Conrad and Graham met for the first time in London in December 1897, and Conrad told Sanderson that "We got on very well. . . . I like him—and I verily believe he likes me" (LL 1, p. 219). Graham read and admired *The Nigger of the Narcissus* when it appeared, and their correspondence continued with Conrad becoming more assured and explicit in his differences of opinion. When Graham suggested that it would be good if so fine a character as Singleton of the *Narcissus* could also have an education, he replied, "Would you seriously, of malice prepense cultivate in that unconscious man the power to think? Then he would become conscious—and much smaller—and very unhappy" (LL 1, p. 214).

These letters drew from Conrad the fullest-ever expression of his philosophical attitudes, though it may be that Graham's utopian optimism caused him to overemphasize the darkness. There is one powerful passage in which he seems to be adapting the Greek concept of the blind Fates and their tangled threads to modern thought, which at that time meant T. H. Huxley's evolutionary determinism, the cooling cosmos, and a general tendency to see life in terms of mechanical metaphors:

There is—let us say—a machine. It evolves itself (I am severely scientific) out of a chaos of scraps of iron

118

and behold!—it knits. I am horrified at the horrible work and stand appalled. I feel it ought to embroider—but it goes on knitting. You come and say: "This is all right: it's only a question of the right kind of oil. Let us use this—for instance—celestial oil and the machine will embroider a most beautiful design in purple and gold." Will it? Alas, no! You cannot by any special lubrication make embroidery with a knitting machine. And the most withering thought is that the infamous thing has made itself: made itself without thought, without conscience, without foresight, without eyes, without heart. It is tragic accident—and it has happened. You can't interfere with it. (LL 1, p. 216)

The serialization of *The Nigger of the Narcissus* was being read by the young Arnold Bennett, and after the last instalment he wrote in his *Diary* for December 6, 1897, "This afternoon, reading in the *New Review* . . . the conclusion of Joseph Conrad's superb book, *The Nigger of the Narcissus*, I had a mind to go on at once with my Staffordshire novel, treating it in the Conrad manner, which after all is my own on a grander scale." It was also being read by a young American writer, Stephen Crane, who like Conrad was fascinated with the world of action, the cost of courage, the idea of a code against which men can measure their worth, and also, like Conrad, with a questioning of the code. As well as that, he shared Conrad's conviction of the meaningless absurdity of the universe, sharpened for him by the ideals he had inherited from his father, who had been a highly literate Methodist minister. When they met it would be "as though we had lived in the same town from childhood" (LE p. 106).

After journalism in New York, and a harsh poetic novel about it, Crane had written of a boy soldier in the Civil War who after first running away from the battle line, is caught up in the collective rush of a charge and carried through to half-conscious heroism—*The Red Badge of Courage*, which had brought him fame at the age of twenty-four. Eager to see real war, he had failed to get to Cuba in 1896 before a revolt against Spain was over, so in 1897 he came to Europe to report on the war between Greece and Turkey. When at last he heard a roll of gunfire he found it "beautiful as I had never dreamed," but he added, "this is one point of view. Another might be taken from the men who died there." It was out of the tension between these two points of view that he made his art.

When the Greeks were defeated Crane moved on to England, accompanied by Cora, "Lady Stewart," the separated American wife of the son of an English baronet, who had been keeping a "high class bawdy house" in Florida when Crane met her on his way to Cuba. He wanted to meet Conrad, and Heinemann's editor, Sidney Pawling, brought them together. Conrad later wrote, "I saw a young man of medium stature and slender build, with very steady penetrating blue eyes, the eyes of a being who not only sees visions, but can brood over them to some purpose."

This first lunchtime meeting lasted until four o'clock, when Pawling "jumped up, saying, 'I must leave you two now'—nearly a whole afternoon wasted, for an English business man," while Conrad and Crane "went out and began to walk side by side in the manner of two tramps." They wandered the streets of London for hours until "suddenly at ten o'clock in the evening Crane demanded insistently to be told in particular detail all about the *Comédie Humaine.*" They had supper at Monico's and finally parted at eleven "without making any arrangements for meeting again" as though they were sure "to run across each other next day" (LE pp. 100–106). This was in October, and in November Crane came to stay at Ivy Walls and Conrad told Garnett, "We talked and smoked half the night. He is strangely hopeless about himself. I like him" (LL 1, p. 211).

The Nigger of the Narcissus came out in book form in December, after Conrad had removed, at Heinemann's personal insistence, all the "bloody"s from his seamen's conversation (EG p. 113)—Eliza Doolittle was still fifteen years away. It brought a warm letter from the distinguished author and critic, Sir Arthur Quiller-Couch, who called it "truthful and heroic." He had "tested it on an old salt" and they had both concluded that "This *is* a book" (EG p. 122). The *Spectator* thought him "a writer of genius," but the *Daily Telegraph* was not so pleased: "Mr. Joseph Conrad has chosen Mr. Stephen Crane for his example, and has determined to do for the sea and the sailor what his predecessor had done for war and warriors. The style, though a good deal better than Mr. Crane's, has the same jerky and spasmodic quality; while a spirit of faithful and minute description—even to the verge of the wearisome—is common to both" (December 8, 1897).

The idea of Crane as Conrad's "example" and "predecessor" became a standing joke between them, for Crane's attitude to Conrad was that of a worshipping disciple, but it had some justification in the sense that Crane had already an international reputation. He quickly became a cult figure in England, collecting an odd band of parasites who wrongly imagined that he was wealthy. Conrad later recalled that "there would always be a great crowd around him and I was absolutely unknown then. One literary critic said, 'Why do you have that man around?' He meant me. I would sit in a corner and wait till Stephen got free of them. . . . He would say, 'I'm glad those Indians are gone.' "*

There seems to have been something of a clash between Conrad and Harold Frederic, London correspondent of the *New York Times*, who had tried to adopt Crane on his arrival, introducing him "as if he had invented the boy." A little older than Crane, he also was the son of an American clergyman, and in a rather coarser way, had very similar attitudes. Frederic lived with, or near, him for the whole of Crane's first period in England, and seems to have been very jealous of his relationship with Conrad. Frederic used his friendship with Frank Harris to enable him to review *The Nigger of the Narcissus* for the *Saturday Review*. He accused Conrad, in his earlier novels, of writing about the "degenerating white man in the East" as a means of appealing to the lowest level of popular taste, and then, in *The Nigger*, of plagiarizing Kipling, while the Nigger himself "wearies the reader from the outset, as one feels he bored and fatigued the writer." It not only does less than justice to Conrad, but to Frederic himself, whose own novel *The Damnation of Theron Ware* is still regarded as a minor classic. He later attempted to placate Conrad by saying that the best passages had been cut out by Harris's assistant, John Runciman, and Conrad replied that he "did not care a hang" (LL 1, p. 231).

The *Saturday Review* was soon to publish another attack

* From an interview reported in *New York Herald*, June 23, 1923.

on *The Nigger of the Narcissus,* by the young poet and critic Arthur Symons, who linked it with Kipling's *Captains Courageous* as being full of "movement, noise, and distraction," but, "Where is the idea of which such things should be but the servants? Ah, there has been an oversight; everything else is there, but that, these brilliant writers have forgotten to put in" (CH pp. 97–98). Conrad was provoked to make a reply, under the form of a defense of Kipling, but it was not printed, and has not been preserved (LL 1, p. 228). Symons repented, and would later become a great admirer of Conrad, but Harris held out against continuing pressure from Cunninghame Graham to publish Conrad, and in his autobiography, still loyal to Frederic's view, he lists Conrad along with Hall Caine and Marie Corelli as one of the overrated idols of the public (p. 338).

Of the two friends that Conrad had made on the *Torrens,* only Sanderson had a home in which Conrad could be welcomed, as at this time Galsworthy was involved with his love for Ada, the wife of his cousin Arthur, a glamorized version of which would provide the main substance of the *Forsyte Saga.* Conrad had passed on to Garnett Galsworthy's first collection of stories, eliciting the opinion that "the author is essentially a clubman," and after the publication of Galsworthy's first novel, *Jocelyn,* early in 1898, which was dedicated to Conrad, the two men met and corresponded with increasing frequency. To a Polish cousin Conrad wrote that "the book is not outstanding but the man is very charming, and likeable, and rich" (NP p. 223).

While Conrad was comforting Galsworthy over the critical opinion that his book was "superficial"—"it is not your business to invent depths—to invent depths is no art either"—his wife was upstairs in confinement, attended by her mother. Jessie says that when the birth pangs began Conrad "departed in a jaunty manner in search of the doctor. Arrived at his house he assured him that there was no need for any hurry and accepted the offer of a second breakfast with a good appetite. We had to send two messengers before they arrived," an action which Conrad described as "most unseemly." Later in the morning, while walking in the garden, he heard a baby crying, and went into the house to tell the maid, "Send that child away at once—it will disturb Mrs. Conrad!" (CC p. 57).

Next morning he added to the end of his letter to Galsworthy, "An infant of male persuasion arrived yesterday. All is going well here. I feel relieved greatly and hope to do some work now." To a relative in Poland he wrote, "He has dark hair, enormous eyes—and looks like a monkey," adding that he would be called "Borys," since although it was a name more common in Russia than in Poland, it was "purely Slavonic yet not too difficult for foreigners to pronounce" (NP p. 223). This choice, rather than that of a thoroughly British name for his half-British child, would seem to indicate that beneath his apparent lack of interest in Polish affairs and his avowed hatred of Russia, lay an inextinguishable loyalty to his Slav inheritance.

The boy would receive plenty of affection when he attained an adequate size, but Conrad had a kind of aversion to infants, combined with an aristocratic conviction that they should be kept out of sight. Soon after the birth, the Conrads, with Jessie's younger sister, were invited to visit the Cranes, who had settled in Surrey in a house they shared with Frederic. Jessie says that Conrad "had taken our tickets, first class, and intended travelling in the same carriage, but here he became most emphatic—on no account were we to give any indication that he belonged to our little party. . . . Soberly we installed ourselves in that railway carriage, and, in due course, he also entered and settled himself in a far corner, ostentatiously concealing himself behind his newspaper" (CC p. 57).

He was put to shame by Crane, who frequently upbraided him for his attitude towards the child, and liked to spend long periods in communion with Borys. Conrad tells how, "glancing out of the low window of my room I would see them, very still, staring at each other with a solemn understanding that needed no words, or perhaps was beyond words altogether." Crane wanted, rather prematurely, to give the infant a dog and to teach him to ride. Of Crane's own dogs, Conrad wrote that "they pervaded, populated, and filled the whole house." Each time they wished to leave or enter his study, Crane left his work to open the door, and "one afternoon on the fifth or sixth repetition I could not help bursting into a loud interminable laugh in which there was the beginning of hysteria" (LE pp. 106–109).

Crane's love for Conrad was accompanied by a wholehearted

123

admiration of his work and respect for his opinions: Conrad's love for Crane had less unqualified admiration, but of the love there can be no doubt, and Garnett gives a picture of them together: "On the few occasions I saw him with Stephen Crane he was delightfully sunny, and bantered 'poor Steve' in the gentlest, most affectionate style, while the latter sat silent, Indian-like, turning enquiring eyes under his chiselled brow, now and then jumping up suddenly and confiding some new project with intensely electric feeling. I can still hear the shades of Crane's poignant friendliness in his cry 'Joseph!' and Conrad's delight in Crane's personality glowed in the shining warmth of his brown eyes" (EG pp. xv–xvi).

How much that cry of "Joseph!" meant to Conrad can be judged from the fact that twenty-five years later, on his visit to America, talking about Crane he said, "Stephen was the first one who ever called me Joseph."* Probably also one of the last, for with the isolation in which he lived, and the British convention of using surnames even among close acquaintances, Conrad seems hardly to have been addressed as "Joseph" by anyone else until he went to America in 1923.

Crane wanted to collaborate with Conrad in a play to be called *The Predecessor*, about "a man impersonating his 'predecessor' (who had died) in the hope of winning a girl's heart," and he insisted that "one of the situations should present the man and the girl on a boundless plain standing by their dead ponies after a furious ride." Twenty years later Conrad would use "the shadow of the primary idea" for his story *The Planter of Malata*, but for the moment he merely expressed a doubt as to "whether we could induce the management of any London theater to deposit two stuffed horses on its stage" (LE p. 116).

* New York *World*, June 3, 1923.

15. *Collaboration*

After completing *The Nigger of the Narcissus* Conrad returned to his struggle with *The Rescue,* interrupting it from time to time with shorter tales to replenish his housekeeping money. Reviewers had repeatedly praised *The Nigger* because, in contrast with conventional stories of the sea, it had "no pirate in it, no wreck, no desert island, no treasure trove," nor did Conrad "seek any adventitious aid by the introduction in mid-ocean of beautiful but athletic young ladies who have been yachting with their papa." All this must have sounded to the author rather like a criticism of his next book, for *The Rescue* was to employ every one of these "adventitious aids," though Conrad hoped to lift them all to "a new aesthetic level" (MB pp. 9–10).

Despite the fact that he had already spent so many weeks sitting in front of blank paper, he was determined to get the book written. Indeed, he had little choice, for he had already sold the serial rights and the American rights, and was receiving a regular allowance to enable him to finish it. The young American publisher F. N. Doubleday had come to England to look for some unrecognized genius who could be acquired at a bargain price, and Heinemann had offered him a half-share in Conrad at $50 a month until *The Rescue* was completed (Doubleday, pp. 150–151). This was an unfulfilled obligation that would weigh on Conrad for years to come, making him feel, as he later said, "like the impenitent thief on the cross."

The struggle continued through the rest of 1897 and on to March of the following year, when he wrote to Garnett, "I sit down for eight hours every day—and the sitting down is all. In the course of that working day of eight hours I write three sentences which I erase before leaving the table in despair" (EG p. 31). It seems absurd that with his memory stocked with half a lifetime of real adventurous experience, Conrad should have spent so many frustrating months trying to invent an improbable romance, but perhaps this was the period of gestation needed for the great things that he was about to bring forth, though at the time he would not see them as such but merely as financially motivated interruptions of his real task—*The Rescue.*

Of these interruptions that would prove to be of such greater value than that which they interrupted, the first was "Youth," a longish short story which gives a brilliant, entertaining, and slightly glamorized version of his voyage in the *Palestine* in 1882. The narrator is a seaman called Marlow who sits in a circle of friends and recalls an experience of his youth, twenty years before. With this simple invention Conrad had come upon something of much greater consequence than he realized. From this beginning—the analysis of his youthful emotions from the standpoint of middle-age—Marlow would be used for the analysis, in ever increasing depth, not only of Conrad's moral convictions, but of his very soul and sensibility, a process that would begin with *Heart of Darkness* and reach its greatest depth and complexity in the flowing energy of *Lord Jim.*

This is one aspect of Marlow, but equally important was the way in which this method of distanced retrospection allowed Conrad to control his material, to select the significant and the symbolic, and to develop those shifts in time that made the finished story a complex work of art. Also, by seeing himself as a seaman talking to a circle of friends, Conrad developed a new rhetoric in which the heavy style of his early books changes to a more colloquial idiom. The initial incompatibility between his intensive reading and the idiom he had exchanged with his fellow seamen is resolved and unified in the voice of Marlow, at once colloquial and sophisticated, shifting from brief Anglo-Saxon abuse to long flights of rhetoric, yet always retaining the rhythms of the spoken word.

Conrad had thus opened the way for a presentation of his own experience and his own inner conflicts that would lead him to write very quickly and virtually without hesitation *Heart of Darkness* and *Lord Jim,* arguably his two best books, and thus put himself, with one leap as it were, in the very front rank of the world's great writers. But of this, as yet, he knew nothing, and having dashed off "Youth" he returned once more to sitting in front of the blank pages of *The Rescue,* a task that reduced him to such despair that by the middle of 1898 he was determined to go to sea again.

He enlisted the help of Cunninghame Graham in getting interviews with the directors of various shipping companies, but his age, his lack of experience in anything but sailing ships and his time away from the sea were all against him, and as he wrote to Graham after a fruitless trip to Glasgow, "the fact is from novel writing to skippering *il y a trop de tirage.* This confounded literature has ruined me entirely. There is a time in the affairs of men when the tide of folly taken at the flood sweeps them to destruction" (LL 1, p. 253).

It was in this extremity that there came the idea of collaboration with some fluent writer. The man who eventually undertook this task, Ford Madox Ford, subsequently claimed that Conrad thought in Polish, turned it into French, and then translated it into English, which is, like many other things said by Ford, hardly credible, but at least indicates what was thought to be the problem. Conrad spoke English awkwardly and with a strong accent, and this led to the belief that he must have had equal difficulty in writing it. Lewis Hind once wrote, "It was a marvel to me then, and always has been, how so un-English a man in temperament, looks, and utterance as Conrad should be able to write such perfect English," and this was a typical contemporary view.

On Conrad's side, it seems that in seeking a collaborator, he was primarily concerned to produce the kind of quantity, and the kind of quality, or lack of it, that would ensure rapid financial rewards. Thus there came about that bizarre conjunction with Ford which Henry James, when he heard of it, described as "like a bad dream one relates at breakfast." In contrast to Conrad's isolation on the outermost edge of English artistic life, Ford, known, until he changed his surname in 1918, as Ford Madox Hueffer, had been born at the center of it. His father, an immigrant from Germany devoted to music and the philosophy of Schopenhauer, had died when he was young, and as a grandchild of the painter Ford Madox Brown he had been brought up with his cousins, the Rossettis, who lived next door in the house where Swinburne was "as like as not, lying drunk in the bath on the top floor." As against Conrad's pessimistic and contemplative nature, Ford was gregarious, talkative, the archetypical anecdotalist and the prolific producer, writing in his lifetime more than eighty books, as well as editing, encouraging, travelling, steering himself to the center of each successive literary movement, often the discoverer, and at least the acquaintance of almost all the literary figures of his time.

Ford had known Edward Garnett and his solicitor brother, Robert, since their boyhood days, and it was through Edward that he met Conrad. Stephen Crane, at Oxted, was quite close to the Garnetts at Limpsfield, and the latter had promised Conrad that he could come for a long visit. Jessie, well aware of her husband's intellectual isolation, made no objection, intending to fill their farmhouse with some of her own relatives during his absence. When Garnett's invitation came, late in the summer of 1898, Jessie saw "unmistakeable signs of intense satisfaction" on her husband's face, and was happy enough with her sisters and her baby until the barns behind the house came to be filled with what she calls a "riff-raff" from the East End of London. They had come for the picking of peas, but stayed on in the barns to await the hop picking. They frightened her so much that she wrote repeatedly to Conrad asking him to take her away, and when there was no response, finally sent a desperate telegram.

Conrad was enjoying himself at Limpsfield. Garnett's son David, then five, recalls that with a basket, sheet and clothes-prop, Conrad made him a boat—"the green grass heaved in waves, the sail filled and tugged, our speed was terrific. Alterations were made and the rig perfected and when, an hour later, Edward came out looking for his guest, he found him sitting in our big clothes basket steering the boat and giving me orders to take in or let out the sail" (D. Garnett, p. 62). A farm near the Garnetts was occupied by a woman who looked after four or five girls rescued from the East End, of whom the most intelligent and strong minded, a girl called Li Whale, rebelled, and came to live with the Garnetts (pp. 58–59). Her character and circumstances bear some resemblance to those of Flora in Conrad's *Chance*, and this was probably his source. The house was also frequented by anarchists and other refugees from Russia, which must have helped Conrad when he came to write on these themes.

Conrad was obviously not very pleased when Jessie's telegram arrived, but he could not avoid the problem any longer, and he found her lodgings at an old mill not far from Garnett's cottage. He met her at the station, and having delivered her there, said, "Good night. I shall be late for dinner as it is. I shall see you no doubt tomorrow." This, according to Jessie, was the worst moment since their marriage—"I determined silently that if he came the next day I would be out, no matter what time it might be. I felt truly vicious, and only the expression of comical concern on my sister's face and the renewed lamentations of the baby recalled me to myself and my usual philosophy" (CC pp. 60–63).

It was probably on this visit that Conrad met Ford, who was then twenty-four, but already married for four years to the former Elsie Martindale, the daughter of a distinguished medical writer. Too lonely in a farmhouse in Kent, the couple had moved to Limpsfield and occupied a cottage next door to Garnett's. David Garnett remembered Ford as "a very young man, tall and Germanic in appearance, with a pink and white complexion, pale, rather prominent blue eyes, and a beard which I referred to when we first met as 'hay on his face' " (p. 36).

In *Return to Yesterday*, Ford describes the first encounter:

Conrad came round the corner of the house. I was doing something at the open fireplace in the house-end. He was in advance of Mr. Garnett who had gone inside, I suppose, to find me. Conrad stood looking at the view. His hands were in the pocket of his reefer-coat, the thumbs sticking out. His black torpedo beard pointed at the horizon. He placed a monocle in his eye. Then he caught sight of me.

I was very untidy in my working clothes. He started

back a little. I said, "I'm Hueffer." He had taken me for the gardener.

His whole being melted together in enormous politeness. His spine inclined forward; he extended both hands to take mine. He said, "My dear feller . . . Delighted . . . Ench . . . Anté!" (p. 52)

Before his marriage Ford had for some time lived with a wealthy uncle in Paris: he had a taste for French literature, and a feeling, rare in England at the time, for the novel as "high art." Moreover, as a Tory romantic, he had no time for the "progressive" views of Garnett, in all of which he would have been at one with Conrad. Working on two or three books, with ideas for a dozen more, he must also have seemed a marvel of fertility. The two men obviously took to each other, so much so that very soon they had decided that Conrad could take over the lease of the farmhouse in Kent that Ford had left, and that they would work together on *Seraphina*, a historical novel about pirates that Ford had already begun. This agreement must have been finalized at some time between September 6, 1898—when Conrad wrote to Wells from Limpsfield to thank him for some comments on "Youth," which had just appeared in *Blackwood's*—and October 11, when Conrad, back at Ivy Walls, wrote again to Wells to tell him with "jubilation," that they would soon be neighbors as "we are coming to live in Pent Farm, which is only a mile or so from Sandling Junction" (LL 1, pp. 248–249).

Conrad had already arranged to go and see some more shipping companies, but with Ford's proposals in front of him, he was probably more relieved than not when nothing came of this, and on September 29 he wrote to Ford, "I've just got back from Glasgow and write without loss of time asking you to conclude the affair with the landlord. . . . This opportunity is a perfect Godsend to me. It preserves what's left of my piety and belief in a benevolent Providence and probably also my sanity" (JB p. 222). Conrad's feelings of relief are partly accounted for by the fact that he was under notice to leave Ivy Walls. A little while before, Jessie had gone with her sister Ethel and the baby to call on the landlord's wife, but arrived just as she was setting out for a drive, so had turned back. As the lady overtook them, she said something that Jessie interpreted as the offer of a lift, and replied, "Oh, no thank you." When her sister told her that the actual words were, "You will come and see me another day?" she knew she had made a *faux pas*, but how great a one she realized only when they received notice to quit (CC p. 65).

Thus, before the end of October, Conrad was settled in Pent Farm, on the sheepdowns of Kent, outside the village of Postling, near Aldington. It was a farmhouse of soft red brick with matching tiles and a few trees, at the foot of a hill, about three miles from the sea. Ford called it "the mournful house under the bare downs." He had leased it in 1896, and restored it to its "original antique condition of great rafters and huge ingles." To Elsie it had seemed large enough with two rooms downstairs, "a huge kitchen" and "five good-sized bedrooms," but to visitors such as Garnett's friend E. V. Lucas it was "a damp dark little farmhouse." Ford left there various Pre-Raphaelite relics including Christina Rosetti's writing desk and a William Morris table that Conrad would use (CC p. 66).

Here Conrad would live for the next nine years and write his best books. Ford had previously rented the house to the artist Walter Crane, who had painted over the front door, "Want we not for board or tent/While overhead we have the Pent," words that remained, according to Borys Conrad, until the house was redecorated in the 1960s. Pent Farm suited Conrad, and he wrote to Cunninghame Graham, "Now I am here I like it. I can write a little" (LL 1, p. 253).

This small section of the south coast was now, quite fortuitously, filling up with great writers. W. H. Hudson was observing the birds in Romney Marsh, Henry James had moved to Lamb House at Rye, and H. G. Wells had just come, for the benefit of his health, to Sandgate. Stephen Crane would soon move to Brede Place, and Kipling was not far away at Rottingdean, but protected by poor roads and their own paranoia, they would not communicate with much frequency or mutual profit. Only Ford, soon to move to Aldington, would go to and fro among them collecting insults and anecdotes.

W. H. Hudson was another of Garnett's protégés, and a friend of Graham's, but he does not seem to have found much common ground with Conrad who was never a lover of nature, and it is only Jessie whom he seems to have found sympathetic.

She recognized him instinctively when he turned up one day at the back door of the Pent, and once, when they met on the Tube in London, they completed three circuits of the Circle Line discussing Hudson's latest work (CC pp. 72, 87).

In the middle of November Conrad made his first visit to Wells's cottage, but Wells was out, so Conrad wrote asking him to call, offering to meet the train at Postling (LL 1, p. 254). Soon after Ford and Elsie came to stay, and they all went to Sandgate again; this time, however, Wells had gone to see the Conrads. When Conrad pressed the doorbell, "an invisible finger kept the button down (or in rather) and the bell jingling continuously to our extreme confusion." The joke about it being the Invisible Man of Wells's latest book would echo long between Ford and Conrad.

The two did eventually meet, and Wells thought Conrad "the strangest of creatures," a view that he claimed to share with Henry James. "He was rather short and round-shouldered with his head as it were sunken into his body. He had a dark retreating face with carefully trimmed and pointed beard, a trouble-wrinkled forehead and very troubled dark eyes, and the gestures of his hands and arms were from the shoulders and very Oriental indeed." He adds that Conrad spoke English strangely, but "not badly altogether": by learning from reading, he had formed "wrong sound impressions of many familiar words" (Wells 2, p. 615).

Studying science under T. H. Huxley had given Wells a strong sense of the conflict and contradiction between the ruthless indifference of Nature and the hopes and needs of humanity, very close to Conrad's view of the world. Wells had expressed this vision with great imaginative power in a sequence of science-fantasies that had already brought him, at the age of thirty-two, fame and comparative fortune. Unlike Huxley or Conrad, however, he was not by nature deep or pessimistic, and he was already beginning to turn into the tireless social reformer of his middle years. Thus at the time of his meeting with Conrad he was moving away from what might have been their common ground, and so, as he said, "We never really 'got on' together. I was perhaps more unsympathetic and incomprehensible to Conrad than he was to me. I think he found me philistine, stupid and intensely English; he was incredulous that I could take social and political issues seriously; he was always trying to penetrate below my foundations, discover my imaginative obsessions and see what I was really up to" (Wells 2, p. 620). It cannot be said that Conrad did not "take social and political issues seriously," but he was equally concerned with "imaginative obsessions" and that self-awareness, rather lacking in Wells, by which one might "penetrate below the foundations."

Conrad had been happy enough over W. E. Henley's warm reception of *The Nigger of the Narcissus* for serialization in the *New Review*, but by July 1898 we find him referring to Henley in a letter to Graham as "a horrible bourgeois." Conrad was not at all pleased when, in October, Henley made a rather strange, and quite unsolicited, intervention on behalf of Ford in the matter of the proposed collaboration. Henley, as a young man, had collaborated with R. L. Stevenson, and had apparently found it painful; he cited also the manner in which young collaborators had been "eaten up" by Dumas. Conrad made a lengthy reply : in the midst of one paragraph, which runs to six hundred words, he says :

> The line of your argument surprised me. R. L. S.—
> Dumas—these are big names and I assure you it had
> never occurred to me that they could be pronounced in
> connection with my plan to work with Hueffer. But you
> have judged proper to pronounce them and I am bound
> to look seriously at that aspect of the matter. When talk-
> ing with Hueffer my first thought was that the man
> there who couldn't find a publisher had some good stuff
> to use and that if we worked it up together my name,
> probably, would get a publisher for it. . . . Were I a
> Dumas I would eat up Hueffer without compunction.
> Was it you who called the old man "a natural force"? He
> was *that;* and a natural force need not be scrupulous. Not
> being *that* I must navigate cautiously at this juncture lest
> my battered, ill-ballasted craft should run down a boat
> with youth at the helm and hope at the prow. . . . (JB
> pp. 217–218)

Wells also took an interest in the proposed collaboration, but on the opposite side from Henley. According to Ford, when he arrived at Aldington, Wells cycled over to tell him that Conrad had a "wonderful Oriental style, as delicate as clockwork," which would be ruined if Ford "stuck his fingers into it" (Ford, 1931, p. 224). The partnership would not, in fact, be very fruitful in the production of either money or great literature, but it rescued Conrad from a state of extreme isolation, providing him with someone to listen to his tales and help with his day-to-day problems.

When he wrote, Conrad disciplined his imagination by severe standards of "realism," but it seems that when talking he liked to fantasize in a style that can be guessed from the contents of the book that Ford put out shortly after his death, *Joseph Conrad: A Personal Remembrance*. Much of the color may be Ford's, but one can hardly doubt that the basic material of its almost wholly fictional content was spun by its hero.

We have his youth in Poland—"a long white house, in the dark, with silver beeches in an avenue or, ghostly in groups. Indoors was Conrad, right through adolescence, for ever reading in the candle-light of an immense stately library, with busts on white plinths and alternate groups of statuary, in bronze. His uncle would be in a rather subterranean study at the other end of the vast house—writing his memoirs" (p. 74).

Or Conrad in Marseilles, in the French Navy, which he left "with the rank of—he was specific as to that—of *Lieutenant de Torpilleurs de la Marine Militaire Française.* During that time, on the French flagship *Ville d'Ompteda,* he had witnessed the bombardment of a South American town. . . . he painted red the port of Marseilles, intrigued for Napoleon III, hired, since there was nothing else to be hired, an unpainted four-in-hand from a coachbuilder's yard and drove, buried in actresses and the opera chorus to the races. . . . He would relate the instance of the unvarnished coach with great energy and fire and then, dropping his hands with mock senility, exclaim: '*Alas, tel que vous me voyez* . . . Now I am an extinct volcano . . ." (p. 82).

There are comparable scenes with Conrad as Lingard, outwitting the Dutch as he smuggles guns to rebel sultans, or in the Congo dying in a native hut. Ford manages to fill nearly two hundred and fifty pages with this kind of poetic material, and perhaps in doing so, indicates the nature of the greatest service that he performed for Conrad. He also undertook such chores as answering letters, taking dictation, correcting proofs, and ghostwriting parts of the articles collected in *The Mirror of the Sea*.

No doubt this collaboration also filled a need for Ford : Conrad's beard, his age, his accent, and his taste for Schopenhauer must all have been reminiscent of Ford's own German father. As a child he had been taken for holidays to Lowestoft, and he liked to imagine that Conrad when there had taken him on his knee and told him stories. It probably explains why, in contrast to his behavior towards everyone else, he was always so patient with Conrad and so willing to serve him. It may also explain his reluctance, despite an abundance of evidence to the contrary, to abandon his image of Conrad as an iron-nerved buccaneer, "a returned Sir Francis Drake emerging from the territory of the Anthropophagi and the darkness of the Land of Fire." Neither this, nor his determination to see Conrad as a devoted disciple of Flaubert, takes us very far, but Ford does convey very well the kind of nervous irritation in which Conrad lived—"throwing tea cups into the fire"—though failing, perhaps, to appreciate how often he himself was the chief source of it.

Ford is also a witness to the vigilant energy of Conrad in his prime, an aspect that is easily missed by those who study only his correspondence. Conrad used his letters largely to complain, and it may be true, as Karl says, that in them the Conrad house "is a hospital. Doctors—Tebb, Hackney, Mackintosh, later Fox and Jones—are principal characters and reappear in Conrad's correspondence almost as often as do writers" (p. 47), but his letters were not his life.

When Aubry first published Conrad's collected letters in 1927, Ford wrote, "Which was Conrad? The bothered, battered person who wrote innumerable woeful, tactful, timid letters that are here connected by a string of properly noncommittal prose, or the amazing being that I remember?"* The view of Conrad as a "psychologically crippled valetudinarian" presented by Meyer or Karl can only make one wonder, as Ian Watt puts it, how it was that he produced "some twenty volumes of fiction that are marked by gloom, certainly, but also by a moral strength and sanity that remain unrivalled in the literature of our century" (Watt, 1980, p. 25).

* *New York Tribune*, September 18, 1927.

16. *Inspiration*

In July 1880, while Conrad, just qualified as an officer, was looking for a berth in London, the steamship *Jeddah* had been leaving Penang for Mecca with a thousand pilgrims on board. It was a big ship, not very old, and thought to be in perfect condition, and its crew of fifty included six British officers. The captain, part-owner of the vessel, had commanded it successfully for the past five years; his first officer was Augustine Podmore Williams, then twenty-eight.

The voyage was uneventful until, nearing the Gulf of Aden, on August 2, the *Jeddah* ran into a gale, and its two boilers shook loose, so that the engines had to be stopped. After a few days of wallowing in the sea the ship sprang a leak, and constant pumping was needed, the passengers helping with buckets. They were now quite close to Cape Guardafui, but the captain and the mate came to the conclusion that the ship was sinking, and gave orders to prepare the lifeboats. This alarmed the passengers, few of whom could hope to get into them, and at this point the captain's nerve seems to have failed. Williams took charge, and prepared for a secret launching of three boats under the cover of darkness. At 2:30 A.M. the captain and his wife, two other officers, and sixteen Malays entered one of the boats and Williams started to lower it. Some of the pilgrims, waking up to what was happening, tried to stop him, and Williams was pushed into the water. He was pulled into the boat, and when the pilgrims started throwing pans at it, he fired a couple of shots at them, and the boat was rowed away. The party was picked up by a British steamer and taken to Aden, where the captain reported that the ship had sunk, and he and his companions were the only survivors. The next day it appeared in the harbor, towed in by another British ship.

A court of enquiry, held at Aden, published a full report, from which the foregoing details are extracted. Conrad must have heard frequent references to this scandal, which was strongly condemned in editorials around the Empire, and he took the basic idea as the plot for a short story that would eventually grow into *Lord Jim*. He would make the ship and its circumstances wholly different, the only correspondence being in the outward aspect of Williams, whom he had glimpsed in Singapore. This point he confirmed in a conversation with a lady admirer, Mrs. Viola Allen, who had asked about the original Jim:

> "I used to see him in Singapore—a ship's runner he was—nearly six feet tall."
>
> "Yes, an inch perhaps two, under six feet." I interrupted. For a moment—he gaped at me—not recognising the opening words of Jim!
>
> "Yes," he said, "and he had an expression like this"—and he gave a rather lowering frown. "He was a fine looking man of about forty—his name was Williams—but I used that name somewhere else, and so I called him Jim." (ES p. 85n)

The body may have belonged to Williams, but the soul would be entirely Conrad's. He had not in fact used the name "Williams" for any other character, and in any case, "Jim" is given no surname—perhaps in itself an indication of Conrad's closeness to him. Williams was never punished, and always maintained that he had acted rightly in rescuing the captain's wife from the maddened natives. He subsequently served on other ships until, from a preference for life ashore, he became a chandler's representative, and later established his own business (SY pp. 145–147).

It is likely that Conrad began the story of Jim early in 1898 (BM p. 21), and in its original form, the court of enquiry would probably have provided the climax. His only experience

137

of such a court was at the loss of the *Palestine,* so it was probably the recalling of this event for the purposes of "Jim" that led him to write "Youth," or vice-versa. Either way, the two stories belong together, as interruptions of his continuing struggle with *The Rescue.* In a letter to Garnett at the beginning of June 1898, Conrad refers to the sale of "Youth," but lists it after "Jim," as part of a plan to produce a volume for Blackwood which would consist of, "I think, 'Jim' (20,000) 'Youth' (13,000) 'A Seaman' (5,000) 'Dynamite' (5,000) and another story of say 15,000" (EG p. 130). "A Seaman" may be what became *Typhoon,* or possibly *The End of the Tether,* while "Dynamite" was put away, apparently, to appear some fourteen years later as the opening chapter of *Chance* (JB p. 210).

In his letter to Henley about working with Ford, Conrad had emphasized that he "meant to keep the right to descend into my own private little hell—whenever the spirit moved me to do that foolish thing—and produce alone from time to time—verbiage no doubt—my own—therefore very dear." Settled at the Pent, he was now to descend into this private little hell, and from it would rise triumphant with the verbiage of the very *Heart of Darkness*—and then return there to search for the soul of *Lord Jim.*

The difficulty was that now, with Ford on his doorstep and a common task in front of them, Conrad needed an excuse, almost an apology, for descending into his private hell, and both *Heart of Darkness* and *Lord Jim* were done on the pretext of throwing out something for *Blackwood's* to keep the wolf away. In the Author's Note to *The Rescue* Conrad says that he had to interrupt it with *Heart of Darkness* because Blackwood wanted something for their thousandth number, issued in February 1899, but his correspondence shows that he had started it before the invitation came (BM pp. 35–37).

When Conrad began *Heart of Darkness* his conscious intention was probably no more than to throw out a quick story of adventure for the magazine market, which paid much better, in proportion, than did that of full-length novels. "Jim" had been started in this spirit, but put away again in the drawer when Conrad began to sense its real possibilities (LJ, p. viii): now, in its place, he seized on his Congo memories as ready-made material. All he would need to do would be to add a little glamour—the river in a more primitive state, battles with the natives, tribal rites, and hints of horror. The sophisticates might have been looking for the day "when the Rudyards cease from kipling and the Haggards ride no more," but not the British public.

This was how it was begun, and when it had ended Conrad was hardly aware of all that he had accomplished. In a letter to Elsie Hueffer in 1902, when the story finally appeared in book form, he says, "What I distinctly admit is the fault of having made Kurtz too symbolic or rather symbolic at all. But the story being mainly the vehicle for conveying a batch of personal impressions I gave rein to my mental laziness and took the line of least resistance" (JB p. 227).

Evidently this "line of least resistance" was what Conrad needed to escape his self-conscious labors with *The Rescue* and bring up from his "little hell" some of the chaotic shapes that since the time of Nietzsche had been shaking the moral foundations of Europe. In a sense it may be that Kurtz is too easily symbolic, as is also the mythical "darkness" of Africa, and that, as Leavis says, there are places where Conrad "stands convicted of borrowing the arts of the magazine writer"—he was after all writing for a magazine. But these are minor blemishes on an indisputable masterpiece: the gunboat, with its limp flag, rolling on a greasy swell and firing into a continent, the wild landscape littered with upturned railway trucks and lost rivets, the starving savages at the foot of the impeccably dressed accountant, the *Rules of Seamanship* lying in a grass hut, a dying steamboat threading its way through a primeval forest towards a liberal ideal that has suffered a Kafka-like metamorphosis—all this makes a parable so perfect and so prophetic that one cannot wonder at the book's continuing resonance or its profound effect on such younger contemporaries as Scott Fitzgerald and T. S. Eliot.

Conrad sent off the pages to Blackwood as fast as he produced them, so that the first of the story's three instalments was published in February 1899 even as the last was being written. When he had a theme that suited him, Conrad wrote with speed and grace in a flowing rhetoric—sentences that fill whole paragraphs, and paragraphs that almost fill whole chapters—*Lord Jim* has paragraphs that cover four pages. This is surely something akin to the ecstasy in which seers and prophets produced their oracles, though for the skeptical Conrad it was merely a kind of malignant fever, "an exaltation as false as all the rest of it" (LL 1, p. 283).

When *Heart of Darkness* was done, Conrad, still keeping Ford at bay, took out of the drawer the first sketch of *Lord Jim* and perhaps began to see that by bringing in Marlow as narrator, it could become the vehicle for his own spiritual autobiography. Jim has none of Conrad's intellectual qualities —these are given to Marlow, who becomes the instrument of the spiritual vivisection—but there can be little doubt that the sensibility that lies on the operating table is Conrad's own. Like Conrad, Jim is called to the sea by a boyhood reading of adventure stories, and both of them have "a half-crown complete Shakespeare" as part of their minimum luggage (LJ p. 237, PR p. 72). Jim is given to romantic dreams, and he has a sense of honor that is not un-English, but has an extra edge that owes something to Conrad's Polish background:

> There were his fine sensibilities, his fine feelings, his fine longings—a sort of sublimated idealized selfishness. He was—if you allow me to say so—very fine; very fine —and very unfortunate. A little coarser nature would have not borne the strain, it would have come to terms with itself, with a sigh, a grunt, or even with a guffaw; a still coarser one would have remained invulnerably ignorant and uninteresting. (p. 177)

This is a key passage for the understanding of Jim, and of his creator. The other important quality that Jim appears to share with Conrad is a strong tendency towards "sympathetic identification"—for the novelist, an essential qualification, but for the man of action, a fatal flaw. This is the immediate cause of Jim's undoing in the two great crises of his life—first, when the other officers of the *Patna*, having jumped, call on him to jump too, and "I had jumped—it seemed": he feels that "it was their doing as plainly as if they had reached up with a boat-hook and pulled me over" (p. 123). The other occasion is when he is confronted with Captain Brown, who similarly unnerves him and gains his sympathy.

Conrad had spoken to Garnett of that "sense that one's own personality is only a ridiculous and aimless masquerade of something hopelessly unknown," and it is this mysterious "something" with which Conrad is concerned—as Marlow puts it, "that side of us which like the other hemisphere of the moon, exists in perpetual darkness, with only a fearful ashy light falling at times on the edge" (p. 93). This is the real excitement of the book, and Marlow is hardly overstating the case when he asks himself "if the obscure truth involved were momentuous enough to affect mankind's conception of itself." This is a measure of Conrad's ambition, and *Lord Jim* is indeed one of those books that subtly and irreversibly change "mankind's conception of itself."

If the book seems to fall into two halves—the *Patna* incident, and Jim's subsequent career in Patusan—this is because Jim is concerned not only with his "good character" and a point of honor, but also, like his creator, with dreams of glory, and both these themes have to reach their tragic conclusion before his case has been dealt with. As the book passes from a question of betraying the seaman's code to that of fulfilling a dream of power, Marlow is no longer an adequate instrument for probing Jim's sensibility, and we are introduced to Stein, the man who lives "beyond good and evil," who creates his own illusions and lives by them as if they were true. In *Heart of Darkness* Kurtz as "superman" is simply evil, and pathetic, but in Stein we meet him a little more as Nietzsche imagined him in *Zarathustra*. At this altitude, Marlow, understandably, begins to feel a certain dizziness:

> The whisper of Stein's conviction seemed to open before me a vast and uncertain expanse, as of a crepuscular horizon on a plain at dawn—or was it, perchance, at the coming of night? One had not the courage to decide; but it was a charming and deceptive light, throwing the impalpable poesy of its dimness over pitfalls—over graves. His life had begun in enthusiasm for generous ideas; he had travelled very far, on various ways, on strange paths, and whatever he followed it had been without faltering, and therefore without shame and without regret. In so far he was right. That was the way, no doubt. . . .
> (p. 215)

The other and opposing perspective is provided by another man who has lived a comparable life, but stayed within the bounds of convention, the retired adventurer to whom Marlow

141

goes for a judgement on Jim's case. He dwells not in the wilds, but in "the highest flat of a lofty building," overlooking the tightly packed city, and he takes the opposite view : Jim should not have been true to his dream, with all its "illusory satisfaction" and "unavoidable deception," he should have stayed in the ranks : "We must fight in the ranks or our lives don't count."

These two oracles can be seen as speaking for the two halves of Conrad's own soul, and perhaps also as echoing the opposing voices of his father and his uncle. The book seems to give Stein the last word, when in the closing pages, against the criticism of Jim's widow, he affirms that Jim was not false but "True! True! True!" but the story leaves the conflict to continue in the mind of the reader as doubtless it did, lifelong, in Conrad's own.

17. *Typhoon and Other Events*

Out of the shipwreck that had ended Stephen Crane's attempt to reach Cuba at the time of the revolt against Spain in 1896 came his story "The Open Boat," which Conrad greatly admired, though he liked to tease Stephen about the waves that were "barbarously abrupt" (LE p. 102). When, in 1898, the blowing up of an American warship at Havana led to the Spanish-American War, Crane was determined to go there as a war correspondent. He had advanced tuberculosis, and no money, but, as Conrad said, "Nothing could have held him back. He was ready to swim the ocean." Conrad tells how he and Crane spent "a cloudy afternoon" rushing all over London trying to raise £60 for his fare. When all other sources had failed, Conrad took him to David Meldrum at Blackwood's office, where they were kindly received, and Crane was given the money as an "advance" for stories to be written about the war (LE p. 18).

Crane saw a great deal of action in Cuba between April and November 1898, and did not seem anxious to return, but at Oxted, Harold Frederic had died of a heart attack, and Cora, left with his mistress, Kate Lyons, and their three children, was about to be turned out of the house. Conrad tried to persuade *Blackwood's* to provide another advance, but Meldrum advised against it (BM pp. 31–32). By December, Cora managed to borrow enough to send Stephen his fare, and he got back to England just in time for Borys's birthday in January

1899. He was now able to give the boy a dog, which they called "Escamillo"—the toreador's song in *Carmen* was Conrad's favorite, and one of the only two pieces that he could whistle (BC p. 32).

Conrad's great productive period, which began after his move to the Pent in the autumn of 1898, was interrupted by both illness and increased social activity, the two being closely connected—it was usually guests that brought on the gout. Jessie was, by all accounts, an excellent cook and housekeeper, and the Conrads began to return some of the hospitality they had received. Not the Garnetts, who seem to have been allergic to Jessie—but the Fords were invited, of course, and their oldest friends, the Hopes, followed by Galsworthy, Cunninghame Graham and Hugh Clifford. There was also an excursion to Rye, with the Fords, for tea with Henry James. He offered a cup to Elsie before Jessie, which probably reflected his feelings about social priority, but made Elsie worry about whether he thought she was the elder (CC p. 69).

After tea they went for a walk and James's young nephew "Billy" remembered that James took Conrad's arm, leaving Billy to follow behind with Ford: "Hueffer babbled and I didn't listen. I wanted to hear what the great men were saying up ahead," but when he did he found that it was in French (Edel, p. 40). As Ford remembers it, "their phrases could not have been more elaborate or delivered more *ore rotundo*. James always addressed Conrad as '*Mon cher confrère*,' Conrad almost bleated with the peculiar tone that the Marsellaise get into their compliments '*Mon cher Maître*.' . . . Every thirty seconds!" (Ford, 1931, p. 270).

Crane was to live nearer to Conrad, since early in 1899 he moved his various dependents into Brede Place, a great decaying mansion set in the hollow where Harold had pitched his tent before the battle of Hastings. Conrad described it as "given over to rats, ghosts and draughts," but Crane furnished a few rooms "which even then looked bare and empty" (LE p. 112). Frederic's Kate and her ragged children haunted the upper reaches of the house, inspiring in the motherly Jessie Conrad a great desire to "tidy them up" (CC p. 73). James thought them "beautiful young barbarians": he had contributed £50 when their father died (Edel, p. 57).

At the end of 1899, Crane wanted to mark the close of the

century with a great party to which he invited all the leading writers of England—"a distinguished rabble." A lot of them came, but Crane was celebrating on borrowed time and borrowed money, and at the end of the festivities, while entertaining the last unsleeping guests with his guitar, he collapsed, with a tubercular hemorrhage. Cora woke Wells, who rode off on his bicycle, through the rain, to fetch a doctor from Rye. Crane's condition continued to deteriorate, and Cora decided to take him to a German clinic in the Black Forest. Conrad went with Jessie to see him off at Dover, and found him "in a big hotel in a bedroom with a large window looking on to the sea. . . . one glance at that wasted face was enough to tell me that it was the most forlorn of all hopes" (NLL p. 52). He died at Badenweiler on June 5, 1900.

Although Crane himself was always more desperate, financially as well as spiritually, than Conrad, one of his last acts was to write to a Canadian friend asking him to help Garnett to "pull wires" to obtain a Civil List pension for Conrad— "he is poor and a gentleman and proud. His wife is not strong and they have a kid" (Berryman, p. 259). Conrad's difficulties were aggravated by the fact that Krieger, in trouble himself, was now importuning him for the return of a loan of £180. Conrad told Meldrum that these demands were driving him mad, and William Blackwood was persuaded to advance him £100 (BM pp. 49–52).

Garnett shared Conrad's financial worries, and had long since suggested that he should employ an agent, then still something of a novelty. By August 1899, Conrad was persuaded to become a client of J. B. Pinker. Pinker was then thirty-five, a small and energetic man who had worked as a magazine editor and publisher's reader before setting up in business in 1896, with Wells and Oscar Wilde among his first customers. These would be followed by many other famous names. Frank Swinnerton would later describe Pinker as "a rosy, round-faced, clean-shaven, grey-haired sphinx with a protusive underlip, who spoke distinctly in a hoarse voice that was almost a whisper, shook hands shoulder high. . . ." (Hepburn, I, p. 27). For Pinker, Conrad would represent prestige rather than profit, but he was prepared to invest, indeed, to gamble on him, and would let him accumulate ever-increasing debts for the next ten years or more.

Towards the end of 1899, William Blackwood discovered John Buchan, and was immensely pleased with him. He was keen to know what Conrad thought of his first contribution, and Conrad promised to "read it at once and write you *all* I think." He thought it copied from Kipling and disliked it intensely. Meldrum saw it as a "violent antipathy," and crossed Buchan's name off a list for a little dinner party at which Conrad was to be introduced to some of the magazine's contributors (BM pp. 70–73, 113).

All this time, the intense nervous energy that Conrad was putting into *Lord Jim*, along with his illnesses and his fear that he would not be able to feed his family, was bringing him near to breakdown. His letters are full of groans and complaints as of a man who feels himself at the very end of his resources. He tells Sanderson that writing fiction for a living is "a fool's business," for "the unreality of it seems to enter one's real life, penetrate into the bones, make the very heartbeats pulsate illusions through the arteries. One's will becomes the slave of hallucinations, responds only to shadowy impulses, waits on imagination alone." In a second letter, after Sanderson has offered him some comfort, he provides quite another insight into his feelings: "Ah! my dear fellow, if you knew how ambitious I am, how my ambition checks my pen at every turn. Doubts assail me from every side. The doubt of form—the doubt of tendency—a mistrust of my own conceptions—and scruples of the moral order. Ridiculous—isn't it?" (LL 1, pp. 283, 286).

On top of all this, there was Ford, and collaboration to be attended to, Conrad's neglect of which was inducing impatience in Ford and indignation in Elsie. By this time Ford had put aside *Seraphina:* in February 1899 he had told Meldrum that he and Conrad were going to write a great novel about the Ana Baptists, on which he had "masses of information" (BM p. 44), but by the autumn he was simultaneously working on an enormous history of the Cinque Ports and a novel about Oliver Cromwell. He then dropped Cromwell in favor of a satire of contemporary society to be called *The Inheritors,* and in October he gave Conrad the first chapters, asking him to decide whether this or *Seraphina* should be the object of their collaboration (Mizener, p. 51). No answer

came, and in November he sent an indignant letter to which
Conrad replied with apologies, saying that the proposal to
collaborate "came from me under a false impression of my
power of work. I am much weaker than I thought I was,"
but nevertheless, "I am not going to draw back if you will
only consent to sweat long enough" (JB p. 236).

As a result of this, the Fords came to stay for a fortnight,
with late-night sessions in which the two men seem to have
developed a genuine sense of comradeship, though their wives
did not find it so rewarding. Long after Jessie had gone to
bed their raised voices would keep her awake, and Ford
"would relieve his feelings by thumping the oaken beam that
crossed the ceiling below and my small son would stir in his
sleep and mutter sleepily: 'Mama, dear, moo-cows down
there' " (CC p. 66).

Ford's habits were quite incompatible with Jessie's ideas of
good housekeeping, and in her memoirs complaints about his
behavior are almost as frequent as complaints about his poetic
exaggerations. One morning she found her husband's best
suit in a crumpled condition under Ford's bed, as he had used
the blankets to keep out the morning light, and then Conrad's
clothes to keep himself warm; and on another occasion, when
she was cooking the Sunday dinner, Ford having washed a
very greasy Panama hat, put it in the oven to dry just above
the joint (pp. 113, 116).

The collaborators had decided to begin with *The Inheritors*,
an easy social satire attacking "selfishness and falsehood,"
with sub-Wellsian touches of science fiction, but it would
arouse some interest from its caricatures of contemporary
politicians. What Conrad really thought about it he put into
a letter to Garnett, who is also portrayed, sympathetically, in
the book:

> I consider the acceptance of the *Inheritors* a distinct
> bit of luck. Jove! What a lark!
> I set myself to look upon the thing as a sort of skit
> upon the sort of political (?!) novel fools of the Morley
> Roberts sort do write. This in my heart of hearts. And
> poor H. was in dead earnest! Oh Lord. How he worked!
> There is not a chapter I haven't made him write twice—
> most of them three times over. (EG p. 168)

He goes on to say that "joking apart the expenditure of nervous fluid was immense. There were moments when I cursed the day I was born and dared not look up at the light of day I had to live through with this thing on my mind." If he seems to overprotest, it must be remembered that he was writing *Lord Jim*, against monthly deadlines from *Blackwood's Magazine*. Knowing the pain it might cause Ford, he told Garnett to burn the letter, but it was kept, and eventually published, and it did wound Ford, then an old man and given to tears (Mizener, pp. 54–55).

Blackwood's had begun to serialize *Lord Jim* in October, expecting it to be twenty thousand words, enough for three issues, and there are signs that they became a little dismayed when the story stretched on towards one hundred and forty thousand, for which they were paying Conrad £3 per thousand words. There had also been a £200 advance on the book, and they would soon be complaining that they were losing money on him. These worries were, of course, premature: *Blackwood's* would be constantly reprinting *Lord Jim* for the next fifty years. Even in 1947, before the refurbishing of Conrad's reputation that began with the publication of Leavis's *The Great Tradition* (1948), they were bringing out a new hardback edition of 10,500 copies.

There is evidence that after his marriage Conrad kept up some kind of minimal communication with Marguerite Poradowska (JB, p. 171), although no letters of his were preserved by her from June 1895 until April 1900, when she came to stay for a week at the Pent. Unable to provide her with a personal maid, Conrad instructed Jessie to fill the gap by setting out her clothes and brushing her hair, but Marguerite would have none of this, and won Jessie's heart by her warmth and friendliness. She was then in her early fifties, but Jessie described her as "I think, the most beautiful woman I have ever seen" (CC p. 70).

It was on July 20, 1900, that Conrad wrote to Galsworthy:

The end of *Lord Jim* has been pulled off with a steady drag of twenty-one hours. I sent wife and child out of the house (to London) and sat down at 9 A.M. with a desperate resolve to be done with it. Now and then I took a walk round the house, out at one door and in at the other. Ten-minute meals. A great hush. Cigarette ends growing into a mound similar to a cairn over a dead hero. Moon rose over the barn, looked in at the window and climbed out of sight. Dawn broke, brightened. I put the lamp out and went on, with the morning breeze blowing the sheets of MS. all over the room. Sun rose. I wrote the last word and went into the dining-room. Six o'clock I shared a piece of cold chicken with Escamillo (who was very miserable and in want of sympathy, having missed the child dreadfully all day). Felt very well, only sleepy; had a bath at seven and at 8.30 was on my way to London. (LL 1, p. 295).

The pile of cigarette stubs to commemorate the death of Jim is a reminder that Conrad had kept from his days as a seaman a taste for Virginia tobacco, at a time when only Turkish, which could not be chain-smoked, was socially acceptable. He had also the stained fingers of the man who rolls his own.

The trip to London was the first stage on the way to a holiday at Knocke on the Belgian coast, which had been recommended by Marguerite. On the way, the Conrads picked up the Fords, who were already staying at Bruges. Borys was sick on the journey, and it turned out to be enteric fever, of which he nearly died. Conrad told Galsworthy that "the whole hotel was in a commotion: Dutch, Belgians and French prowled about the corridor on the lookout for news. Women with babies of their own offered to sit up, and a painter of religious subjects, Paulus by name, rose up and declared himself ready to do likewise" (LL 1, p. 296). Conrad always tended to protect himself from his own over-sympathetic nature by avoiding the sight of illness, and it was probably Jessie's dissatisfaction with this aspect of his behavior that caused her, for once, to speak well of Ford: "He earned my gratitude and appreciation by the manner he showed his practical sympathy. He was always at hand to shift my small invalid, fetch the doctor, or help with the nursing" (CC p. 71).

The collaborators were supposed to be working on *Seraphina*, but apart from Borys's illness, Conrad was correcting the typescript of *Lord Jim* until August 11 (LL 1, p. 296), by which time he appears to have got the idea of *Typhoon* into his head, the net result being that he collapsed with a severe attack of gout, and the Fords went home without them. Back at the Pent, at the end of August, a further visit from the Fords sent Conrad back to bed with gout and *Typhoon*, which he would complete before the end of the year.

For Conrad, *Typhoon* can be seen as a kind of recuperation from *Lord Jim*, "my first attempt at treating a subject jocularly so to speak," a story full of sense, humor, and courage, with nothing that the ordinary reader could regard as "morbid." If J. B. Priestley has fairly well summed up what was once a common view of Conrad's work, "a sharp and often terrifying vision of man himself, with nothing to guide or help him but the skill he has mastered and a few simple loyalties, moving in a little lighted space above the dark destructive elements," then *Typhoon* is the archetypical expression of it. It is almost as long as *Heart of Darkness*, but seems much shorter, since it has nothing like the same intensity of image and idea.

Typhoon should have pleased William Blackwood, but after the "avalanche" of *Lord Jim*, which had run on until the issue of November 1900, he evidently felt that his readers had had enough of Conrad for a while, so the story went to Heinemann, who was still waiting for the completion of his promised volume.

Conrad followed *Typhoon* with *Falk*, another brilliant story of similar length, which he finished in May 1901 (LL 1, p. 300). The idea of the survivors on a drifting ship being driven to cannibalism he took from "a short paragraph in a newspaper" (AK p. 118), using his own experience with the *Otago* in Bangkok to provide the background. Although the way that the story deals with the themes of self-preservation and sexual desire seem, by modern standards, extremely restrained, it was rejected by all the magazines and had to wait to appear in *Typhoon and Other Stories* in 1903.

In his account of their time in Belgium, when Borys was ill, Ford refers to "the scared face of Amy Foster, maid, who had never been abroad," and in his next story, "Amy Foster," Conrad combined the face of their servant with the face of his wife during his fever on their honeymoon, and an anecdote found by Ford in his researches on the Cinque Ports about a shipwrecked foreign sailor. All this makes a story of considerable poetic power, expressing in parable, and hyperbole, Conrad's own experience of isolation and his own emotions as a "bloody furriner"—the dark side of his relationship with England.

All through this year there were short spells of collaboration in an attempt to finish *Seraphina*, now renamed *Romance*, which repeatedly put Conrad into a state of nervous prostration, followed by apologies to Ford on behalf of his nerves, "which, as you may have perceived, are and were devilishly attuned to the concert pitch of gloom and absurd irritation" (JB p. 272). *Romance* was not completed until March 1902 (BM p. 146). It has a rather self-conscious, and self-defeating, idea of "romance," but it is competently written, and Conrad hoped that at least it would be financially successful. To a limited degree it was: the first edition was sold within a month, and as Conrad wrote to Galsworthy, "that is better than anything of mine has ever done." Once it was out of the way, Conrad could regard Ford with more affection, and after a few weeks of peaceful isolation he wrote, "I miss collaboration in a most ridiculous manner. I hope you don't intend dropping me altogether" (Mizener, p. 76).

During a stay with Ford over the Christmas of 1901, Conrad had begun a short story called "Tomorrow," in which Ford evidently had a hand (JB p. 269). It is a powerful little parable that shows how a strong hope, unfulfilled, can turn to madness, and then spread its contagion. It made up the quota for *Typhoon and Other Stories*.

Sometime early in 1902, Wells had brought George Bernard Shaw to the Pent, Conrad's only reference to the incident being in a letter to Garnett in August—"four or five months ago G. B. S. towed by Wells came to see me reluctantly and I nearly bit him" (EG p. 181). According to Wells, Shaw told Conrad:

"You know my dear fellow, your books won't *do*"—for some Shavian reason I have forgotten—and so forth.

I went out of the room and suddenly found Conrad on my heels, swift and white-faced. "Does that man want to *insult* me?" he demanded.

The provocation to say "Yes" and assist at the subsequent duel was very great, but I overcame it. "It's humour," I said, and took Conrad out into the garden to cool. One could always baffle Conrad by saying "humour." (Wells 2, p. 620)

Shaw's feeling that Conrad's work "wouldn't *do*," like Conrad's feeling that Wells's wouldn't do, was no doubt connected with the incompatibility of the reformers and the "aesthetes" that would culminate in Wells's savage attack on James in *Boon*. For Jessie, always proud of her cooking, the reason why the reformers would not do was their reluctance to eat. Shaw insisted on "Van Houten's cocoa and a dry biscuit," while Wells limited himself to "a glass of milk and two aspirins from his waistcoat pocket" (CC p. 75).

Constance Garnett was continuing her translations, and in June 1902, after looking at her *Anna Karenina*, Conrad wrote that the translation was "splendid," but "of the thing itself I think but little, so that her merit shines with a greater lustre." This is only one of several strangely disparaging comments that he made about Tolstoy. On another occasion he accuses him of being "anti-sensual" (EG p. 244), apparently failing to appreciate that this was but a reflection of his rich sensuality, a quality that Conrad conspicuously lacks. In this, of course, he was joined by James, who spoke of "loose baggy monsters," but perhaps they both needed to play down Tolstoy a little in order to be able to believe in themselves.

Graham introduced to the Conrads the artist William Rothenstein, who became a regular visitor, painting pictures of Borys and his toys, and also a formal portrait of Conrad, Jessie insisting that unlike his picture of W. H. Hudson, in which the head "appears to be floating in a mist," there should be some shoulders visible (CC p. 72). Rothenstein, highly regarded by his contemporaries, and later knighted, would be influential in obtaining for Conrad grants from literary funds.

18. *Two Eventful Years in Costaguana*

In the Author's Note to *Nostromo* Conrad says that "after finishing the last story of the *Typhoon* volume it seemed somehow that there was nothing more in the world to write about." Indeed, from "Youth" through to the end of *Lord Jim* he had been using up both his seafaring experience and his inner substance at such a rate that he might well feel that he had almost exhausted them. There now began a new phase in his writing, in which the personal color is less concentrated, and there is more of a purely novelistic imagination: *Nostromo* can be seen as its greatest monument.

Conrad still owed Blackwood another thirty thousand words to complete the volume he had promised them, its other components, "Youth" and *Heart of Darkness*, having long since been set up in type. In March 1902 he set out to clear the debt in one go with *The End of the Tether*, whose considerable length may thus have been determined by factors other than the strictest artistic necessity—Blackwood would soon be complaining that the story was rather "slow in development." Even so, the way in which the reader gradually becomes aware that Captain Whalley is blind, and must then wait breathlessly for the outcome, makes compulsive reading. The story conveys very powerfully that conflict between social ideals and primal instincts that was one of Conrad's deepest concerns.

Whalley is the very embodiment of that "fidelity" upon which the merchant service depends, but his instinctive love for his daughter proves stronger, and forces him to betray it.

The expectations of William Blackwood and his readers were hardly compatible with the depth of Conrad's work, but Conrad himself seems to have been slow to realize this. Blackwood had also resented Pinker's intrusion into to what he regarded as a paternal relationship, particularly since Pinker kept pushing up the prices. When Conrad, obsessed with financial worries, made the first instalment of *The End of the Tether* the occasion for requesting a further "advance" of some £300, he was summoned to a meeting at Blackwood's London offices, where the concealed resentments came out. Conrad was told not only that he overvalued his work, but that altogether he was a conceited failure on whom, so far, *Blackwood's* had lost money, that he indulged in "an endless analysis of affected sentiments," that he missed his datelines, and hid behind the excuses of an artistic temperament. And, in particular, that though they had had one whole instalment of *The End of the Tether*, the story did not yet seem to have begun. Conrad went home deeply wounded and eventually wrote a long reply, of which a couple of pertinent paragraphs are enough to convey the mood:

> I admit that after leaving you I remained for some time under the impression of my "worthlessness," but I beg to assure you that I never fostered any illusions as to my value. You may believe me implicitly when I say that I never work in a self-satisfied elation, which to my mind is no better than a state of inebriety unworthy of a man who means to achieve something. . . .
>
> I am long in my development. What of that? Is not Thackeray's pennyworth of mediocre fact drowned in an ocean of twaddle? And yet he lives. And Sir Walter himself was not the writer of concise anecdotes I fancy. And G. Elliot [sic]—is she as swift as the present public (incapable of fixing its attention for five consecutive minutes) requires us to be at the expense of all honesty, of all truth, and even of the most elementary conception of art? But these are great names. I don't compare myself with them. I am *modern*, and I would rather re-

call Wagner the musician and Rodin the sculptor who both had to starve a little in their day—and Whistler the painter who made Ruskin the critic foam at the mouth with scorn and indignation. They too have arrived. They had to suffer from being "new". And I too hope to find my place in the rear of my betters. But still my place. My work shall not be an utter failure because it has the solid basis of a definite intention— first: and next because it is not an endless analysis of affected sentiments but in its essence it is action (strange as this affirmation may sound at the present time) nothing but action—action observed, felt, and interpreted with an absolute truth to my sensations (which are the basis of art in literature) —action of human beings that will bleed to a prick, and are moving in a visible world. (BM pp. 152–156)

And so on. Conrad's defense is moving, in places magnificent, and there is not a word that time has failed to justify, but it did not solve his financial problems. Fortunately, Sir Hugh Clifford had interested Edmund Gosse in obtaining help from the Royal Literary Fund, and in June 1902 Gosse wrote to James asking for his support. James's testimonial says that Conrad's work approaches to "the truth and beauty of the French Pierre Loti." *The Nigger of the Narcissus* is "the very finest and strongest picture of the sea and sea-life that our language possesses," while *Lord Jim* "runs it very close." This view of *Lord Jim* must raise doubts as to whether James had actually read it, but the letter served its purpose and Conrad received a grant of £300 (BM p. xxvii).

After the interview with Blackwood, it would be something of a point of honor with Conrad to get the next instalment of *The End of the Tether* away on time. He was only a few days late with it, on June 23, 1902, when a paraffin lamp he had left burning on Ford's William Morris table blew up and "before I could run back into the room the whole round table was in a blaze—Books, cigarettes, MS. alas! The whole second part of 'End of the Tether' ready to go to Edinburgh" (JB p. 278). The instalment, of about four thousand words, was not needed until the August issue, and Conrad does not seem to have been in a desperate hurry to rewrite it, but Ford subsequently made a good anecdote out of it, describing how he helped, both of them working day and night, while the household stayed up keeping soups warm, "until finally a horse was saddled in readiness for an early morning gallop to catch the mail train" (Ford, 1924, pp. 242–243). The story would run on longer than originally planned, and in October he would still be late with the last instalment, so that "I had three hours sleep for two nights and for the third no sleep at all going to bed as I am in a state. I may describe it as frenetic idiocy" (EG p. 183).

He now returned once more to *The Rescue*, but after grinding out a few more words he sent it off to Ford for what he hoped would be "the only real work of Rescue that will ever be found in its text" (JB p. 286). Evidently not, for it is one of the few works of this period in which Ford never claimed to have had a hand. Conrad's tendency to postpone the instalments of *The End of the Tether* and his inability to sit down any more in front of *The Rescue* can probably be attributed to the fact that he was already meditating on what would become the longest and most complex of his works, *Nostromo*.

When he began this book early in 1903, it seems that as with *Lord Jim*, he was thinking only of a short story, which would be set in South America, but "concerned mostly with Italians" (LL 1, p. 315). This is consistent with his source, which as he explains in the Author's Note, was an anecdote about an Italian who steals a lighter of silver on the eve of a revolution. This is in fact the whole "plot" of *Nostromo*—Conrad merely fills in the details of where the silver came from, and how the revolution went, but, as it turned out, at some length.

He took most of the minor scenes, incidents, and people from two good travel books, *Venezuela* by Edward B. Eastwick and *Seven Eventful Years in Paraguay* by G. F. Masterman, together with incidents from the autobiography of Garibaldi (WS pp. 156–158). He had also, through Graham, been introduced to Santiago Pérez Triana, a Colombian diplomat resident in London, and this provided him with the source for his one convincing South American character, the essential "anchor-man" of the book, Don José Avellanos (LL 1, p. 338).

Nostromo himself is, as Conrad says, based on Dominic

Cervoni, while Decoud, who as the book goes on, replaces Nostromo as its essential hero, expresses Conrad's own sensibility—his voice becomes virtually indistinguishable from that of the author. One of the book's successes is Captain Mitchell, a kind of more articulate McWhirr of *Typhoon*, who speaks for the England of Marryat and *Blackwood's Magazine*. Dr. Monygham is extrapolated from Masterman, who was himself a doctor, and was imprisoned and tortured in Paraguay. Gould is probably based largely on Cunninghame Graham.

It would appear from what Conrad says both in letters at the time and in the Author's Note, that he did not write *Nostromo* according to a preconceived plan, but let it grow in his storyteller's mind in rather the way that *Lord Jim* had done. This is supported by the fact that the shifts in time do not quite "add up," and Guerard remarks that "it has been my experience each time I have tried to disentangle the time-scheme of *Nostromo*, to come up with a different result" (p. 21). Since Conrad was carrying the whole thing in his head, the book had to be written, as far as possible, in long uninterrupted spells, and when, despite Jessie's precautions, an interruption came, the results were catastrophic:

> The whole world of Costaguana, men, women, headlands, houses, mountains, town, *campo* (there was not a single brick, stone, or grain of sand of its soil that I had not placed in position with my own hands) : all the history, geography, politics, finance; the wealth of Charles Gould's silver mine, and the splendour of the magnificent Capataz de Cargadores. . . . All that had come down crashing about my eyes. I felt I could never pick up the pieces—and in that very moment I was saying, "Won't you sit down?" . . .
> "I am afraid I interrupted you."
> "Not at all."   (PR p. 100)

Once begun, *Nostromo* went ahead at a great pace—it had to, or it would all have tumbled down. As Conrad put it in a letter to Wells, "I go on as I would cycle over a precipice alone on a 14 in. plank. If I falter I am lost" (LL 1, p. 311). In April 1903, Ford came down for a final proofreading of *Romance*, which no doubt brought down the whole world of

Costaguana again, and the effect on Conrad's nerves can be judged from Ford's story that on the way to London with the proofs, when he tapped him on the shoulder to announce that they had reached Charing Cross, Conrad, who had been on the floor making final revisions, "sprang to his feet and straight at my throat" (1924, p. 157).

It was also during this period that he met Sir Henry Newbolt, author of "Drake's Drum," and that pure distillation of the public-school spirit, "Play up, and Play the Game." In his account of the meeting Newbolt begins in the manner then acceptable for an English gentleman summing up a foreign specimen—"the man himself did not disappoint me. One thing struck me at once, the extraordinary difference between his expression in profile and when looked at full face," and so on, but then he almost got bitten. Asked why he was not staying longer in London, Conrad replied that he was too frightened of the people: "He leaned forward with both hands raised and clenched. 'Yes, terrified: I see their personalities all leaping out at me like *tigers!*' He acted the tiger well enough almost to terrify his hearers" (Sherry, 1972, p. 87).

Back at the Pent, Conrad cycled on across the plank and in November wrote again to Wells:

> *Romance*'s gone into 2nd ed: I hear. That no doubt does not mean much but still it is better than any of my other books did do. Is *Men in the Moon* doing well for you—I mean *really* well? After all, my dear boy, for all our faith in good intentions and even in our achievements, a paper-success (as I call it) is not a strong enough tonic. I say so because for me writing—*the only possible writing*—is just simply the conversion of nervous force into phrases. With you too, I am sure, tho' in your case it is the disciplined intelligence which gives the signal—the impulse. For me it is a matter of chance, stupid chance. But the fact remains that when the nervous force is exhausted the phrases don't come—and no tension of will can help. (LL 1, p. 323)

"The conversion of nervous force into phrases" provides an epigrammatic summation of Conrad's art, and his distinction between the apparent "chance" of what came to him and the "disciplined intelligence" of Wells, conveys the essential difference between what he was doing and what Wells was doing. One does not feel that he was speaking with any intentional irony—merely with envy.

Early in 1904 came the tragic event that would change Jessie's life, and that of the family. She had been anxious about her heart, and in January she and Conrad went to London for a consultation, to be told that there was nothing to worry about. Then, after shopping in Kensington High Street, Jessie was on her way back to Galsworthy's apartment when she slipped the cartilage of both knees and fell on the pavement, seriously injuring a knee that had been in a previous accident. She and Conrad returned to the Pent, but her condition forced them to come to London again for extended treatment (AK p. 50, CC p. 89).

Ford was then living at 10 Airlie Gardens on Campden Hill, and the Conrads, after staying with Galsworthy, found rooms a little farther down at 17 Gordon Place (Mizener, p. 85). The cost of Jessie's treatment added to Conrad's financial burden, made worse in February by the failure of his bankers, which required him to pay off an overdraft of £200 (LL 1, p. 326). Thus with *Nostromo* unfinished, but already being serialized in *T. P.'s Weekly*, Conrad felt forced to attempt also a series of newspaper articles on life at sea, dictating them to Ford in the evenings after a day's work on the novel. These pieces, eventually collected in *The Mirror of the Sea*, vary in interest and quality. Much of a chapter called "Rulers of the East and West" reads as if written by Ford, though the experience behind it can only be Conrad's. He told Wells, "This must save me. I've discovered that I can dictate that sort of bosh without effort at the rate of 3,000 words in four hours. Fact. The only thing is to sell it to a paper and then make a book of the rubbish. Hang! So in the day *Nostromo* and, from 11 P.M. to 1 A.M., dictation" (LL 1, pp. 326–327).

They also kept up some social life, with "at homes" and invitations to Galsworthy, James, and others. One guest, the critic Lewis Hind, congratulated Conrad on the way in which *T. P.'s Weekly* was advertising his name on posters all over London, which Conrad took as a deliberate attempt to insult him (Ford, 1924, p. 214). Ford is no doubt exaggerating when he says that it upset Conrad so much that he could not write the next weekly instalment, so Ford had to do it for him. Ford did later sell a passage of the book fifteen pages long, written in his own handwriting, but its complex relationship to preceding passages indicates that it was almost certainly dictated by Conrad.

The Conrads returned to the Pent in March, with Jessie not much better, and Conrad continued to "cycle over the precipice" with *Nostromo* until on August 30, 1904 he wrote to Ford:

> Phoo! I am weary. For more than a month I have been sitting up till three A.M.—ending with a solid 36 hours, (in the middle of which I had to wire for the dentist and have a tooth drawn!! . . .) It broke!! . . .!! Till at 11.30 *I* broke down just after raising my eyes to the clock.
>
> Then I don't know; two blank hours during which I must have got out and sat down—(not fallen) on the concrete outside the door.
>
> That's how I found myself; and crawling in again noted the time; considerably after one.
>
> But I've finished. There's no elation. No relief even. Nothing. (JB p. 293)

To Garnett, he summed it all up: "*Nostromo* is finished, a fact upon which my friends may congratulate me as upon a recovery from a dangerous illness" (LL 1, p. 335).

19. *Father Takes Command*

Of the two years that he spent in the writing of *Nostromo*, Conrad says in the Author's Note, "On my return I found (speaking somewhat in the style of Captain Gulliver) my family all well, my wife heartily glad to learn that the fuss was all over, and our small boy considerably grown during my absence." Borys was now six, and father and son seem to have been very happy in each other's company, Conrad encouraging the boy in all kinds of pranks and protecting him from too much maternal protection. He did not want to push him along his own painful path: soon after Borys's birth he had written to Garnett that he hoped to make a bargeman of him, "strong, knowing his business, and thinking of nothing. That is *the* life my dear fellow. Thinking of nothing! O! bliss." Later, however, when this policy had proved rather too successful, he would complain to Jessie that he "had no literary curiosity and showed almost a dislike of printed matter" (AK p. 5).

The dips of the downs encouraged a boy to get on to wheels, and when Borys was still "at a very early age," with the help of the gardener, Conrad made a go-cart that could be pushed to the top of the hollow in which they lived, and allowed to descend at dangerous speed. It was followed later by a pedal car, "constructed in secret by the village wheelwright" and produced as a birthday surprise (BC pp. 18–20).

Mrs. George found it hard to forgive her daughter for

marrying so extremely foreign a foreigner, and Conrad's relations with his mother-in-law seem to have been of the conventional, and conventionally comic, kind. The Pent had outside toilets, and on what Borys believed to be the last occasion on which his grandmother came to stay, Mrs. George had to go out there during the night—one of those nights on which Conrad was in Costaguana until after two in the morning. He took his rifle to investigate, and trailed Grandma twice round the house before she made a bolt for the toilet, where Conrad "having as he thought, run the intruder to earth, burst into the building shouting: 'Come out you ————, Damn you' " (BC p. 25).

The family did their weekly shopping at Hythe, and Ford tells of Conrad trying to persuade a grocer there to give him three years' credit on the strength of his future success. Hythe was about six miles away, over hills and through winding lanes, an hour's trip in the dog cart. Borys recalls an occasion when the mare stumbled and fell, so that his father "sailed through the air in a crouching posture like some huge frog, and came to rest squarely on the mare's head. My Mother, being much heavier, merely toppled over the splash board and landed upon the animal's hindquarters." Realizing the danger, Conrad "remained firmly seated upon the animal's head and called out to her, 'Scramble away from her legs, Jess, she can't kick you while I remain here' " (BC p. 28).

Conrad was introduced to motoring through Major Ernest Dawson, a fellow contributor to *Blackwood's* who became a family friend. His brother, A. J. Dawson, was a pioneer motorist, and Conrad, never very happy with horses, soon became an enthusiast. The Conrads began to hire cars regularly from a garage at Folkestone, and on one occasion made an expedition as far as their old friends the Hopes at Stanford. After crossing on the ferry from Gravesend to Tilbury, they knocked down a seaman in a busy street, and were attacked by the crowd, who tried to pull the driver off the car. Borys says that "then, as always in cases of dire emergency, my Father took command. He descended from the car; brisk orders were given which were smartly obeyed by the seamen in the crowd, and in a few moments calm was restored, the crowd was pushed back and the victim carefully lifted and

162

laid on the pavement. Fortunately his injuries proved to be trivial" (BC pp. 42–43).

After treatment for her leg, Jessie remained laid up at the Pent for some months, and in October 1904 returned to London for another spell in a nursing home. She says that "it was typical of Joseph Conrad with his inherent extravagance" that the night before she went in "they had some thirty guests to supper, including E. V. Lucas, Augustus John, and other literary and artistic names now forgotten" (CC p. 89). Her own philosophy, as Borys sums it up, was "complete imperturbability and apparent lack of emotion, an unassailable placidity that was almost frightening at times."

After some painful examinations of her knee, it was decided that an operation was necessary. While it was in progress Conrad and Borys paced the pavement "in the chilly mist of a November morning." The street must have impressed itself on Conrad, for it would apparently become the location of the embassy in his next book, *The Secret Agent*—"in its breadth, emptiness, and extent it had the majesty of inorganic nature, of matter that never dies. The only reminder of mortality was the doctor's brougham arrested in august solitude close to the kerbstone. The polished knockers of the doors gleamed as far as the eye could reach, the clean windows shone with a dark opaque lustre. And all was still." Borys remembers that "he clutched my hand firmly, a gesture very rare with him," and then apparently retreating even further into subconscious behaviour, he found himself with his arms round the neck of an underfed dray horse, and gave the carter half-a-crown to buy it an extra feed of corn (CC p. 90). This, presumably, becomes that underfed animal of a "truth more cruel than caricature" that takes Winnie Verloc on her cab ride through the city in the same book. The owner of the brougham by the curb was not, apparently, very efficient: Borys says "I believe it is true that the surgeon concerned made a mess of the job," and Jessie was crippled for life (BC p. 44).

As soon as his wife was able to move, or at least to be moved, Conrad wanted to get away from the English winter. Galsworthy and Ada were in Italy at Amalfi, and early in January 1905 Conrad set off for Capri. It was a complex operation, requiring a tenuous chain of bookings by ship and train, with chairs to be waiting for Jessie at each change, as she had to be lifted everywhere, at one moment dangling over the water, at another left clinging to the ledge above the door of a train. Conrad expressed anxiety in bursts of anger, chiefly with the nurse they had hired, who ended up in bed being nursed by Jessie. At Naples they were delayed five days by bad weather. When the ferryboat reached the island, a gang of seamen were mobilized by Conrad, and Jessie says, "I was hoisted over the side of the vessel and passed by willing hands down the gangway into the small boat lying alongside. I simply shut my eyes and let myself go. Still in the wooden chair, I was landed on the 'Granda Marina,' without a pause as it seemed to me. Poor Joseph Conrad was loud in praise of the feat—'It took a sailor to do things properly.' The dear man seemed to have forgotten his agitation during the process" (CC pp. 91–95).

Conrad had hoped to produce "sixty thousand words" to pay for the expedition (LL 2, p. 9), but the desiccated island, blown upon by the Sirocco, did not suit his nerves, the family with whom they lodged were numerous and noisy, and in the end all that he wrote was one essay, called "Autocracy and War." They visited and were visited by the Galsworthys, and Conrad made friends with Norman Douglas, who lived there, and also with a Dr. Cerio, who attended Jessie, played chess with Conrad, and lent him books about the naval war in the Mediterranean at the time of Napoleon, a subject on which, two years before, Conrad had expressed his intention of writing a novel (BM p. 158). He would brood upon this for many more years before beginning, and leave the task unfinished when he died. A Polish expatriate on the island, Count Zygmunt Szembek, told Conrad of an "abominable adventure" in Naples that would be retold as "Il Conde" in Conrad's *A Set of Six* (AK p. 127).

"Autocracy and War," by far the best of Conrad's few essays, was originally intended to be "a sort of historical survey of international politics from 1815," which would bring home the guilt of Prussia (LL 2, p. 13), but it so happened that just at that moment came the defeat of Russia by Japan, which so excited him that he almost forgot about the Germans, and produced a song of triumph not unlike that of Isaiah at the fall of Babylon:

> This dreaded and strange apparition, bristling with bayonets, armed with chains, hung over with holy images; that something not of this world, partaking of a ravenous ghoul, of a blind Djinn grown up from a cloud, and of the Old Man of the Sea, still faces us with its old stupidity, with its strange mystical arrogance, stamping its shadowy feet upon the gravestone of autocracy, already cracked beyond the repair by the torpedoes of Togo and the guns of Oyama. . . . The task of Japan is done, the mission is accomplished; the ghost of Russia's might is laid" (NLL pp. 89–90)

Only at the end of the essay does he return to Poland's other enemy, Prussia, where, in effect, he prophesies the First World War as the inevitable outcome of German energy and ambition, and "democracy, which has elected to pin its faith to the supremacy of material interests, will have to fight their battles to the bitter end." It provides an interesting commentary on the implicit philosophy of *Nostromo* and the theme that echoes in the ideals of Charles Gould, and the nightmares of his wife—"material interests." For Gould, "action" was necessary because only in action could he find the "illusion of a mastered destiny." In the essay this aphorism is applied also to nations, with the pessimistic conclusion that for the state, aggression is the only form that the action can take (NLL p. 109; cf. *Nostromo*, p. 66).

One of the jobs that Ford had done for Conrad during their stay in London had been to extract the dialogue from Conrad's story "Tomorrow," so that they could turn it into a one-act play, renamed *One Day More* (LL 2, p. 17). While Edward Garnett's father had been Keeper of the Printed Books at the British Museum, Sidney Colvin, later knighted, was Keeper of the Prints and Drawings, and it is probably through this connection that Conrad came to know Colvin. Considerably older than Conrad, Colvin had been a friend of Robert Louis Stevenson's, and had edited the letters of Keats. At the center of the cultural establishment, he would prove a valuable friend, and on this occasion he persuaded the Stage Society to put on Conrad's play. Conrad wanted to attend the rehearsals, so the family left Capri early in May, returning by sea.

On the ship, Jessie noticed that Conrad was in a state of agitation, continually emptying his pockets when he thought that she was not looking. When she demanded the reason, "with his usual extravagant gesture and flinging away his freshly lighted cigarette, he rose and paced the length of the cabin before he said, abruptly, 'I left my damn' wallet on the table in that cafe the other day. Every blamed cent. Well, it's no use crying over spilt milk, we shall have to wait in Marseilles till I get some more sent to us, that's all. Don't pull that face. It's gone, I tell you, and whining over it won't help any.' " Jessie found it, along with two letters that she had given him to post, in his waistcoat, but she adds that as he subsequently distributed it all in largesse to the crew, they had to wait anyway (CC pp. 102–103). They spent the time with Marguerite Poradowska, who had come to Marseilles to meet them—but missed an intended meeting with Conrad's French translator, Robert d'Humières (SD p. 248).

With any income from *Nostromo* absorbed by the numerous advances he had already obtained from Pinker, Conrad was again financially desperate, but Rothenstein had persuaded Gosse to obtain a further grant, from royal funds, this time for £500. Sir Henry Newbolt was to act as trustee, and pay the money out in small sums according to Conrad's needs. Conrad took this as an insult, and angered Gosse by saying so. Rothenstein made peace between them, and Conrad had no difficulty in demonstrating his needs—his first application, including £100 to be sent to Capri, debts to three doctors and a host of local tradesmen, was enough to use up almost all of the grant, and he would still be in debt. Newbolt suggested that he should rather declare himself bankrupt, but Conrad replied, rightly no doubt, that this would be a betrayal of people who had trusted him, and make his position worse for the future (Karl, pp. 579–585).

One Day More was performed at the Royal Theatre on three successive evenings from June 25. Conrad wrote to Galsworthy, "As to the success of my thing, I can't say anything. I've heard that some papers praised it and some ran it down. On Tuesday when we went (like the imbeciles we are) there was some clapping but obviously the very smart audience did not catch on. And no wonder! On the other hand the celebrated 'man of the hour,' G. B. Shaw, was ecstatic and enthusiastic. 'Dramatist,' says he" (LL 2, p. 21).

Although he would occasionally be tempted by dreams of making a fortune from it, Conrad hated the stage: any play seemed to him "an amazing freak or folly," while to watch the players "breeds in my melancholy soul thoughts of murder and suicide—such is my anger and loathing of their transparent pretences" (LL 1, p. 213). Films he liked no better —"the movie is just a silly stunt for silly people." This temperamental distaste can be seen as closely connected with the nature of his talent: no doubt he was right to see the stage as a kind of evil temptation, for it is at the opposite pole from his kind of subtle and excursive analysis. Subsequent experience has shown that to make a play or a film from one of his stories requires so much rewriting that whatever its merits as entertainment, it usually bears little resemblance of the original.

20. *Secret Agents*

Conrad returned to the peace of the Pent, but for some months failed to find further inspiration. Jessie attributed this to the poor sales of *Nostromo*, which had come out in book form in October 1904. It had not been well received by the critics, and even those who called it a work of genius had suggested, quite correctly, that it would not be popular. Jessie says that Conrad was "bitterly disappointed. This was the only time I saw him display any feeling about the fate of his books. And I didn't wonder at it, because I knew how much effort, what an amount of vitality and nervous force he had expended in writing that book" (AK p. 53). In fact he would never again match the abundant vitality of the period that ended with *Nostromo:* from now on there would be shorter sentences and smaller paragraphs, more reason and convention, less deep energy.

After using crutches for a time, Jessie was able to move about on her own, though she would always have trouble with stairs—"I could move and I did move, not exactly like a cripple but with difficulty, as though dragging an invisible weight riveted to my leg" (AK p. 52). Conrad's gout was now beginning to have a permanent effect on his hands, provoking bursts of irrational irritation : servants stayed or went according to their ability to put up with it.

In those days, in the Kentish countryside, the police seem to have been almost as distant, and as little relied on, as in the

168

American West, and although Conrad had his gun, the family's isolated position was rather frightening for the London born Jessie. Apart from a crazy gardener who nearly murdered Borys, and occasional aggressive tramps, her worst experience was when a mentally unstable German arrived in the area with a gun, believing that Conrad had slandered him in his books. Conrad's favorite villain was the German hotel-keeper Schomberg, who appears in *Falk*, *Lord Jim*, and other stories, and as sometimes seems to happen with authors, he took flesh and came to seek his creator.

Jessie had put Conrad into bed with a bad attack of gout when:

> There was the tinkle of a bicycle bell, and looking round I beheld a stoutish stranger ride into the yard, dismount and lean his cycle up against the wall, while he came purposefully towards me.
>
> "I 'ave gom to make zee acquaintance of Mr. Conrad."
>
> I answered rather shortly that this was impossible as my husband was very ill in bed, and not allowed to see anyone. The stranger stuttered with excitement, and declared in guttural tones: "I gom again, I will come many times." He glared at me in truly vengeful manner, and as I turned my back upon him, his hand flew to his hip pocket in a significant gesture.

The next morning the stable lad told them that the man had been prowling round the house, and then a local farmer sent them a note to say that the man had been lodging with them, and had declared his intention of shooting Conrad at sight. All day, no one came to the house, and Jessie was too frightened to go out and seek for help. The next day they heard that the German had been captured after killing a soldier in Folkestone. He had escaped from the care of a sister in the West country, and had a book with passages in *Falk* marked in red ink (CC pp. 81–83). It may be that this bizarre incident contributed to the plot of *Victory*, in which Schomberg inspires an evil emissary who suddenly appears on the hero's island intent on murdering him.

Conrad's imagination could make tragedy out of less than this. Once when their stable lad had stayed out very late to help to find some lost hounds, Conrad told Jessie, "That fellow's committed suicide, my dear. I heard of a case just like it on board once." When she protested, he added, "You don't know these young men; his whistling and being, or appearing, happy is nothing to go by." After much running to and from the village, and sending of messages to the family and police, the Conrads were slowly walking back to the Pent by the light of the moon when "we heard in the distance a loud guffaw that ended in a strangled effort to restrain it" (CC pp. 109–110).

During the latter part of 1905, Conrad completed *Gaspar Ruiz*, a "powerful" but relatively shallow novella that uses up the leftovers of his South American reading, which must have included Darwin's *The Voyage of the Beagle*, as this is apparently Conrad's source for an Indian attack on a fort (WS p. 138). He also wrote a trivial tale, "The Brute," based on what Captain Blake had told him about the *Apse Family* in 1884. Meanwhile, he was meditating on the themes of anarchy and revolution, which were just outside his personal experience but very much part of his background: he brings to them an intellectual analysis that seems so much in conflict with buried emotions that the results are often deep and disturbing.

In "An Anarchist" Conrad uses an idea that he will take up again in *Under Western Eyes*—that of the young man who wishes to be an unnoticed conformist, but who is, through strange misunderstandings, regarded as a rebel. No doubt it reflects, in a magnified manner, some of his own feelings as a youth in Poland, where his father's reputation led him to be regarded as a potential agitator. His next story, "The Informer," is set in England, and uses bits of gossip he had picked up from Ford, whose Rossetti cousins, while still at school, had been actively involved with the anarchists. The "Lady Amateur" of the story resembles Helen Rossetti, whom Conrad had met on one or two occasions (WS p. 213).

Conrad was doubtless fascinated by a movement in which middle-class children made tea for the men of violence and aristocratic idealists such as Cunninghame Graham fought the police in Hyde Park alongside psychotic killers, but it cannot be said that he really helps us to understand the social and psychological issues that lay behind it. *The Secret Agent* is a deep and disturbing book, but it is not a serious study of the anarchist movement, and most of Conrad's material came straight from newspapers and magazines (WS Chs. 20–32).

At the end of 1905, as the winter deepened, Conrad was ill, Jessie was pregnant, and Borys was just recovering from some skin poisoning that had followed scarlet fever. Conrad felt that they all needed some sunshine, and took them to a hotel at Montpellier, in the south of France. Here he was happy, playing boats with Borys in the Public Gardens, taking him for tram rides, or sitting in a cafe. The boy had daily lessons in fencing and riding, and his father wrote to Pinker to boast of his skill, adding, as he remembered who was paying for it, that the lessons were very inexpensive (LL 2, p. 31).

It was in the midst of this soft sunlight that Conrad began *The Secret Agent,* making his descent into the City, "cruel devourer of the light, darkness enough to bury five million lives." As had happened before, the novel began as a mere short story, but already by March 5 he was telling Pinker, "Alas, it'll be longish." The original impulse may have come, as he says in the Author's Note, from the "utter absurdity" of an attempt to blow up Greenwich Observatory in 1894, but he was soon carried beyond the absurdity of anarchism into the deeper irrationality that lies everywhere beneath the conventions of day-to-day living—anarchism becomes but another aspect of the general absurdity of life, acted out in the drama of the Verloc family in a way that is only incidentally, and as it were symbolically, connected with theories of anarchy.

A little frightened, perhaps, in the end, by what he had done, Conrad, in the Author's Note added much later, set up all kinds of diversions, overprotesting his "sincerity," and generally trying to assure his public that he did not intend to commit "a gratuitous outrage on the feelings of mankind."

In his youth Conrad had spent many hours walking the streets of London, not like Dickens, happily at home there, but in utter isolation; in the Author's Note he says, "I had to fight hard to keep at arm's length the memories of my solitary and nocturnal walks . . . lest they should rush in and overwhelm every page." They are distilled into a dark poetry that expresses, as in *Heart of Darkness,* the experience of an alien explorer. It is an underfed cab-horse that is said to illus-

171

trate "the proverb that 'truth can be more cruel than caricature' if such a proverb existed," but the whole city is presented, like a working model in a glass case, as if to illustrate
this "proverb."

In March 1906, Galsworthy published *A Man of Property*,
and Conrad was asked to review it for the *Outlook*. It brought
loyalty to a friend into conflict with artistic conscience, and
conscience just won. Conrad filled most of the space with
vague generalities, but had to say that "in this world of
Forsytes (who never die) organised in view of acquiring and
preserving property, Mr. Galsworthy places with the sure in-
stinct of a novelist a man and a woman who are no Forsytes,
it is true, but whom he presents as in no sense the adversaries
of the great principle of property," and concluded, "Mr.
Galsworthy may possibly be found disappointing by some, but
he will never be found futile by anyone, and never uninter-
esting by the most exacting. I myself, for instance, am not
so sure of Bosinney's tragedy. But this hesitation of my mind,
for which the author may not be wholly responsible after all,
need only be mentioned and no more, in the face of his considerable achievement" (LE pp. 125–131). This, one can
imagine, was rather less than Galsworthy would have hoped
for, and in a subsequent letter we find Conrad appeasing him
at some length (LL 2, p. 32).

After the family's return from Montpellier in April, Jessie
found the primitive conditions at the Pent rather too difficult,
and Ford, still in London, suggested that they look for a place
at Winchelsea, offering them the use of his house while they
did so. Conrad accepted, against the advice of Jessie, who
found this period very difficult, since the Fords came down
every weekend, and seemed to Jessie to be unfairly combin-
ing the advantages of being both the hosts and the guests.
After a final quarrel about whether the kitchen door should
be left open, to reduce the heat for Jessie, or shut to keep the
kitchen from the sight of their guests, Conrad was "forced
to take his head out of the sand," and they returned to the
Pent (CC pp. 112–115).

While at Winchelsea, Conrad was persuaded to help with
what Ford called "a rather larky collaboration," a story called
The Nature of a Crime, written quickly with the idea of

anonymous publication. Conrad never liked it, but Ford did, and would eventually publish it himself, as no one else would, when he became editor of the *English Review* in 1908.

It was probably during this stay at Winchelsea that Ford introduced another local resident, Arthur Marwood, who would soon become Conrad's closest friend. The younger son of a baronet, Marwood was a cultured right-wing radical of the kind that Conrad found most congenial. In appearance, he was, according to Ford, "the heavy Yorkshire squire with his dark hair startlingly silver in places, his keen blue eyes, his florid complexion, his immense expressive hands and his great shapelessness," but he "possessed upon the whole, the wisest and most serene intelligence of any human being I have ever met" (Ford, 1931, p. 372). Although he was trained in mathematics, ill health had ended Marwood's career as a statistician: he had married his nurse and developed an interest in literature. Conrad would use him as the original for his "well connected but rustic Mills" in *The Arrow of Gold* (LL 1, p. 40n), and in appearance and background he is fairly obviously the source for Tietjens, the hero of Ford's best three books. Some of the discursive sections of Conrad's *Chance* probably give a fair selection of his conservative wisdom (see Ch. 23).

The Conrad's second child was due to appear in August 1906, and for this occasion the Galsworthys, in Italy again, lent them their house in London. Although it was nominally well up to strength in servants, Galsworthy's conscience had compelled him to staff it with women who, like his wife Ada, and her fictional equivalent, Irene, had suffered from allegedly brutal husbands. The men had been sent to Australia at Galsworthy's expense, while the wives lived below stairs, but were not, as Jessie put it, "at all satisfactory from the servant point of view."

Because of Jessie's condition a car was hired, on doctor's orders, to carry her "in the greatest comfort" from the Pent, but when they arrived, Conrad, "ill and desperately irritable," was so upset that his favorite bed-side book had been left behind that, two days later, Jessie volunteered to hobble back by train and fetch it. She had forgotten that it was Sunday, when the trains were few, and returned five hours later than expected to find Conrad in trouble with an angry Doctor Tebb, who thought the whole thing incredible. When he had gone, Conrad said, "Of course, Tebb doesn't know you my dear. You're not one of those frail, hysterical women, who go to pieces at the mere idea of a little exertion."

She went to bed, but two days before the birth when guests were due for lunch, "the derelict servant woman" due to cook "turned up her toes with a bad headache," so once more Jessie "rose to the occasion." When she did produce the baby, whom they named John, Conrad thought he looked Italian, and was a little worried: Borys sighed and said, "Well, I must give him half the dog and half the cat. And I'll let him sleep in Mum's bed." This was a reference to the occasion when he had been told that he was too old to sleep there himself, and had asked why, in that case, his father was allowed to do it (CC pp. 118–119).

In December 1906 the Conrads again set off for Montpellier, meeting Marguerite in Paris. On the way across France, Jessie left a bundle of baby's clothes on the floor of the carriage, which Conrad stumbled over and then threw out of the window, but when they arrived the sunshine restored him, and there was no more gout for a couple of months (CC p. 122). He wrote at this time his remarkable novella *The Duel*, the source of which was, according to Aubry, an artillery officer Conrad met, though another version of the tale had appeared in America in 1858 (SD p. 350; JB p. 343). It is the story of two French officers living in conflict through the whole of the Napoleonic era, of whom one, the thoughtful D'Hubert, who cannot escape the obligations of "honor," even though aware of their utter absurdity, obviously speaks for the author.

In February, still at Montpellier, Borys caught measles, and after that, whooping cough, which he passed on to the baby, and Conrad's gout returned. The children's coughs grew worse, and the doctor, suspecting tuberculosis, advised the family to go to Switzerland. On the way, at Lyons, every hotel, after hearing the children cough, decided it had no room, until at last "the cough hung fire just long enough."

At Geneva the Hotel de la Roseraie, where Conrad had always stayed, declined to take them in, and the best they could find were rooms on the top floor of another place, where the stairs made Jessie a virtual prisoner. Borys was now recovering, but John was growing worse, and on May 18, Conrad wrote to Pinker, "We started by medical advice, counting on the change of climate to check the disease, but it has developed on the road in a most alarming manner. The poor little devil has melted down to half his size. Since yesterday morning he has had a coughing fit every quarter of an hour or so and will not eat anything" (LL 2, p. 48).

In the midst of this Conrad was rewriting *The Secret Agent*, making it about thirty thousand words longer than the original version. This was now being serialized in America by a magazine called *Ridgeway's*, which subtitled itself as "A Militant Weekly for God and Country," and presumably thought that with this exposure of anarchy, it was striking a powerful blow at the radicals. Some of Conrad's friends, less militant for God and country, also thought so, and we find him writing several defensive letters, such as one to Galsworthy in which he says that he is being "misunderstood": "After all you must not take it too seriously. The whole thing is superficial and it is but a tale. I had no idea to consider Anarchism politically, or to treat it seriously in its philosophical aspect" (LL 2, p. 33).

John began to improve, but then Borys developed rheumatic fever, and on June 6, Conrad wrote to Galsworthy describing how, for the first time in a month, the baby had smiled, but Borys was crying out in the next room as pain awoke him from a feverish doze, while he was trying to "elaborate a little more" the conversation between Verloc and his wife: "By Jove! I've got to hold myself with both hands not to burst into a laugh which would scare wife, baby, and the other invalid—let alone the lady whose room is on the other side of the corridor!" (LL 2, p. 52).

It was July before the children were well enough to go out into the garden, and Borys "for a long time seemed to be wearing the clothes of some other bigger and plumper person." There was a pool with a fountain, and Borys had a model yacht that Marguerite had given him. Father and son "amused themselves by making docks, and constructing bridges across from side to side. Joseph Conrad would be perfectly patient at this kind of game for hours on end." In August the family set off for home. To teach Borys about time zones, Conrad told him to keep his watch on Swiss time while he would put his own on British, as a result of which he made them miss their dinner to go to the station an hour too early (CC pp. 127–128).

The first priority now was to seek a house better suited to Jessie's condition. After failing to find anything nearby, Conrad went to Bedfordshire to look at a farmhouse called the Someries at Luton Hoo, the estate of the diamond magnate Julius Wernher. To their subsequent regret, he decided immediately to take it. When Jessie was sent ahead to prepare for her husband's official arrival, she found pigs in the kitchen, the well unusable, and droves of bullocks, but no milk. Conrad arrived in the evening and "made what he declared was the most reasonable demand—his dinner." After he had had it, he told her, "Not as well served as usual, my dear. You must see to it. Put your foot down at once" (CC p. 130).

After the birth of John, Jessie no longer had the time to do Conrad's typing, and a succession of secretaries came and went until they found Lilian Hallowes, whom Borys describes as "a tall willowy female, then I think, about thirty, with a supercilious manner and a somewhat vacant expression," who would stay until Conrad died. It has been suggested that with Peter Ivanovitch in *Under Western Eyes* Conrad was satirizing Tolstoy (JB p. 372), but in the account of Peter's methods of dictation, Conrad was evidently satirizing himself: "First of all you have to sit perfectly motionless. The slightest movements you make put to flight the ideas of Peter Ivanovitch. You hardly dare to breathe. As to coughing—God forbid" (p. 147). Of Miss Hallowes, Borys says she survived only because she "possessed the ability to sit quite silent and motionless in front of her machine, hands resting tranquilly in her lap, for long periods" (BC p. 14). With gout now stiffening his fingers, it was a relief to Conrad to dictate long passages, but inevitably, it affected the quality of his style.

That autumn *The Secret Agent* was published. Conrad had hoped that as a "thriller" it would have "an element of popularity in it," but it was not the average man's idea of a good read, nor even, as it turned out, the average critic's. They were not encouraged by either "the subtlety of his mental processes" or the "moral squalor of the tale," and could explain it only by the rumor that he was "the son of a Revolutionist" (PR p. viii). There were of course sympathetic

176

notices from the more intelligent, including, as always, Edward Garnett, but *Country Life* was indignant that Verloc should be made to appear almost human, when everyone knew that such people were "the most unmitigated blackguards." They also thought it most improper that he should be legally married, "instead of forming one of the slight and fleeting attachments which are more common in the order to which he belongs" (CH p. 187). The *T.L.S.*, on the other hand, went, more admirably, but almost as absurdly, on the opposite tack: in the past terrorists had been treated only in a sensational manner, but "then comes Mr Conrad with his steady, discerning gaze, his passion for humanity, his friendly irony, and above all his delicate and perfectly tactful art, to make them human and incidentally to demonstrate how monotonous a life can theirs also be" (CH p. 184).

Conrad had a copy sent to Henry James, cautiously keeping his head down: "The covers are deep red I believe. As to what's inside them I assure you I haven't the slightest idea. That's where Hazlitt's Indian Juggler has the pull over a writer of tales. He at least knows how many balls he is keeping up in the air at the same time" (LL 2, p. 55).

At the Someries that December, Conrad passed his fiftieth birthday in a state of gloom. He and Jessie hated the house, and the situation did not suit him—"you have no idea of the soul corroding bleakness of earth and sky when the east wind blows"—and with *The Secret Agent* no more successful than *Nostromo*, his debts grew deeper. In January 1908 he wrote to Galsworthy of the "inspiration killing anxiety" of having to think, "Is it saleable? There's nothing more cruel than to be caught between one's impulse, one's act, and that question, which to me is simply a question of life and death" (LL 2, p. 65). In a subsequent letter Conrad mentions that although he has not been spending more than £650 a year, he now owes Pinker £1572.

21. *The Advantages of Barbarism*

With the making of money now "a question of life and death," Conrad turned again to *Chance,* which he had first begun as long ago as 1905 with the idea of producing something the public would like. As with *The Rescue,* however, his heart was not in it: when it came to a choice between God or Mammon he could never resist the temptations of the spirit, and he would soon be abandoning *Chance* for another book about revolutionaries.

In his review of *The Secret Agent* Garnett had suggested that Conrad transcended his British contemporaries through possessing a certain understanding of human nature that he shared with the great Russian novelists as part of a common Slav inheritance. This oft-repeated conviction of Garnett's, with which posterity would largely agree, angered Conrad every time it was aired. For him, Poland was a Western, Catholic nation, culturally linked to France, while he himself was a British master mariner whose temperament differed only incidentally from that of others of his class (LL 2, p. 336). This is probably one of the factors that influenced him to write *Under Western Eyes.* He would show us what the Russians are like, and as the title emphasizes, he would see them through Western eyes.

Although he himself had escaped from Russian "autocracy," he was always aware of its effects on the lives of those he had left behind. In particular, letters from his uncle in

178

1892, when Conrad was on the *Torrens,* had described the predicament of his Bobrowski cousin Stanislaw, who had been arrested "accused of some political or rather social propaganda" and was kept for months in the Warsaw Citadel without trial—"the exceptional *ad hoc* procedure is carried out in secrecy and an exceptional penalty may be imposed on the poor devil, ruining his present life—for he was just about to finish at the University—and possibly even his whole future." In another letter written later in the same year Tadeusz confirms these fears: "whichever way it goes he is a lost man —especially as he has studied law—he could never become either a government official, a solicitor, or a notary—not even in Kamchatka!! His whole life has gone off the rails together with all the hopes and confidence I had placed in him" (NP pp. 162, 168).

Tadeusz described Stanislaw as having "a worthy character," but as being "very presumptous and rather a doctrinaire. Possibly he has, in fact, ultra-democratic notions which, however, he keeps to himself either out of consideration for his paternal uncle or else not wishing to 'cast pearls before swine.' He is rather reserved and cold." This student, "rather reserved and cold," who may or may not have concealed "ultra-democratic notions," caught in a way that made him "a lost man whichever way it goes," was seized by Conrad and christened "Razumov." Abandoning *Chance* again as "a jaded horse" that could "no longer be made to gallop," he rode off on what would become *Under Western Eyes.*

In an introduction to a German version of *The Secret Agent,* published in 1926, Thomas Mann suggested that Conrad's choice of England, his commitment to British values and British limitations, implied a loss that debarred him from rivalling the great Russian writers. He gained reason, moderation, and intellectual freedom, but lost what Mann calls ironically "the advantages of barbarism." It may be true that Conrad tried to suppress, or disguise these "advantages," but *Under Western Eyes* makes it evident that they were not altogether lost. Conrad may have begun with the intention of identifying himself with his narrator, a pair of wise Western eyes through which we may look with irony on the barbarism of the East, but as the story goes on it is Razumov who takes control. The narrator is reduced to editing his confession, and

so becomes no more than his mouthpiece. He stands unnoticed when the hero finally confronts Natalia with the
truth, until at the end Razumov says, in astonishment, "How
did this old man come here?" It is not after all the Russians
who are to be pitied, but England, the dull country that has
"made a bargain with fate."

Reviews of *The Secret Agent* had emphasized some dis-
turbingly "un-British" elements in Conrad's work, and even
before *Under Western Eyes* was completed, this appearance
of foreignness was increased by the publication, in August
1908, of *A Set of Six*, which contained, as well as *Gaspar
Ruiz* and *The Duel*, four shorter stories, none of which except "The Brute" has any British scenes or characters, and
all with violent or subversive themes. Conrad had escaped
from the iron hand of Russian autocracy, but the soft palm
of British prejudice was now beginning to squeeze him almost
as cruelly. In a review in the *Daily Mail* he was called "a
heartless wretch with a pose of brutality," and that was not
all:

> There is a fellow in the *Daily News* who calls me—
> God only knows on what provocation—a man without
> country and language. It is like abusing a tongue-tied
> man, for what can one say? The statement is simple
> and brutal; and any answer would involve too many feel-
> ings of one's inner life, stir too much secret bitterness
> and complex loyalty to be even attempted with any hope
> of being understood. I thought that a man who has
> written the *Nigger, Typhoon, The End of the Tether,
> Youth* was safe from that sort of thing. But apparently
> not. If I had made money by dealing in diamond shares
> like my neighbour here, Sir Julius Wernher, of Ham-
> burg, I would be a baronet of the UK and provided both
> with a language and a country. (EG p. 212)

Never far from the edge of paranoia, Conrad was seriously
affected by these repeated suggestions that he was some kind
of undesirable alien, the degree of public esteem he had gained
with stories like *Typhoon* only making them the more disturbing. From this time onwards he seized on *The Mirror of
the Sea* as his refuge and defense. It was made up of news-

paper articles that he had once described as "rubbish" and "bosh," but for the rest of his life he would build it up as his major work, the revelation of his inmost soul, referring often to the "sincerity" of its tone, and keeping copies of it to present to any distinguished people who came to see him. Thus, in the Author's Note added to *The Secret Agent* he refers to it twice, and in a Note added to the *Mirror* itself he speaks of it as "a very intimate revelation" full of "sincere disclosures," laid bare with "the unreserve of a last hour's confession. . . . This book written in perfect sincerity holds back nothing— unless the mere bodily presence of the writer." Is it so surprising that, from this point onwards, critics have detected a decline in the depth and astringency of Conrad's work? Several books have been written on the subject of his "Achievement and Decline," to quote the title of one of them, but their authors largely ignore these social pressures.

Ford had now obtained Marwood's financial support for a new literary journal, the *English Review*, which, while the money lasted, would be filled with all the best writers in the country. Conrad was to do reviews and a series of memoirs, later published as *A Personal Record*, which would be as "sincere" and as revealing as *The Mirror of the Sea*. Ford was editing it from rooms over a fish and poultry shop in Kensington, where manuscripts overflowed into the garden and were nibbled by the fishmonger's rabbits, while the rooms were so full of people that once a week Ford would take a pile of papers and his assistant to the Empire Theatre at Shepherd's Bush to make decisions in the comparative quiet of a variety performance (Mizener, pp. 161 ff.).

The need for more space, and perhaps Ford's fond memories of Jessie's hospitality, caused him suddenly to descend on the Someries for the final putting together of the first issue. Jessie says that she has often wondered "where he would have found anyone else so accommodating, and I had almost said foolish." He arrived almost unannounced, bringing with him his secretary and editorial assistants: "there were six bedrooms, but these were not enough. . . . Lights blazed from every room downstairs . . . orders, directions, or suggestions were shouted from room to room. It was an uproar all night, and the next day the house was in chaos. My monthly stock of provisions was soon devoured, and the great trouble was that we had to use lamps and candles" (CC p. 131).

Conrad, preoccupied with the fate of Razumov, disappeared to his own study, and remembered it more objectively when he wrote to Ford in 1923, "I shall never forget the cold of that night, the black grates, the guttering candles, the dimmed lamps—and the desperate stillness of the house, where women and children were innocently sleeping, when you sought me out at 2 A.M. in my dismal study to make me concentrate suddenly on a two-page notice of the *Ile des Pingouins*" (LL 2, p. 323).

With continuing stress and increasing fame, Ford seems to have grown rather arrogant. He quarrelled with almost all of his contributors, and finally with Conrad. The latter fell behind with the instalments of his memoirs, under the usual plea of "gout," and in the issue of July 1909, Ford put in a notice referring to "the serious illness of Mr. Joseph Conrad," who was not amused. He also disapproved of Ford's Russian brother-in-law, David Soskice, who had been brought in as business manager, and told Galsworthy, "A Russian has got hold of the E. R. and I cannot contribute any more" (JB p. 350).

There was also trouble between Ford and Marwood. Elsie, ill and neglected at Winchelsea, had turned to Marwood for sympathy, and then wrote to Ford saying that he was "making advances." Ford, although not inclined to believe her, had his own reasons for being at odds with Marwood, and made it the occasion for breaking off their relations with a savage letter. Conrad, who had listened to Elsie, and found her accusations incredible, took Marwood's side, telling Ford that Marwood was "a gallant *homme*" whom he would not give up for the sake of a "ruffian" (Mizener, pp. 183–184). It would be 1915 before Conrad and Ford made peace again.

Conrad had come to hate the Someries so much that early in 1909 he decided to rent a small cottage at Aldington. He was to go and stay with friends while Jessie supervised the move, and she tells us that he refused to allow any carpets to be taken up or pictures taken down before he had departed with his guests. When it was pointed out that some furniture had already been put in the van, he had it brought out and replaced. As a result the exasperated removal men could not get away that night, "and I had eight men to feed and sleep" (CC pp. 134–136). Borys had begun to attend a local school at Luton, so he was left there as a boarder when the family moved.

Soon after settling in at Aldington, Conrad had a visit from Charles Marris, the man who had succeeded Craig as captain of the *Vidar*. As copies of Conrad's Malayan stories had filtered East the people "out there" had begun to wonder, as Conrad put it, "Who the devil has been around taking notes?" He had then been known as "Korzeniowski," so the author's name did not provide an immediate clue, but in the end someone guessed that "it must have been the fellow who was mate on the *Vidar* with Craig" (LL 2, p. 103). Marris, the son of a seaman from Yorkshire who had married a Maori, was a "soft-eyed black-bearded man married to a Patani girl of good family, with a house in Penang on the beach and a small plantation of rubber trees" (LL 2, p. 109). For Conrad, it brought to life again the scene of his early tales, and from what had seemed dead earth he would gain another crop. He told Pinker that these men "feel kindly to the chronicler of their lives and adventures. They shall have some more of the stories they like" (LL 2, p. 103). From this would come "The Secret Sharer," one of the best things that he did, as well as what is almost certainly the worst, *Freya of the Seven Isles*.

Using his own experience on the *Otago* to provide the background, Conrad took the plot of "The Secret Sharer" from an incident on the *Cutty Sark* in 1880, in which the chief mate, John Anderson, killed a black with a capstan bar. Whether or not he knew the details of the story, Conrad does not stick to them, making his protagonist a much more sympathetic figure than the violent Anderson. He exploits and explores that almost compulsive tendency towards "sympathetic identification" that seems to have been a central feature of his own psychology, and had provided the two critical turning points in the story of Jim. The tale is so convincing, and in every detail so clearly seen, that one can well understand how Jessie thought it must all be true, and "bitterly reproached" him for never having told her about it (CC p. 77).

He made the sending in of this saleable story the occasion

for requesting a further advance, but Pinker replied that he had had nothing to sell for two years, and was unwilling to increase the debt until *Under Western Eyes* was completed. He did, however, offer Conrad a wage of £6 a week, if he would promise to provide "regular supplies of manuscript." Pinker had unwittingly come upon the point where the styles of a British businessman and a Polish aristocrat are at their antipodes. Conrad took it as the worst insult that he had ever received, and boiled over in a long letter to Galsworthy in which he said that he was going to throw his manuscript onto the fire:

> It is outrageous. Does he think I am the sort of man who wouldn't finish the story in a week if he could? Do you? Why? For what reason? Is it my habit to lie about drunk for days instead of working? I reckon he knows well enough I don't. It's a contemptuous playing with my worry. If he had said—No. I will stick to the lot— I would have been hurt. But this gratuitous ignoring of my sincerity of spirit and also in fact is almost more than I can bear. I who can hardly bear to look at the kids, who without you could not have held the boy at school even—I wouldn't finish the book in a week if I could—unless a bribe of six pounds a week is dangled before me!—I sit twelve hours at the table, sleep six, and worry the rest of the time, feeling the age creeping on and looking at those I love . . . (JB pp. 359–360)

With an intense effort he completed *Under Western Eyes* before the end of January 1910, but it brought him to the very edge of insanity. In a state of extreme nervous tension, he decided to deliver the manuscript himself, and tell Pinker what he thought of him. He drove Jessie's pony cart to the station at such a rate that he broke the springs on the way; calling at his publishers, he started an argument in the course of which "he placed his elbows against the arms of the big leather armchair and pushed the sides out"; at Pinker's office, his excitement made his inflections so unintelligible that Pinker requested him to "speak English, if you can." He walked out, and went to spend the night with Galsworthy, where "incredible as it seemed, he pushed the foot out of the bed in an excess of nervous strength."

184

He went home the next day determined to destroy the manuscript of *Under Western Eyes*. He sent Pinker a pre-paid telegram to find out whether he had a complete copy, and when the answer "No" made him "unaccountably elated," Jessie realized what was happening and surreptitiously locked up the manuscript: "I was not a little disconcerted to hear his voice the next moment speaking in smooth, level tones from the window seat behind me. 'Mind what you do with that key, don't mislay it.' "

She managed to keep him calm for the rest of the day, and early next morning he got out of bed and curled himself up in an out of the way corner of the house. He was angry when she suggested sending for the doctor, but a little later she heard him whisper, "I think . . . perhaps, you . . . had better let Dr. Hackney come . . . if he comes at once." She was horrified to see that "his throat was swollen out level with the end of his chin, and in a moment he rambled off in evident delirium" (CC pp. 140 ff., AK pp. 135 ff.).

For days he lived in the world of Razumov, raved in Polish, or argued with the shade of Pinker, and his treatment, in the course of which he almost died, was an extraordinary case of medical confusion. Three different doctors, one from Hythe and two from London, were attending him, each independently prescribing drugs without knowing that the others were involved, while Conrad secretly poured all their medicine down the drain, and was given alternately aspirins by his nurse and whisky and hot water by his wife, who seems on this occasion to have shown an uncharacteristic lack of common sense. He kept the manuscript at the foot of the bed, and Jessie told Pinker that "he lives mixed up in the scenes and holds converse with the characters" (BM p. 192). He thought they were plotting to have him put in an asylum, and ended up by saying, "I know what is wrong with me, but I'm not going to tell them. I'm not going to do half the dam' doctor's work for him." Jessie finally confessed the whole business to Dr. Hackney, and it was arranged that all three doctors should meet.

Their cottage was close to the church, where the bell often tolled for a parishioner who had died. Conrad knew the Prayer Book service from having said it over men who had died at sea, and repeated the words over and over again, making Jessie vow that never again would they live near a church (CC pp. 140–146). The illness lasted about three months, and it was May before Conrad was again writing to friends, and to Pinker to tell him that "as it can't have escaped your recollection that the last time we met you told me that I 'did not speak English to you' I have asked Robert Garnett [Edward's solicitor brother] to be my mouthpiece—at any rate till my speech improves sufficiently to be respectable" (JB p. 373). He told Galsworthy that coming back to health again was "very much like coming out of one little hell into another" (LL 2, p. 108).

Jessie had been searching for a better house, and as soon as Conrad was well enough she took him to see a place called Capel House at Orlestone. It was another Kentish farmhouse, larger than the Pent, and about eight miles to the west of it, in flat fields, bordered by an orchard and woods of dwarf oak trees. They moved there in June, and once again Conrad felt, "I can work here."

It was a sign of his recovery perhaps, but equally, of his financial desperation, that as soon as he had moved in he accepted an invitation to do reviews for the *Daily Mail* on books that they sent him, at five guineas a time. After he had done two or three—they are collected in *Notes on Life and Letters* —a case of murder intervened. Crippen, the famous poisoner of his wife, was arrested by means of the newly invented wireless, on a liner in the middle of the Atlantic, and the editor of the *Daily Mail*, evidently regarding Conrad as a kind of nautical expert who was now on the payroll, wanted him to write about it. Conrad did not have a telephone, so the editor rang up the landlord of the Railway Hotel at Ashford, who was in his bath at the time, and told him to hire a car and fetch Conrad. Conrad was in bed with a fresh attack of gout, but he got up and went to the hotel wondering what tremendous issue was involved. After soothing his nerves with a cup of black coffee, he went to the phone. Borys, who was with him, remembers his "growing expression of indignant astonishment as he listened," followed by a violent refusal. The family expected the gout to grow worse, but apparently his anger was so great that it cured it. It cured him also of writing for the press (BC pp. 65–66).

186

22. *A Profound Suspicion*

During the last half of 1910, Conrad wrote a short novel, *A Smile of Fortune*, based on his voyage to Mauritius in 1888. If in one sense it is a kind of long-delayed revenge for his humiliation over Eugénie Renouf, it also reflects the mood of the weeks he had spent hearing the bell toll, and even introduces the words of the burial service, when the narrator attends the funeral of a child. It reads rather like a poetic presentation of Schopenhauer. For the German philosopher, love was a trick of nature, an illusion by which the continuation of the species is made to appear as a promise of happiness for the individual—"he serves the species under the delusion that he is serving himself. In this process, a mere chimera, which vanishes immediately afterward, floats before him, and as motive takes the place of reality."

In the story, the island, as the narrator approaches it, floats before him as a "blue pinnacled apparition, almost transparent against the sky," but after his ship arrives he is introduced successively to the death and burial of a baby; the captain who has been in love with the painted figurehead of his ship, for whom Jacobus, the ship's chandler, offers to "procure" a new one; the brother of Jacobus beating up his illegitimate son, and the story of Jacobus's past, in which a degrading affair with a circus woman has left him with a daughter. This is the prelude to the presentation of the daughter to the narrator, amid the seductive scents and colors of a tropical garden, along with the request to purchase a cargo of potatoes. The girl fascinates him with an illusion of depths and mysteries that are entirely created by his own idealization of her. Then the spell is broken, and he departs in an odor of rotting potatoes, which make his fortune when he returns to Melbourne to find a potato famine.

For the character of Alice, Conrad owes an obvious debt to the girl in Maupassant's "Les Soeurs Rondoli" who is described, often with virtually identical phrases, as similarly sensuous and slovenly. Conrad, however, covered this up by claiming to have known her, and even made Jessie jealous of her (AK p. 139). He also spoke of her in the same way to Aubry, his subsequent biographer, who says that Conrad once asked him, in regard to the occasion when the narrator kisses Alice, "Do you think that Jacobus had seen something?" adding that he himself never knew (LL 1, p. 113).

In a letter to Galsworthy about *Under Western Eyes*, he had expressed the fear that "perhaps no magazine will touch it," not just because it was "gloomy," for "the novels of Hardy, for instance, are generally tragic enough and gloomily written too," but because of his "foreignness." Certainly, Pinker seems to have had difficulty in selling it, but eventually it was agreed that it should be serialized in the *English Review*, where Ford had now been replaced by Austin Harrison. In October 1910, Norman Douglas brought Harrison along to meet Conrad, and Frank Harris came too, as he was curious to see what Conrad looked like.

Harris received his regulation copy of *The Mirror of the Sea*, and later wrote, "I had thought from his photograph that his forehead was high and domed, but it was rather low and sloped back quickly. He was a little above middle height and appeared more the student than the sea captain. Both he and his wife were homely, hospitable folk without a trace of affectation. But Harrison's presence prevented any intimacy of talk" (Harris, p. 770). Harris seems to have acted very much in character, upsetting Conrad by ringing for more coffee on his own initiative, and furthering his ideas of "intimacy" by making some improper remark to Jessie, which "brought Norman Douglas to his feet with a bound." He escorted Jessie to safety, and Conrad was not told (CC p. 77).

Early in 1911, Conrad completed *Freya of the Seven Isles*,

based on an anecdote he had heard from Marris, and subtitled, perhaps with intentional irony, "A Story of Shallow Waters," after which he had another relapse for about two months, and then began to work hard at *Chance*. Despite his original horror at the idea of a "wage" from Pinker, poor sales of *Under Western Eyes* did little to reduce his debts, and he allowed Robert Garnett to make an arrangement by which he would receive £4 for every thousand words, of which £3 would be paid on delivery, and the balance upon completion of the book (JB p. 379).

After failing to win a scholarship at Tonbridge School, Borys was enrolled with H.M.S. *Worcester*, a training ship for the Merchant Service. His shortsightedness, which required spectacles, would normally have disqualified him, but a visit to the captain by Conrad and his journalist friend Perceval Gibbon resulted in a special arrangement (BC p. 70). After delivering him there at the end of September 1911, Conrad wrote to Galsworthy, "Poor Mons. B. looked to me a very small and lonely figure on that enormous deck, in that big crowd, where he didn't know a single soul. It is an immense change for him. Yes. He did look a small boy. I couldn't make up my mind to leave him and at last I made rather a bolt of it" (LL 2, p. 135). Borys says that "it seemed that everyone in the ship spent a large part of their time yelling 'Four eyes' and I was the butt of all hands during the first term," but eventually, with some tactful support from the chaplain, he settled in, and his health improved (BC pp. 72–74).

When *Under Western Eyes* was published in October, Edward Garnett wrote, as always, an extremely sensitive and appreciative review for the *Nation*, but apparently in a private letter to Conrad, accused him of "putting hatred into the book." In a lengthy reply Conrad says, "You are so russianized, my dear, that you don't know the truth when you see it—unless it smells of cabbage-soup when it at once secures your profoundest respect. I suppose one must make allowances for your position of Russian Ambassador to the Republic of Letters" (EG p. 232).

Garnett's wife, Constance, sent a sympathetic criticism, and drew from Conrad a very honest confession of ignorance: "I am quite aware that it does not go very far. But the fact is I know extremely little of Russians. Practically nothing.

. . . In the book as you must have seen I am exclusively concerned with ideas" (EG p. 234). In the light of his intense involvement with Razumov, and his months of raving, the suggestion that the book was "exclusively concerned with ideas" can be seen only as another "movement of instinctive secrecy," analogous to his public dissociation of himself from the personality of Lord Jim.

It was at about this time that the Conrads bought their first car, an elderly two-seater Cadillac with a single-cylinder engine at the back, and Conrad had a third seat added behind on iron legs so that they could carry a groom. Each time Borys was due to come home on holiday, Conrad made the long trip to Greenhythe to fetch him in the car, allowing him the great pleasure of driving it home. On one occasion, when Borys came by train, and was met by his father at the local station, the car came down the hill very fast, made a circuit of the station yard at the same speed, and charged up the hill again until it ran into a grass bank. Looking underneath, Borys found a disconnected brake cable, and his father "never made any subsequent comment upon the event" (BC p. 75).

Almost all of Conrad's friends were younger than himself, men who still had reputations to make. His late start as an author inevitably reduced his "literary age," but as time passed he seemed to like his companions to be ever younger, and this may be connected with the increasing reticence that followed the reception of *The Secret Agent*. Younger men would be less likely to notice that *The Mirror of the Sea* was only a shiny surface, or to ask the kind of questions that hardly arise until maturity has brought some degree of self-awareness. It implies underneath, an enormous loneliness. Set down in England, Conrad had tried very hard to adopt English tastes, English limitations, and English friends, but below it all he could never cease to be a Pole, a "barbarian," a pessimist, and a profound psychologist. One often hears in his work echoes of Nietzsche, who might almost have been speaking for Conrad when he wrote in the preface to *Human, All Too Human*:

My writings have been called a school of suspicion. . . . Indeed I myself do not think that anyone has ever

190

looked at the world with such a profound suspicion . . . and he who realizes something of the consequences involved in every profound suspicion, something of the chills and anxieties of loneliness to which every uncompromising *difference of outlook* condemns him, will also understand how often I took shelter in some kind of reverence, or hostility or scientificality or levity or stupidity, in order to recover from myself and as it were obtain temporary self-forgetfulness.

Richard Curle, who would become the most intimate, and the most perceptive, of his younger friends, wrote after his death, "Nobody ever really discovered what went on inside Conrad's brain, or pierced very profoundly—even the friends for whom he had the fewest reservations—into the isolated silences of his ultimate convictions. All that one caught were glimpses of the stirring pool, but beneath the surface there was a solitary Conrad, inexplicably removed from any human being. The deepest layers lay far out of sight" (Curle, p. 38).

After Conrad settled at Capel House, two of his more frequent visitors—apart from Marwood, who was twelve years his junior—were Francis Warrington Dawson, a young American of thirty-two, and an earlier acquaintance, Perceval Gibbon, a lively young author and journalist with a powerful motorcycle, both man and machine being much loved by Borys. Gibbon's idea of curing Conrad's depression was "fresh air," and "he rushed me about on the side-car motorbike, storming up hills and flying down vales as if the devil was after him. I don't know whether it was particularly good for the nerves, but on return from these excursions I felt ventilated, as though I were a bag of muslin, frightfully hungry, and almost too sleepy to eat" (CC p. 152).

Dawson, from the American South, had attitudes rather like those of Captain J. Y. M. K. Blunt, who had so impressed the young Conrad in Marseilles. He was a frequent visitor, and for a time rented a cottage near Capel House. An effective journalist, he saw himself as an author, and would eventually publish a novel dedicated to "my friend Joseph Conrad," with a "preface" made up of sentences from four letters Conrad had written to him (CD p. 113–114).

Another friend was Arthur Symons, the symbolist poet

191

and critic. After worrying Conrad with his early, inept reference to *The Nigger of the Narcissus* as having no "idea," he had been fascinated by *Heart of Darkness* and *The Secret Agent* and had worried Conrad again by writing of him as a man with an "unlawful soul" who delighted in death, cruelty, and the shedding of blood. Conrad wrote to tell him that he was not to be confused with Mr. Kurtz—"the fact is that I am a much simpler person. Death is a fact, and violent death is a fact too. In the simplicity of my heart, I tried to realize these facts when they came in. Do you really think that old Flaubert gloated over the death of Emma, or the death of Matho, or the last moments of Félicie?" (LL 2, p. 70).

The two men corresponded, met, and discovered a shared belief in the blackness of things, summed up in lines that Symons wrote for the title page of Conrad's next collection of short stories, *'Twixt Land and Sea:*

> Life is a tragic folly
> Let us laugh and be jolly
> Away with melancholy
> Bring me a branch of holly
> Life is a tragic folly.

It was Symons who early in 1911 introduced to Conrad the American poet Agnes Tobin, to whom he dedicated *Under Western Eyes*. She had lived in France, in the circle of Verlaine and Huysmans, and she brought along to Capel House André Gide, who had long admired Conrad's insight into the irrational aspects of human nature. This meeting was important for Conrad, because Gide agreed to supervise the systematic translation of Conrad's works into French, of which a beginning had been made by H. D. Davray in 1902, with help from Robert d'Humières (Karl, pp. 612–614). Gide also provided John Conrad with an early Meccano set, with which father and son would spend many happy hours (AK p. 5).

Agnes Tobin also introduced the American collector John Quinn, who had an infallible eye for what was not yet, but soon would be fashionable, in both art and literature. Over the next few years he would pay a total of about $10,000 for all the manuscripts that Jessie could dig out, and though it was but a fraction of what he would sell them for, it came just when the money was most needed (CC p. 165).

The loss of the *Titanic* in 1912 tempted Conrad to write two long essays in which his contempt for both ocean liners and the idle rich could be freely indulged:

> You build a 45,000 ton hotel of thin steel plates to secure the patronage of, say, a couple of thousand rich people, you decorate it in the style of the Pharoahs or in Louis Quinze style—I don't know which—and to please the aforesaid fatuous handful of individuals, who have more money than they know what to do with, and to the applause of two continents, you launch that mass with 2,000 people on board at twenty-one knots across the sea —a perfect exhibition of the modern blind trust in mere material and appearances. . . . (NLL p. 218)

In the autumn of 1912, Richard Curle, then twenty-four, wrote an appreciation of Conrad's work which he passed on to Garnett, before publication, for Conrad's opinion. Conrad was very pleased with it, and replied, "Would Curle come to see me? That criticism is something and no mistake. All that went before seems mere verbiage in comparison" (EG p. 240). The article appeared in a magazine called *Rhythm* in November, and Conrad wrote again to Garnett in praise of it. What he liked about it was that it sought to combat the popular view of him as a "writer of the sea," and saw him as introducing into England qualities of "realism" that had previously been found only on the Continent. Here was a man who had the right kind of respectful sympathy, and Conrad encouraged him in his intention of writing a full-length study. This would be published in 1914, with the prophetic conclusion that "Conrad's day is at hand and once his sun is risen it will not set."

There were already signs of the dawn at the end of 1912, when *A Smile of Fortune*, "The Secret Sharer," and *Freya of the Seven Isles* appeared in one volume as *'Twixt Land and Sea*. It was more successful with both the critics and the public than anything written since *Typhoon*, and on November 5, Conrad wrote to Garnett, "Thanks for your letter on the 3 tales—very much of sorts. I daresay Freya is pretty rotten. On the other hand the Secret Sharer, between you and me, is *it*. Eh? No damned tricks with girls there. Eh? Every word fits and there's not a single uncertain note. Luck my boy. Pure luck. I knew you would spot the thing at sight. But I repeat: mere luck" (EG p. 243).

23. *Chance*

In November 1912, Joseph Retinger, a young Polish aristocrat come recently from Kraków to open in London a bureau on behalf of the Polish National Council, was on his way to Kent to meet a fellow countryman who had made a considerable reputation, and very little money, as a novelist in England. Of the man who was waiting for him in the chilly dusk when he got out of the train at the little station of Hamstreet, Retinger says:

> He was unmistakeably Polish, even to his old fashioned sort of brown greatcoat, like the one my father used to wear when he was a child. He seemed, indeed, a typical Polish landowner from the Ukraine. . . . A trifle too short in build, he was over-broad of shoulders. His head was powerfully sculptured in rough, sharp contours framed with unruly hair and a strong, wiry but short beard. His nose, almost aquiline, was somewhat broadly, one might say carelessly carved. His eyes, grey-brown and clear, slightly watering in a strong light, were underlined by wrinkles, which under his right eye had become veritable furrows from supporting a stiff monocle. . . .
>
> I went straight up to him, and he greeted me in Polish in what surely must have been the most drawling, singing voice that ever came out of the Ukraine. (Retinger, p. 55)

On the way to Capel House, Conrad continued to talk in Polish, "liberally interspersed with French and English words" and "so engrossed in what he was saying that he forgot completely, and with alarming results, that he was driving a car." Of the house, Retinger says:

> From a diminutive hall one passed directly into the dining room, one wall of which was entirely occupied by an old-fashioned fire-place, in which a vast heap of small dried twigs waited for the dinner to be lit into a most entertaining crackling fire. From there one passed into the drawing room, which served as Conrad's study. This was a well-shaped large room, well lit and cheerful, the walls hung with a few pictures, among them a bluish reproduction of Hunt's *Hope* (although Conrad disliked the pre-Raphaelites), several old faded photos representing his father and mother, his uncle Bobrowski and others. . . . A piano stood there on which his wife used sometimes to play, and by the window his large desk. Opposite the fireplace a comfortable couch, with a side-table on which, as soon as dinner was over, his wife used to place a bottle of whisky, a siphon, biscuits and cheese. (p. 57)

Retinger came with an introduction from Arnold Bennett, who had known him in Paris (LL 2, p. 142), and he would attempt, rather late in the day, and with limited success, to reactivate Conrad's interest in Polish affairs. A man of extraordinary energy and talent, he had been educated in the same school as Conrad, in Kraków, and after graduating in law, had arrived in Paris at the age of eighteen, and became a *Docteur ès Lettres* at the Sorbonne in 1908. His cousins, the Godebskis, were at the center of French literary and artistic life, and he became a close acquaintance of Gide's.

After returning to Kraków, where he married and founded a literary magazine, he accepted the task of opening a Polish Bureau in London to make propaganda and influence statesmen in the cause of Polish independence. He was only twenty-four, but he regarded himself as Poland's ambassador to Europe, and always insisted on meeting no one less than the president or the prime minister. At first his charm and intelligence won him extraordinary success, but his taste for political intrigue took him too far, and he was expelled from France towards the end of the First World War. After that he would use his talent for cloak-and-dagger diplomacy to fight the American oil companies in Mexico, and only in the Second World War would he really come into his own, rescuing General Sikorski, with a borrowed airplane, after the fall of France, and taking him to Churchill, as a result of which the Polish forces came to England. He continued as Sikorski's personal advisor, and concluded his active career by parachuting into Warsaw, at the age of fifty-seven, to join the partisans.*

All through 1912, Conrad was hard at work on *Chance*, sometimes producing as much as twelve thousand words in a fortnight (LL 2, p. 128). It was also a time of close association with Marwood. Curle says, "They met every week, and I have never listened to more able talk. Marwood was the profoundest critic I ever knew: his thought acted like a grindstone to sharpen the edge of Conrad's genius" (p. 72). Jessie also testifies that "my husband would always accept his criticism, if not exactly without argument, at least with a reasoned and considered one. I can trace Arthur Marwood's influence in most of the books written during the period of his close friendship" (CC p. 117).

It may well be that this continuing dialogue influenced the contents of *Chance*, for much of it is taken up with discussions between Marlow and a Dr. Watson-like narrator who remains anonymous. He reports Marlow's reports of what other people have said and produces a plethora of aphorisms and opinions which while they maintain a high standard of conservative intelligence, make the book rather longer than it needs to be. This multiplication of narrators produced a famous comment by Henry James in which he likens it to "the successive members of a cue from one to the other of which the sense and interest of the subject have to be passed on together, in the manner of the buckets of water for the improvised extinction of a fire, before reaching our apprehension; all with whatever result to this apprehension, of a quantity to be allowed for as spilt on the way." It was probably a reflection of Conrad's lack of confidence in dealing with matters quite outside his own experience: he felt that he had very little in the buckets, so

* For details of Retinger's career see *Joseph Retinger: Memoirs of an Eminence Grise*, edited by John Pomian.

he found himself, with a kind of instinctive cunning, setting up the spilling apparatus in order to justify the lack of water reaching the fire.

Unlike the best of his earlier books, *Chance* was a conscious endeavor to please the public. Conrad now believed that to be successful a novel had to be based on some public issue such as "labour or war" (LL 2, p. 49). It was the time of suffragettes and the feminist movement, so he had seized on the problem of "woman" as something timely—"All about a girl, and with a steady run of references to women in general all along. . . . It ought to go down" (JB p. 381). It really reaches its emotional climax with Anthony's rejection of Flora's love at the same moment that for reasons of moral idealism, he marries her, but after that the book goes on to melodrama and a happy ending—indeed, two happy endings. Conrad had once praised James's way of ending things—"a certain lack of finality, especially startling when contrasted with the usual methods of solution by rewards and punishments, by crowned love, by fortune, by a broken leg or a sudden death" (NLL p. 18), but the broken leg is about the only one of these "usual methods" that is omitted from the end of *Chance*.

The book was completed on March 25, 1912, "at 3 A.M." (LL 2, p. 138), some seven years after it had been begun. It had grown out of a story about Mr. Powell to be called "Explosives" (LL 2, p. 18), and this itself may have been developed from a story called "Dynamite" to which Conrad referred in a letter of 1898 (EG p. 130). Thus, in the first chapter, Powell is introduced as though he were to be the hero, and the kind of epilogue in which he reappears to marry the widowed Flora was presumably added in order to balance the attention he receives at the beginning. For this purpose, Captain Anthony is disposed of in a manner so arbitrary as to appear absurd, while the load of dynamite, which like Mr. Powell, the ship had acquired as it were by "chance," plays no part in the plot.

Serialization in the *New York Herald* had begun in January 1912, but Conrad continued to revise *Chance*, and it was not until June 1913 that he sent the final manuscript to Pinker with a letter in which he says, "It's the biggest piece of work I've done since *Lord Jim*. As to what *it is* I am very confident. As to what will happen to it when launched—I am much less

confident. And it's a pity. One doesn't do a trick like that twice
—and I am not growing younger—alas! It will vanish in the
ruck." (LL 2, p. 145)

One can understand Conrad's fears. This was his first attempt to write a book about life in England, and it was a bid
for popularity, with obvious debts to Dickens. It was longer
than anything he had written since *Nostromo*, and as he
rightly guessed, he would never find such energy again. If it
did vanish in the ruck, he would have nothing ahead of him
but a decline into poverty and despair.

But *Chance* was not destined so to vanish : the reviews were
good, and the sales were reasonable—it sold over thirteen
thousand copies in the first two years, compared with four
thousand for *Under Western Eyes*. It was almost equally successful in America, where it was helped by a sales campaign
by Doubleday, the publishing house that had inherited Conrad from another company it had taken over in 1908. In the
1890s Frank Doubleday had lost some money on him over
the unfinished *Rescue*, and had left Conrad with his partner
McLure when the two had split at the end of 1899. More recently, however, Doubleday had been persuaded by his young
associate Alfred A. Knopf to read *Lord Jim* and was now convinced that "in Conrad we had a great author, though not one
of his books had sold, I think, more than two thousand copies"
(Doubleday, p. 122).

Pinker, thinking that Frank Doubleday would not wish to
risk more money on Conrad, had already sold the rights· of
Chance to his rival George Doran, but such was Doubleday's
new and well-timed faith in Conrad that he not only bought
back *Chance*, but also the rights and the plates for half a dozen
of Conrad's earlier books, scattered among as many different
American publishers. Knopf wrote Conrad an enthusiastic letter about the big deal, and received a cool reply : "I am very
glad to hear that Doubleday, Page & Co has bought two of
my vols. from Mr. Doran. It is a sign of interest. But the fact
remains that Mr. Doubleday might have had all my books
up to date in his hands if he had cared. Other people bought
them and I haven't heard that they have been ruined by it"
(LL 2, p. 146).

When after all this Doubleday actually saw the manuscript
of *Chance*, he was disappointed : compared with *Lord Jim*, he

found it hard to read, and thought it unlikely to be popular, but even so, "I think we sold eight or ten thousand copies, which was astonishing for Conrad at that time" (p. 123). The relative success which for Conrad began from this time can be seen as due not so much to the particular merits of *Chance*, which would never be very popular, but to the fact that public taste had now caught up with the great books of his early years. It was *Lord Jim* that was selling—between 1914 and 1919, Blackwoods would print nearly sixty thousand— and the collections containing *Heart of Darkness* and *Typhoon* would be almost equally popular.

Unfortunately for Conrad, in the "private hell" from which these things had come, the temperature had cooled, and as the first good news came in, he wrote to Galsworthy: "*Chance* had a tremendous press. How I would have felt about it ten or eight years ago I can't say. Now I can't even pretend I am elated. If I had *Nostromo, The Nigger, Lord Jim*, in my desk or only in my head I would feel differently no doubt" (LL 2, p. 152). It was too late to be more than a bittersweet success, but at least it would save him from financial worry for his remaining years, and it also led to a reconciliation with Pinker. With the main cause of friction now removed, and age making Conrad more appreciative of a cheerful and uncomplicated companion, the two would become ever more affectionate, until by the 1920s Pinker and his wife would be the Conrads' closest friends.

Now, at the end of 1913, as he reached the age of fifty-six, Conrad could feel that, not without elements of "chance" and irony, he had achieved some kind of success, and he might say with Stein, as at last he grasped his long-awaited butterfly: "I took long journeys and underwent great privations; I had dreamed of him in my sleep, and here suddenly I had him in my fingers—for myself! In the words of the poet (he pronounced it 'boet') —

> *So halt' ich's endlich denn in meinen Handen,*
> *Und nenn' es in gewissem Sinne mein'* "* (LJ p. 212)

---

* "Now at last I hold it in my hands/ And call it, in a certain sense, my own." The quotation is from Goethe's *Torquato Tasso*, which, according to Morf, was one of the set books at Conrad's school (p. 52).

PART THREE

SUCCESS

24. *Victory*

With the completion of *Chance* in 1913, the slowly flattening parabola of Conrad's achievement begins its downward curve. At fifty-six he was prematurely aged and a continuing decline in health would inevitably affect both the quality and the quantity of what he wrote. He seems also to have lost that concern for his appearance that had once made him dress so elegantly, and those who met him in later life speak of a formally correct, but rather dowdy appearance, while at home he worked in pajamas or various degrees of undress. At meal times, especially when there was company, he recovered his nervous vitality, expressed both in animated speech, and as a kind of displacement activity, in rolling little pellets of bread which he threw with great force, sometimes hitting the guests, or their soup.

As a sign that he had in some sense "arrived" he now attracted the attention of that most notable of literary lion-hunters, Lady Ottoline Morrell. She was a friend of James's, and suggested that he might introduce her:

> Henry James held up his hands in horror and was so perturbed that he paced up and down the grey drawing-room. I remember best some of his exclamations and expostulations: "But, dear lady . . . but dear lady . . . He has lived his life at sea—dear lady, he has never met 'civilized' women. Yes, he is interesting, but he would

not understand you. His wife, she is a good cook. She is a Catholic as he is, but. . . . No, dear lady, he has lived a rough life, and is not used to talk to—" an upward movement of the arms had to describe who—and it was, of course, myself. (Gathorne-Hardy, p. 240)

It may be that despite the intensity of his effort, James never quite mastered the subtleties of British snobbery, or was he merely trying to protect Conrad? Anyway, Lady Ottoline was not at all discouraged. After consulting Desmond Mac-Carthy on how to dress, and being advised to wear something "smart and rather elaborate," she arrived at Hamstreet Station to be met by Borys, and found Conrad ready at the door. In contrast to her expectations, he had "the air of a highly polished and well-bred man." She was fascinated by his eyes, "tragic and worn and suffering," but also with something "wicked" in them, so that she was "vibrating with intense excitement inside."

She wanted her friend "Bertie" Russell to share the experience, and shortly afterwards took him along. Russell was even more impressed, and describes the encounter in equally erotic and mystical terms: "We seemed to sink through layer after layer of what was superficial, till gradually both reached the central fire. It is an experience unlike any other I have known. We looked into each other's eyes half appalled and half intoxicated to find ourselves in such a region. The emotion was as intense as passionate love, and at the same time all-embracing. I came away bewildered, and hardly able to find my way among ordinary affairs" (Russell, p. 84).

Conrad had doubtless plunged him into some existential vision of the fundamental irrationality of things such as Stein does for Marlow in *Lord Jim*, and Russell added that Conrad "thought of civilized and morally tolerable human life as a dangerous walk on a thin crust of barely cooled lava which at any moment might break and let the unwary sink into fiery depths." Russell's mathematical rationalism may seem far removed from Conrad's complex and conservative way of seeing things, but he admired Russell's uncompromising atheism, and his emphasis that the Universe had not been providentially designed for the benefit of man. Later in 1913, when Russell sent him a volume containing his essay on "The Free Man's

Worship," which proposed that we should "worship only the God created by our own love of the good," Conrad wrote, "You have reduced to order the inchoate thoughts of a lifetime and given direction to those obscure *mouvements d'âme* which, unguided, bring only trouble to one's weary days on this earth" (SY p. 235).

One might have expected the author of *Lord Jim* or *The Secret Agent* to have expressed some doubt as to whether what man can regard as the "good" was so plain or so generally agreed as Russell's proposals seem to imply, but Conrad had now turned his back on that "vast and uncertain expanse, as of a crepuscular horizon on a plain at dawn" into which he had once ventured with Stein, had retreated with Jim's other assessor to that "highest flat of a lofty building" where "the light of his shaded reading-lamp slept like a sheltered pool, his footfalls made no sound on the carpet, his wandering days were over. No more horizons as boundless as hope, no more twilights within the forests as solemn as temples, in the hot quest of the Ever-undiscovered Country over the hill, across the stream, beyond the wave. The hour was striking! No more! No more!" (LJ p. 338).

Despite Conrad's desire to share with Russell the worship of the "good," and to see himself reflected only in *The Mirror of the Sea*, what Arthur Symons had once called his "unlawful soul" seems to have made itself felt not only in his writings but also in his presence: Ottoline Morrell was not the only one to be fascinated by it. She mentions that the mother-in-law of W. R. Inge, the literary Dean, who had met Conrad in Canterbury, told her, "I am afraid he might drag me down to Hell and I don't want to go there," to which Ottoline had replied, "I would willingly go with Conrad" (Gathorne-Hardy, p. 242).

Indeed, he seems to have provided middle-class matrons with a convenient object for their fantasies. Jessie describes a railway journey from London in the company of two well-dressed ladies, one of whom told the other that Conrad was not married, and went on to say how she had slept with him at various house-parties. Jessie restrained her impulse to interrupt until she was met by Conrad at the carriage door, and then announced "with what I hope was becoming dignity, 'I am Mrs. Joseph Conrad, madam, and have been now for nearly twenty years, and I am the mother of Mr. Conrad's two sons' " (CC p. 161).

Conrad continued his study of the Napoleonic age with the hope of beginning his long projected novel of the war at sea, and somewhere among this material he found a bizarre anecdote about a mechanical bed that could be used to kill its occupants, which he turned into "The Inn of the Two Witches." He was not aware that Wilkie Collins had already used it for a story called "A Terribly Strange Bed," a point he mentions, misquoting the title, in the Author's Note to *Within the Tides*, in which it is collected.

From early in 1912 Conrad had been working on another Malayan story, with the provisional title of "Dollars," which would grow into *Victory*. As it grew he changed the story line, and used the original plot for a short story called "Because of the Dollars," which, along with *The Planter of Malata*, he completed by the end of 1913. The latter is an odd novella developed from the idea that he had discussed long before with Stephen Crane, when they had planned a play to be called *The Predecessor*. Conrad says his story became "the mere distorted shadow of what we used to talk about in a fantastic mood." He is speaking, perhaps, for both Crane and himself when he says of its hero, Renouard, that "he had not seen a single human being to whom he was related for many years, and he was extremely different from them all." Like other Conradian heroes, such as Lingard in *The Rescue*, he is put into a kind of moral and mental paralysis by the appearance of an attractive upper-class woman, and he ends up by swimming out to sea, "with a steady stroke—his eyes fixed on a star."

Some of the scenes take place in the editorial office of "the only literary newspaper in the Antipodes," where a "poet from the bush" lies drunk on the floor, a point that was not missed by the editor of the Sydney *Bulletin*, who wrote to deny the charge. Conrad apologetically replied that such things "do happen in London, though, where—as you know—everything happens" (LL 2, p. 171).

All through the first half of 1914 he worked hard at *Victory*, and had it finished by June (LL 2, p. 56). It was thus one of those books that flowed out of him with something like the compulsion of his early achievements, and it conveys very powerfully the kind of pessimistic vision with which he had overwhelmed Bertrand Russell. As with Decoud in *Nostromo*, the voice of the hero is virtually indistinguishable from that of the author, but now it is the voice of despair. Heyst is a man who has had no "youth" and expresses that Schopenhauerian world-denial that had always occupied one half of Conrad's soul: the other half, filled with a sense of continuing life and ready to give a romantic affirmation to even its darkest aspects, seems in *Victory* to be dimmed with age. There is some attempt to symbolize the forces of life in Lena, the girl whom Heyst attempts to rescue, but she is pale, and the author weighs the odds against her. Evil intelligence and brute force, rather too easily incarnated in the three invaders of the island, are allowed to win—and then destroy themselves.

The relationship between Heyst and Lena, so difficult, because both, in different ways have been so deprived, is convincingly drawn, and through the mind of Heyst, the story is given great philosophical subtlety. In *Lord Jim*, Conrad had analyzed his own sensibility by means of Marlow, who speaks for his critical intellect, but in *Victory* it is the hero himself who embodies this intellect, thus causing something of a breakdown in Conrad's usual methods of narration—he soon abandons the critical narrator who opens the story and identifies himself entirely with Heyst, for whom the world is a senseless "shadow show" in which the laborers are paid only with "counterfeit money."

There is an attempt at a final affirmation—"Ah, Davidson, woe to the man whose heart has not learned while young to hope, to love—and to put its trust in life!" but this is made against the whole weight of authorial comment, and of the evidence of the events. It reflects, no doubt, a precarious balance in Conrad's own mind. Life is a business in which the rewards do not cover the expenses, and the more sensitive you are the greater the cost; nevertheless you must endure, and behave with "decency." When the "for" and "against" are tottering on the scales, Conrad shrugs his square shoulders and casts his deciding vote on the side of "life." But whereas in such earlier books as *Nostromo* the affirmation is instinctive and colors the whole of the material, in *Victory* it is too explicit, and too late, to carry conviction.

The death of Lena, marking the virtual completion of the book, occurred, according to Jessie, on May 19, 1914:

He had been having many troubled days fighting his way to the end of it. He had been very erratic, and had taken his meals mostly alone for two or three weeks. I had been forced to warn callers off, for although he would have been hardly aware of them, there was the possibility that he would need my presence or would wander in search of me insufficiently clad. . . . I stood talking to the gardener in low tones, when the window above me was thrown violently open and Conrad thrust his head out. His voice was hoarse, and his appearance dishevelled; the gardener lifted a scared face. "She is dead, Jess." (AK pp. 143–144)

Whatever the critics might say—they would be, on the whole, respectful, without being enthusiastic—Pinker had no problems with *Victory*. Before it was completed he had sold the serial rights for £1000, and obtained an advance of £850 on the book (LL 2, p. 154).

25. *Poland Revisited*

From the time of their first meeting in 1912, Joseph Retinger had been trying hard to enlist Conrad in the cause of Polish independence; he had not found it easy. By early 1914, however, Conrad had been persuaded to lend his name to documents setting out the Polish case, and had agreed, after much procrastination, to take his family to Poland. They were to stay with Retinger's mother-in-law, in the Russian zone, near Kraków—"the invitation received at first with a sort of dismay ended by rousing the dormant energy of my feelings. Cracow is the town where I spent with my father the last eighteen months of his life. It was in that old royal and academical city that I ceased to be a child, became a boy, had known the friendships, the admirations, the thoughts and the indignations of that age" (NLL p. 145).

He was understandably apprehensive about digging up what had been so long and so deeply buried, and just before leaving he wrote to Galsworthy, "In 1874 I got into a train in Cracow (Vienna Express) on my way to the sea, as a man might get into a dream. And here is the dream going on still. Only now it is peopled mostly by ghosts and the moment of awakening draws near" (LL 2, p. 157). He had agreed to go when *Victory* was finished, but he was still revising it in July 1914, and time was running out for travels in Europe. The assassination of Archduke Ferdinand had occurred on June

28, and the final Austrian ultimatum to Serbia came on July 23. Like most other people in England, Conrad underestimated Germany's determination not to let Austria back down, and refusing to be put off by "alarmist rumours," the party of Conrads and Retingers left Harwich on a British ship for Hamburg on July 25 (LL 2, p. 157).

Conrad had wanted to go by ship so that he could give his sons a taste of the sea and perhaps do a little showing-off, but when he tried to treat the captain as a fellow seaman, the man turned out to be a rather stupid Germanophile who thought Conrad a Frenchman and a liar, and treated him in an increasingly contemptuous manner—"thus Conrad failed to impress his sons and ourselves. Really the scene was painful" (Retinger, p. 128). The ship was full of Schombergs going home to get into uniform, and even when Conrad found an American family with whom he could converse, they turned out to be German-Americans who burst into song when they saw the first lights of the Fatherland (NLL p. 160).

Conrad says that he travelled through Germany with his eyes closed, but Borys, now sixteen, tells of a day in Berlin where at the zoo the attendant became "somewhat hostile when he realized we were British." In the morning, boarding the train for Vienna, Jessie was jostled by a porter "damning the English," and when her lameness held up the train the guard "ended up by spitting contemptuously on the platform" (BC p. 67). They went on to Kraków the same day, arriving at night. Jessie found that the "odour of stables and bad draining was somewhat sickening" and Conrad had to remind her "rather sharply" that "This is not England, my dear" (AK p. 68).

They settled in at the Grand Hotel, and after supper Borys and his father went out with Retinger to see the city by moonlight. Conrad told Retinger that he wanted to see again the central square, the Rynek, and led the way through the narrow streets without hesitation until he stood "at the corner of the place in his greyish suit, an old-fashioned bowler hat on his head, awry as in moments of excitement. Borys in his heavy spectacles, with an eager face, listening to his father and myself. . . ." Retinger adds that when they returned to the hotel, "he kissed me on both cheeks, the ancient Polish custom, which I had never seen him do before, and which in fact he held in detestation. I swear he did it unconsciously" (Retinger, pp. 130–131).

Retinger's wife, Otalia, had gone straight to her home in the Russian zone, but the others had to wait for visas, and on a day "full of majestic, warm, August sun" they climbed the hill to the Wawel, the cathedral fortress where Poland's kings are buried. Retinger says that Conrad was deeply moved, and "as we emerged from the cool interior of the Cathedral he said to me : 'Dear Joseph, it is a great happiness to me that at last I have come here with my wife and sons and have shown them that *il y a quelque chose derrière moi*' " (p. 134).

At the hotel Conrad met by chance an old school friend, Konstantyn Buszczyński, who embraced him in a manner that made Jessie feel "not a little embarrassed by the scene." A former classics scholar, he had retired to his estate and developed a new strain of sugar beet, the seed of which he exported, "not only with profit (and even to the United States), but with a certain amount of glory which seemed to have gone slightly to his head" (NLL p. 176). He took them to his estate the next day, and it was here, while the friends were talking, and Jessie was happily looking out over sunlit fields of sugar beet, that their hostess ran in 'to tell them that War had come —"They are commandeering the horses—already the soldiers are taking them out of the ploughs." On the way back they passed carriages from which the horses had gone, and apparently it was only respect for Jessie's lameness that saved Buszczyński's car from being commandeered. At the hotel they found the manager already in uniform and the rooms filling up with officers (BC p. 86).

Rather than attempt to return to England and risk being "caught in some small German town in the midst of the armies," Conrad decided to join other refugees in an exodus to Zakopane, a small town in the mountains near the Slovakian border, where the widow of Charles Zagórski kept a pension. Here, he told Galsworthy, they would be "out of the way of all possible military operations" (LL 2, p. 158). Retinger, having failed in an attempt to rescue his wife from the Russian zone, left for London, using his wits to bluff his way through the German areas. Otalia subsequently got across the border, and joined the Conrads at Zakopane (CC pp. 171–174).

Luggage had been lost on the way, leaving Conrad with only white flannel trousers and a dinner jacket, and Jessie with two nightdresses, one of which she gave to Otalia. Madame Zagórska gave them a warm welcome at her overcrowded house. The place was full of distinguished refugees, and despite a general shortage of money, clothes and food, Conrad seems to have enjoyed the life of cafe conversations and late-night discussions. It was fine cloudless weather, but as August wore on, increasingly cold. Jessie was house bound, not only through lameness, but because Conrad borrowed her warmer clothes to go out in.

Retinger's friends were working to get them out of the country, and eventually obtained permission for them to return to Kraków with the hope of going on to Vienna. On September 15, they set out from Zakopane at midnight to drive across the mountains to catch a morning train at Chabowka. Jessie had filled one suitcase with newly washed clothes and the other with food. There were roadblocks in the villages, but they had with them "a fat, influential Polish friend." On the train, Conrad and the friend shared a compartment with a wounded officer and his servant, while Jessie and the boys were put with the chauffeur of a Grand Duke.

The station at Kraków was "a maze of wire, filled with the blue-grey figures of Austrian soldiers," and they spent the day in the buffet, "with trains of sick prisoners arriving and wounded soldiers all over the floor." Late that night they boarded a train for Vienna, with broken windows, no cushions, and "reeking of blood and phenol." They spent two days on it, Jessie feeding them out of her suitcase (CC pp. 180–185).

Walter Hines Page, who in 1900 had replaced McClure as Doubleday's partner in the American publishing firm, was now the American ambassador in London. When, through Pinker, he heard of Conrad's predicament, he got in touch with the ambassador in Vienna, Frederic C. Penfield, who was able to use some pressure to help the Conrads on their way.

Through all this Borys remembers his mother as "calm and placid always," but when they found a hotel in Vienna, she says that "the bandage I had been wearing round my sick knee had cut so deeply into the swelling that I felt sick when I first removed it." She managed to fix Conrad's gout medicine, bind his tender ankle, and put him to bed. They were kept in

Vienna for eight or nine days, under police supervision, but not confined to their rooms. On their walks, Conrad and Borys went into a shooting gallery to find that instead of the usual targets there was a cinema film of charging British soldiers, with a prize if you hit one: "We have to go through with it, Boy. To retreat now would draw too much attention, but take care you don't hit any of those fellows." Borys managed to miss with all his five rounds, and then had to use up his father's, as Conrad could not bring himself to shoot (BC p. 95).

Although Penfield was unable to obtain written permission for the Conrads to leave, he won some kind of verbal assurance that they could move in the direction of the Italian border without being detained. He told them that if they were stopped anywhere, they were to send him a telegram using the words "Short of Cash," and he would then take further steps. They set off in a train crowded with soldiers, and Conrad's attempts to make room for Jessie to put up her damaged leg led to various quarrels until "a fresh traveller, a young officer—who seemed to have indulged a little freely—flung an insult in German across the carriage. I trembled for the result, although it was only by the tone I understood an insult had been intended. Some intuition must have made it plain to Joseph Conrad that a countryman of his was speaking. In the next second they were clasping hands and exchanging facts that proved that the young man was the son of a landowner from the same province. He was greatly awed when he discovered that he was travelling with the great author, for Poland revered the name of my husband" (CC pp. 185–187).

At Udine, on the Italian frontier, the Conrads found that the Austrian troops had been replaced by Germans, and a Prussian N.C.O., after looking through their papers, contemptuously turned them away from the train. Conrad's attempts to argue with him in German only caused him to lose his temper, and they had given up in despair when Conrad was inspired to take out his British passport, open at the page that was stamped with the German visa they had been given for the outward journey: the man then assumed a friendly expression, clicked his heels, and found them a compartment. Borys added that according to Walter Page, "soon after we left Vienna, orders came from Berlin to detain Joseph Conrad and his family" (BC pp. 97–98).

They spent a few days in Milan, awaiting money from England, and then caught a ship from Genoa. It was a Dutch vessel on the way home from Java, and this time Conrad had no trouble in making friends with the captain. He and Borys spent much time on the bridge, and were thrilled by the sight of three British destroyers steaming in line. Jessie says that Conrad was now showing the effects of the long strain, and daily growing more lame :

> One day he decided to seek the ship's doctor. As so often happened, he unloaded his symptoms on the first man he met, who listened gravely, and then remarked concernedly : "I should consult the doctor, Sir, if I were you." The mistake disturbed the invalid not a little, but his next venture was still too impulsive. This man was apparently in a hurry : "Pardon me, Sir, I am the purser, the doctor is below."
>
> By this time Joseph Conrad was discouraged and instead of asking again for the doctor he retired to his cabin in high dudgeon. (CC p. 188)

They arrived at Tilbury on November 3, 1914, more than three months after leaving. Since most of the passengers were foreign, there were interpreters waiting for them : everyone was closely questioned, and their baggage searched. Jessie was very nervous, since she was carrying concealed letters and papers from Poles at Zakopane with relatives in Britain, and when she was questioned, started off with the only German word she knew, *Donnerwetter*. There were also confusions with the luggage that bothered Conrad, and a lady passenger said to Jessie, "Look at that excitable old gentleman, a foreigner, making all that fuss about his luggage."

"Madam, that excitable old gentleman is my husband."

26. *The Shadow Line*

In 1905, in his essay on "Autocracy and War," Conrad had treated with contemptuous irony the commercial rivalries and chauvinistic attitudes that were threatening Europe with war, but he had also been very definite in putting the greatest blame on Germany. He had concluded "the once-famous saying of poor Gambetta, tribune of the people (who was simple and believed in the 'imminent justice of things') may be adapted in the shape of a warning that, so far as the future of liberty, concord, and justice is concerned: '*Le Prussianisme —voilà l'ennemi!*' "

Thus Britain at war with Germany, the ancient oppressor of Poland, was a situation in which Conrad need have no misgivings about the justice of the cause, and with his strong liability to "sympathetic identification" he was inevitably caught up in the fervor of patriotism that possessed the whole country. His friends from the Mont Blanc restaurant in Gerrard Street were going into uniform: Perceval Gibbon as a war correspondent and Richard Curle in the air force, while Cunninghame Graham would go back to South America to buy horses for the army.

By the summer of 1915, even Ford Madox Ford was in uniform—"I cannot imagine taking any other course. If one has enjoyed the privileges of the ruling class of a country all one's life, there seems no alternative to fighting for that country if necessary." He did it thoroughly, joining the in-

215

fantry as an elderly and inefficient subaltern, and he made it
the occasion for seeking a reconciliation with Conrad, requesting him to be, with Violet Hunt, his literary executor. He also
asked if he could have Conrad's old binoculars to take to war,
and received an affectionate reply :

> I answer at once the question of the glasses. The pair
> you may have remember knocking about at the Pent has
> in the process of time (and by some help from John's
> hand) dissolved into the primitive elements. . . . Yes
> *mon cher!* Our world of 15 years ago is gone to pieces;
> what will come in its place, God knows but I imagine
> doesn't care.
>
> Still what I always said was the only immortal line in
> *Romance:* "Excellency, a few goats," survives—esoteric,
> symbolic, profound and comic—it survives. (LL 2, p.
> 169)

Thus, although it would cause him to go through many
deaths, Conrad could hardly oppose Borys's determination to
be a soldier as soon as he was seventeen. His poor eyesight
prevented him from sharing with his friend Conrad Hope the
glory of the Royal Flying Corps, but he succeeded in getting
a commission in the Royal Army Service Corps, and was in
uniform by the beginning of October 1915 (BC p. 104). He
was refused a short leave before departing for France as
"owing to certain sins of omission, I was temporarily far from
popular," but while taking a convoy of trucks to Woolwich,
he managed to steal a few hours to say goodbye :

> I arrived in the small hours of the morning and tapped
> on the study window where a light was still burning.
> J. C. accepted my unexpected arrival quite calmly but,
> having asked for an explanation and been told the true
> facts, screwed his monocle into his eye and treated me to
> the most savage glare I ever remember; then, patting me
> on the shoulder, he said : "Go up to your Mother for five
> minutes then come down to me, you must be under weigh
> again in an hour." (BC p. 105)

From this time on Conrad lived in the alternate convictions
that his son was wounded or dead. When some disabled men
from a nearby hospital turned up to meet the famous author,

he retreated upstairs and left Jessie to give them tea, whispering, "Perhaps Borys will come home like that!" On another occasion Jessie returned from a visit to the surgeon in London to find the maid in tears. She told him that Conrad had spent the day in Borys's room, though no telegram had come. When tackled by Jessie, he said, "Can't I have a presentiment as well as you? I *know* he has been killed" (AK pp. 14–15). Capel House was right in the path of German airships on their way to drop bombs on London, and Jessie told of an occasion in 1915 when "a big Zeppelin passed so low over the house that I could distinctly see the heads of the men leaning out of the gondolas" (CC p. 192).

Two recent friends, introduced by Richard Curle, were Sir Ralph and Lady Wedgwood, and in a letter to them in January 1915, Conrad said, "It seems almost criminal levity to talk at this time of books, stories, publication. This war attends my uneasy pillow like a nightmare. I feel oppressed even in my sleep and the moment of waking brings no relief, on the contrary" (LL 2, p. 168).

This was the atmosphere in which he worked on a short book that was to be the one masterpiece of his declining years, *The Shadow Line*. He returned once more to the Gulf of Siam, the voyage of the *Otago*, the moment when he had wondered "how far I should turn out faithful to that ideal of his personality that every man sets up for himself secretly." In *Lord Jim* he had, imaginatively, failed, but this time he was, in imagination, highly successful. He chose to call the story "exact autobiography," but it is a sophisticated work of art in which the actual voyage of January 1888, described in Chapter 7, is used merely as the base for an exciting and amusing tale that brings its protagonist through great sufferings and seemingly supernatural obstacles.

The former captain of what becomes a "death haunted ship" is made into an evil power, and by planting his body in the Gulf, on latitude 8°20′, Conrad gives the metaphorical "shadow line" a geographical location where the ordeal can reach its climax. By distancing it as an early experience of the narrator, he can treat it with skeptical irony, and then by quoting from a fictional diary kept at the time, plunge us back into the immediacy of the horror. His wartime emotions are near the surface, and the psychological probing may not be very deep, but as experience extrapolated into art *The Shadow Line* matches "The Secret Sharer" as one of his most accomplished stories.

While he was writing it, his closest friend, Arthur Marwood, lay dying in his farmhouse at Stowting, and after several visits from Conrad through the winter, Marwood passed away in May 1916, at the age of forty-seven (Curle, pp. 172–173). As Curle says, "His death made a gap in Conrad's life that nobody else could fill."

In the summer of 1916, however, amidst the encircling gloom, a bright angel appeared, for whom there can be no better introduction than a scene from the memoirs of Jessie:

> One Sunday Miss A—— was staying with us and a French Red Cross Officer and his wife came down to lunch. Our American friend was at once aware of the Frenchman's interest—and incidentally, so was his wife. Miss A—— seated herself before the fire like an idol. M. Paul Vance immediately seized a pair of tall vases full of flowers and solemnly placed them before the figure on the rug, making at the same time a deep obeisance. There was a sniff of disgust on the part of the wife and a rather vexed laugh from Joseph Conrad, who at once held out his hand to assist his guest to rise, and upset both the vases in the process. (CC p. 196)

"Miss A——" was a Mrs. Deems Taylor from Arizona who travelled, widely, under her maiden name of Jane Anderson. Her father, "Red" Anderson, had been an associate of Buffalo Bill's, and later marshal of Arizona, when it was still a territory. Retinger says that his breakfast consisted of "a bottle of whiskey and a 2 lb. steak," and his revolver had twenty-eight notches, not including Mexicans (Pomian, p. 38). Of Jane, he says, "Brilliant and beautiful, she turned the heads of many conspicuous and famous men both in Europe and her own country. Exceptionally gifted, a good newspaper woman and a short-story writer of more than average talent, she had a marvellous capacity for listening and understanding" (Retinger, p. 82).

Come to England to report on the war, she began by captivating the newspaper magnate Lord Northcliffe, and being an admirer of Conrad's books, she obtained from Northcliffe a letter of introduction. M. Paul Vance's gallant gesture aptly symbolizes the male reaction wherever she appeared, and during her contact with Capel House, not only Conrad, but Borys and Retinger also fell in love with her. Retinger finally won, but at the cost of his marriage, his friendship with Conrad, and almost his life, since he nearly committed suicide in the early stages of their relationship, and almost became the twenty-ninth notch on her father's gun at the end of it (Pomian p. 39).

Rita, the heroine of Conrad's next book, *The Arrow of Gold*, would be seen, like Jane, "sitting cross-legged on the divan in the attitude of a very old idol or a very young child," and the fact that the "Rita" in this tale bears no resemblance to the "Rita" of his earlier version in *The Mirror of the Sea* supports Retinger's contention that it is Jane whom he here portrays.

Jane's first attempt to meet Conrad through Northcliffe was not successful. Conrad was just beginning a bad attack of gout, and he did not in any case think much of Northcliffe. He "wrote to Miss A—— declining courteously to receive her on the grounds of ill-health," but this star-crossed destiny was not so easily to be turned aside, or as Jessie puts it, "here a curious coincidence intervened." The American sculptor Joe Davidson had been to Capel House to do a bust of Conrad, and later invited the author to its exhibition in London. On similar grounds of health, Conrad declined, but sent Jessie, who met there another American, whom she invited to Capel House for lunch, as he had offered to take a message to Borys in France. He accepted on the condition that he could bring with him a young lady who had been going to lunch with him. "The moment they entered the house," says Jessie, "and almost before he introduced her by the name of Miss A——, I had guessed the identity of our visitor" (CC pp. 195–196).

From this time onwards, Miss A—— was an all-too frequent visitor, and in August in a letter to Curle, Conrad says, "We made the acquaintance of a new young woman. She comes from Arizona and (strange to say!) she has an European mind. She is seeking to get herself adopted as our big daughter and is succeeding fairly. To put it shortly she's quite yum-yum. But those matters can't interest a man of your austere character. So I hasten away from these petty frivolities to inform you that we had Lord Northcliffe for a Sunday afternoon. . . ." (LL 2, p. 173).

Then Miss Anderson went to France to see the war, and Conrad had his own military duties. At fifty-eight he could not hope to fight, but he could not bear to be left out, and eventually he was given the opportunity to make a series of visits to naval stations on the East Coast. They were involved in secret operations against enemy submarines, so nothing of their work could be directly reported, but it was thought that Conrad could encourage them, and the country, with generalized accounts of the dangers and hardships of their task.

He began at Dover, and worked northwards, driving himself to and from Capel House in a second-hand Model T Ford that Jessie would hear chugging through the lanes long before it arrived, and sending Pinker accounts of his hotel expenses to reclaim from the Admiralty (CC pp. 198–200). In September 1916 he visited Lowestoft, where once he had sailed with the *Skimmer of the Sea*, and went out with the mine-sweeper *Brigadier* on one of her patrols.

Meanwhile, Jane Anderson had returned from France as an invalid, overwhelmed by too close a contact with the horrors of the war—no doubt that touch of physical cowardice that adds conviction to Conrad's portrait of Rita in *The Arrow of Gold* is also part of his debt to Jane. She came to Capel House to recuperate, where as Jessie says, "she made an interesting invalid." Despite strong feelings of jealousy, Jessie liked her genuine concern about Borys, and appreciated her presence while Conrad was away on his naval assignments—"I was sufficiently interested in her to be glad of her company, and anything was better than having no one to talk to." Conrad seems to have taken it for granted that Jessie would accept the situation—he referred to Jessie and Jane as "stable-mates," and in a letter to Jessie, when Jane was depressed, he said, "The dear Chestnut filly is obviously put out. I am trusting the dearest dark-brown mare to steady that youngster in her traces. See?" (Karl, p. 790).

Conrad was due to visit a station of the Royal Naval Air Service at Yarmouth, and as both Jane and their son John were recovering from illness, it was decided that they would all go to Folkestone for a holiday, Conrad to join them from Yarmouth. By this time Jane seems to have been suffering seriously from boredom, so she told Jessie that Conrad was in love with her, and had given her a letter in which he declared his passion. As Jessie subsequently came to realize, this claim, though not entirely unfounded, was largely inspired by a wicked desire to see what would happen. The story seemed to be confirmed by the fact that Jessie had had none of the frequent notes and telegrams that Conrad usually sent her, but this was because Jane had been intercepting them.

Meanwhile, at Yarmouth, Conrad had embarked on what for a man of his temperament must have seemed like the promise of certain death, a patrol over the North Sea in one of the primitive flying machines of the R.N.A.S. Although it was not very suitable for an open cockpit, he apparently refused to be parted from his bowler hat, so it was bound on with a silk scarf (BC p. 111). He flew in a Short seaplane for an hour and twenty minutes, and once it had attained its altitude, he felt a "sense of security so much more perfect than in any small boat I've ever been in; the as it were, material, stillness, and immobility . . . the illusion of sitting as if by enchantment in a block of suspended marble." Coming down on the water, he was shocked by its hardness—"I was aware, theoretically, that water is not an elastic body," but this was "the illuminating force of a particular experience" (NLL p. 212).

A somewhat analogous experience awaited him at Folkestone, where Jessie had taken care to meet him alone at the station. She was greeted with the question, "Where is your stable-companion?" and caught "a disappointed expression on his face." He could not understand Jessie's mood, nor realize that she had received none of his telegrams.

> "My flight was every bit as dangerous as any other observers might have been, and yet you greet me like this. I am disappointed in you. Very disappointed."
>
> "Your flight of fancy do you mean? I heard a great deal about that."
>
> "You have been so reasonable before and a real sport. I had no idea you would have taken my flying in so tragic a manner."
>
> "Flying? What do you mean? It is the first I have heard about it."

221

By this time, Jessie began to realize what had been happening, and with her husband's agreement, the "fair American" was asked to leave. When the Conrads were moving from Capel House in 1919, Jessie would drop a book and find a letter:

> The fair American lady had told a little white lie when she said she had burnt the letter she had received from my husband. The letter that would have proved all that she said. It was a very high flown epistle . . . I still held it in my hand when my husband came into the room.
>
> "What have you got there?" I held it out in silence. Before I could say a word he had flung it on the fire, and turning to me suggested a way of procuring something I had expressed a wish for. A usual form of penitence, that followed no accusation and no apology. (CC pp. 207–208)

Returned to town, Miss Anderson collected Joseph Retinger and went for another visit to France where, deprived of the father, she sought the son. Entertaining Borys in Paris, she caused him to overstay his leave and get into trouble with the Military Police, from which she got him out again by ringing up some generals, while Retinger, sick with jealousy, had taken to his bed. Back at his unit, rather bemused, and very much in debt, Borys wrote to tell his father about it, and he says that the reply was "prompt and characteristic. First he informed me that he had taken steps to put my finances in order and then expressed the hope that the enemy would keep me sufficiently preoccupied to enable me to get Jane out of my system" (BC p. 122). In a letter to Pinker, Conrad wrote, "If he must meet a 'Jane' it's better he should meet her at nineteen than at twenty-four" (JB p. 408). Or, one might add, at fifty-nine.

27. *Les Valeurs Idéales*

Conrad's North Sea adventures with the Navy reached their climax in October 1916, when from Granton Harbour, near Edinburgh, he went on a little ship that mended the torpedo-net defences, and then for a voyage on a "Q-boat," one of the armed vessels disguised as innocent merchant ships that went out to hunt for submarines. They were all steamships, except for one elderly sailing vessel, H.M.S. *Ready*, which was extremely vulnerable, should the enemy suspect it. Conrad insisted that this was the ship on which he must sail, though he had to appeal to the Admiralty, over the head of the local commander, before he won his case. He asked for Pinker, rather than his family, to be told if the ship did not return, and wrote:

> I have no nearer friend on whom I could lay the painful task. I believe I have your approval; Borys isn't likely to be angry with my memory; Jessie understands and John knows nothing of course. As to these last I know you will do all you can to make their fate as tolerable as it can be made.
>
> That much to be said, tho' don't imagine I have gloomy forebodings, nothing of the kind. Still it is no use ignoring the fact that the vessel has made three trips already and she may have been spotted. Also there are spies about. The prospect of an expedition of this sort

gives a curious force to the idea of spies. It drives home
one's conviction that they do exist. (LL 2, pp. 175–176)

Before the adventure was over the idea of spies would be
given an even more "curious force," but at the beginning
Conrad very much enjoyed being under sail again, and had a
message transmitted to Pinker :

Dear Friend,
All Well.
Been practice-firing in sight of the coast.
Weather improved.
Health good.
Hopes of bagging Fritz high.
Have dropped a line to Jessie.
Don't expect to hear from me for ten days. (LL 2, p.
179)

Evidently his health did not continue to be good, and before
the ship was due to return, the captain decided to summon a
fishing boat to put him ashore at Bridlington, where he was
promptly arrested as a spy. He eventually managed to establish his identity, but was ordered to report to his local police
station with his documents of naturalization. He believed that
he had long since lost them, and fell into a state of almost
hysterical panic for several days, unable to sleep, and refusing
to tell Jessie what the trouble was. Eventually, a local police-
man came to ask about the documents, and only then did Conrad tell Jessie. She obtained the papers from the bank, where
she had sent them long before, and took them herself to the
police station at Ashford, where the constable, who was in the
midst of shaving, told her to leave them on his desk. She returned to find Conrad halfway down the drive, and still in a
state of madness, but she gradually "coaxed him into a calmer
state of mind" (CC pp. 202–203). For Conrad it must have
seemed like the breaking into reality of subconscious fears, the
alien depth of which is evidenced by the fact that he had been
unable to confide in his wife.

In 1916, he wrote two short stories, both concerned with
the horrors of war. The first, called "The Warrior's Soul," is
from the Napoleonic age, and deals with a Russian soldier who

kills a fatally wounded Frenchman, from pure compassion, and is then accused of brutality. Conrad told Colvin that it was based on an incident from the *Memoirs* of Phillipe de Ségur (JB p. 406). The other, called "The Tale," reflects his experience of the Navy's secret battle. In a North Sea fog the captain of a British warship comes upon a neutral Scandinavian vessel that he suspects of fuelling German submarines. After searching it, he can find no evidence of guilt, but he has such a strong intuitive conviction of it that when the ship's captain insists that he is just lost in the fog, he sets him a course that will take him onto the rocks. He thinks of it as a "test" that will expose the captain's lies, but against his expectations, the ship takes the suggested course, and is lost, so that he is left with an ineradicable burden of guilt. It is not, one imagines, quite what the Admiralty had expected him to write about their heroes.

In fact, he seems to have found it impossible to do very much about this. There was a short humorous account of his flight in the seaplane that appeared in a little magazine for airmen in 1917, a note on the "The Dover Patrol" that was not published until after the war, and another on "The Unlighted Coast" that did not appear until after his death. They are collected in *Last Essays*, and the two stories in *Tales of Hearsay*, both posthumous volumes.

Under the pressure of Retinger's enthusiasm, Conrad wrote "A Note on the Polish Problem" for the Foreign Office, based on a draft provided by his friend. Later, in 1919, he would produce a longer article, "The Crime of Partition," which Retinger says contains "passages almost literally translated" from an article of his own in French (p. 149). Both are collected in *Notes on Life and Letters*. They suggest that for the political future of Poland, as for the war effort in England, Conrad wanted to do his duty, but could not bring to the task much of his heart or his diminishing store of spirit.

Early in 1917 he took some interest in a dramatized version of *Victory*, and intended to collaborate with the same author, Macdonald Hastings, on a stage version of *Under Western Eyes* (JB p. 409). Borys, now nineteen, had his first leave from France, and Jessie says, "I looked at him with a certain wonder. He had developed physically, and looked strangely mature in every way. Only his manner with me remained

what it had been in his school days. I had fifteen days of fearful joy" (AK p. 95).

The Shadow Line, after serialization, was published in
March 1917. Sidney Colvin was asked to review it, and was
evidently puzzled as to whether to treat it as fact or fiction.
After assuring him that it was "exact autobiography," and
giving him some fairly precise instructions on what to say,
Conrad adds:

> I have been called a writer of the sea, of the tropics, a
> descriptive writer, a romantic writer—and also a realist.
> But as a matter of fact all my concern has been with the
> "ideal" value of things, events and people. That and
> nothing else. The humorous, the pathetic, the passionate,
> the sentimental *aspects* came in of themselves—*mais en
> vérité c'est les valeurs idéales des faits et gestes humains
> qui se sont imposés à mon activité artistique.**
>
> Whatever dramatic and narrative gifts I may have are
> always, instinctively, used with the object—to get at, to
> bring forth *les valeurs idéales* (LL 2, p. 185).

At first sight this might seem little more than another attempt on Conrad's part to make himself more morally respectable, and to give to his work a theoretical significance that
could hardly have been consciously intended when he felt
compelled to write; but it is not a statement of intent, it is
what he sees as he looks back, and it is perhaps the most perceptive comment that he ever made about his own work. He
has not been simply an upholder of *les valeurs idéales*, but
concerned rather, as he says, to "get at" them, to "bring them
forth" from their hiding places and lay them out for inspec-
tion. If one adds that it was only by rigorous self-analysis, a
kind of spiritual self-vivisection, that he got at and brought
forth these things, then one has isolated an important aspect
of his achievement. Nothing has been taken for granted:
ideals, social codes, and dreams of glory have been brought
into conflict with a hostile or indifferent nature, and with the
irrational elements in the human psyche, as in *Heart of
Darkness* or *Lord Jim* or else, as in *The Secret Agent* or *Under Western Eyes*, personal ideals and aspirations have come

* —but in truth it is the "ideal values" in human behavior that
have been the determining influence on my writing.

into conflict with the cruel and irrational elements in organized society, and in the process everything is put in question. Much of this was undiscovered country for English literature. British writers might examine their characters against social codes and moral values, but never to the degree that Conrad does, had they questioned the codes and values themselves: they knew what was good and what was evil; but at bottom, Conrad never knows, and it is this that has given his work, in the second half of the twentieth century, its feeling of contemporary relevance.

It is also plain that for the sake of social acceptance, continuing sales, and his own peace of mind, Conrad was determined to play down these deeper implications. We can see him working hard at this in 1917, when he began to write a series of Author's Notes for a collected edition of his works, a task that he would continue intermittently until 1920. In every case they strengthen his defenses rather than take us behind them, and they continually emphasize the factual elements in his stories, as if he were being accused of not telling the simple truth, and is trying to prove that he did nothing else. In this respect, he was, of course, the victim of his own propaganda. He had continually put it about that his stories were "true," and so felt compelled on every occasion to try to justify it.

In so far as this question affected Conrad's personal integrity, it seems that he thought in terms of "truth to my own sensations," a phrase that presumably meant something more exact than mere "poetic truth," though hardly less elastic. When forced to concede that something he had written was not quite literally true, he would insist that it was "true, remorselessly true to the writer's own sensations" (CD p. 84), and in his defence to Blackwood in 1902 he had spoken of "absolute truth" to one's "sensations" as "the basis of art in literature." This is a problem that would become even more acute with the publication of his next book, *The Arrow of Gold*.

Of the literary friends whom Conrad met from time to time at the Mont Blanc restaurant in Soho, Edward Thomas was probably the strongest admirer of his work, and in one review had called Conrad a "lord of language." At that time Thomas was known primarily as a critic, and he had been producing his own poems for only a little while when, moved by a patriotism that, like Conrad's, was rather different from that of the press and the politicians, he volunteered for active service in the Artillery.

During the winter of 1916–17 Thomas was at "Tin Town," an artillery training base on the Kentish coast near Lydd, not far from Capel House. Conrad ferried him in his Model T Ford, and Jessie recalled his last visit, confirming what others have written about the "air of gentle finality" that marked him at this time—"His calm was ominous and hopeless, yet withal he was not by any means dismal or dull." A few days later, when Conrad was coming down from London, Thomas got into the train on his way back to the camp: "So we meet at least once more, my dear Conrad" (CC pp. 199–200). He was in the trenches by February 1917, and was killed early in April.

While Conrad had been on his way to Poland in July 1914, the English writer Hugh Walpole had been about to begin a critical study of him. Walpole, then thirty, had already published half-a-dozen novels, and become an intimate of Henry James. The book on Conrad was delayed by the outbreak of the War, as Walpole went to Moscow as a kind of self-appointed war correspondent, and was soon visiting the front in Poland, on the opposite side of the lines from Conrad in Zakopane (Hart-Davis, pp. 116, 127).

Walpole fell in love with Russia, more particularly with a Russian painter, and would stay on there under various guises until the Revolution in 1917, but he had a set of Conrad's works sent out to him, and completed the study by May 1915. After his return, Sir Sidney Colvin arranged a meeting with Conrad, and this was the beginning of a friendship. Shortsighted, naive and optimistic, with a great aptitude for literally falling on his face, Walpole seems to have welcomed Conrad to fill the gap left by the death of James in 1916, while for Conrad, Walpole was the kind of cheerful, talkative companion that he liked to have around in his later years. In March 1919 Walpole would put in his diary, "The usual delightful but rather tiring day, as Conrad insists on talking the *whole* day through, never reads or walks or sleeps." What did he talk about? "Money and gout" (Hart-Davis, pp. 186, 286).

228

28. *The Faculty of Invention*

In August 1917, Conrad began a magazine story about two women in Marseilles, a "Royalist *femme galante*" and her peasant sister (JB p. 409). This seems to have been a throwback to his unfinished *The Sisters*, which on Garnett's advice he had given up in 1898: it would now grow into *The Arrow of Gold*. Meanwhile, the worsening state of Jessie's knee required another period of treatment in London, and the family took a flat in Hyde Park Mansions, off Edgware Road. Jessie was now under the care of a famous surgeon from Liverpool, Sir Robert Jones, for whom she developed a great affection. At this time, he was, like everyone else, in uniform, but kept up his private practice.

In London, meeting friends amidst the nightly noise of Zeppelins and antiaircraft guns, Conrad seems to have been sufficiently distracted from his worries to be able to work, and every morning he dictated more pages of *The Arrow of Gold*, though without much faith in what he was doing. In December he wrote to Sanderson, "You can imagine what sort of stuff it is. No colour, no relief, no tonality, the thinnest possible squeaky bubble. And when I've finished it, I shall go out and sell it in the market place for twenty times the money I had for the *Nigger*" (LL 2, p. 198).

Jessie's leg was put into a cruel device called a Thomas' Splint in the hope of avoiding another operation, and with its aid she was just able to walk. Early in 1918, Borys came on leave, and they went to the theatre, and to a restaurant where Conrad threw his coat over the arm of an American admiral under the impression that he was the commissionaire (BC pp. 126–127).

Back at Capel House, Conrad completed *The Arrow of Gold* on June 4, 1918, though he would go on revising it until October (JB p. 410n.). It is a strange, uneven, but very readable book, in which Conrad's memories of Marseilles, his familiarity with French literature, his impressions of Jane Anderson, and some reading up of Carlist affairs are put together to produce a colorful concoction quite unlike anything else that he wrote. What is most extraordinary is that with a daring worthy of the Polish cavalry, he claimed that it was all literally true—never before had he overcalled his hand quite so recklessly.

The hero is a young man called "M. Georges," like the name that Conrad had used, or been given, when he had sailed on the *Saint-Antoine* in 1876, but he is pictured here as a wealthy young dilettante and adventurer of such reputation that the highest foreign representatives of the Carlist court must seek his aid. They introduce him to the Pretender's beautiful young mistress, in the hope that she can win him to their cause, for only he could undertake the desperate mission upon which the fate of the Spanish War depends. He accomplishes the task, off-stage, and after he has rescued her from a psychotic attacker with a scimitar, she declares her love. They go away to a rose-embowered retreat, from which he emerges again to fight a duel—also off-stage—with the jealous American, J. Y. M. K. Blunt. Meanwhile the royal courtesan, feeling unworthy of him, goes away, leaving him only her golden arrow. He was cautious enough to add that he had subsequently lost it in a storm at sea.

Conrad's claim that this was autobiography inevitably aroused suspicion, but he stuck to it, and reaffirmed it when he added an Author's Note in 1920—"I venture this explicit statement because, amidst sympathetic appreciation, I have detected here and there a note, as it were, of suspicion." The story's omissions and inconsistencies are, he says, further evidence of its truth, for "in the case of this book I was unable to supplement these deficiencies by the exercise of my inventive faculty. It was never very strong; and on this occasion its use would have been exceptionally dishonest."

Once again Sir Sidney Colvin was asked to review the book, and as with *The Shadow Line*, he was worried about whether or not it was "true." He had read *The Mirror of the Sea* and noticed, as anyone must, that the pre-Jane Anderson "Rita" portrayed there bears no resemblance to the "Rita" of *The Arrow of Gold*. Conrad replied that the *Tremolino* incident in *The Mirror of the Sea* was literally true, but the Rita was "by no means true," whereas the Rita of *The Arrow* was "true fundamentally." Of the Allègre affair, he said that it was "I understand, a fact, of which I make an extended version," but on receiving a second letter from Colvin admitted that "Allègre is imagined from a glimpsed personality of no fame or position." Rather than continue to patch this fragile web, Conrad decided to appeal to Colvin as a "man of the world":

> Your question raises a delicate problem. A man of your *savoir-faire*, your sense of literary *convenances* and your *homme-du-monde* tact, is best fit to judge how the autob'al note, if struck, may affect the world—and the man.
>
> With all deference then I would venture to suggest that the view of its being a study of a woman, *prise sur le vif* (obviously, you may say) and also the story of a young, very young, love told with a depth of emotion pointing to experience is what you perceive, what impresses you. . . . Perhaps you could discover a "personal note of youth" both in the (so to speak) innocence and completeness of this love affair. . . . Pardon me if I have said too much. I rest in your affection and in your comprehension which I have never doubted. (LL 2, pp. 224–225)

By the summer of 1918 it had become evident that another operation on Jessie's knee could not be avoided, and in July the Conrads returned to London. Borys and John, now at a prep school in Surrey, were given leave, so that after her operation Jessie had daily visits from her two sons. "My pain was intense, and the seven weeks I lay, or rather reclined, with my sick limb held in a vice, were the most nightmarish I can remember." To show her gratitude to Sir Robert Jones, she bought two "realistic" female dolls and made clothes for them, as a present for his two granddaughters. When the surgeon saw them he said, "Do they disrobe?" Jessie's answer that they did "afforded him some satisfaction, and immediately he began to disrobe both very thoroughly. There was something tenderly pathetic in that uniformed figure with his skilful fingers busily unbuttoning those tiny garments." Then Conrad came in and said, "A most unseemly display, my dear. Most unseemly, let me tell you." She adds that "he turned away in disgust and made one or two hurried walks up and down the room. I could see his exasperation in the set of his shoulders and the movement of his hands" (CC p. 209).

It was not until the middle of October that they could return to Capel House, where Jessie was put in a small room on the ground floor. Back in France, Borys had been buried by the debris from a salvo of shells, and after a time in Rouen was moved to the Neurological Hospital in South London, and finally sent home. It would be some years before the damage to his nerves was fully healed.

The war was now over, but the continuing illness of his wife and his elder son, and then the death of a maid, were too much for Conrad, and he made a temporary retreat from the world. At the time of Borys's twenty-first birthday, in January 1919, Jessie received a letter from him:

Dear Heart

My soul is weary for the sight of you. I hope you will have a possible night. What a comfort it is to have the two kids with us in these trying times—and especially the big kid, who twines himself round my heart even more than when he was a small child.

I worry about you all, and I fret at being laid up on his twenty-first birthday. What must be will be—and after all, I have all possible confidence in the future. Good night, dearest, and give me a friendly thought before you go to sleep

YOUR BOY

This letter came from a room at the top of the house where he had shut himself up for three weeks (CC p. 213).

When he returned he dug up again his biggest piece of unfinished business, *The Rescue*. This adventure of Lingard and a lovely lady that had tortured him through all the years of his early career had been about half-done when he had abandoned it in 1903. Up till this time he had spent seven years trying to make it something great, an analysis of a courageous man of action whose conscious idealism masks an ambitious egoism, while his humble origins and isolated life make it difficult for him to respond to the love of a sophisticated woman. Writing to Ford in 1898 he was dreaming of "how fine it could be if the thought did not escape—if the expression did not hide underground, if the idea had a substance and words a magic power, if the invisible could be snared into shape. And it is sad to think that even if all this came to pass—even then it could never be so fine to anybody as it is fine to me now, lurking in the blank pages in an intensity of existence without voice, without form—but without blemish" (JB p. 223).

Now, Conrad was simply concerned to get rid of it. He cancelled out certain early passages that suggest the complexity of Lingard, and the ambiguity of his attitudes (Moser, pp. 146ff.), forgot his fears that the original plot was rather ridiculous, and steamed ahead to produce another piece of light literature as colorful, as competent, and as fundamentally unconvincing as *The Arrow of Gold*.

In March 1919 the Conrads were given notice to leave Capel House, and moved temporarily to a furnished house called Spring Grove in the village of Wye, between Ashford and Canterbury. From here on May 25, Conrad wrote to Curle, "I've just finished *The Rescue*." He had been working against time, as its serialization in a weekly called *Land and Water* had already begun, and he would extensively revise it before it appeared as a book in the following year.

Conrad went out with Borys on high-speed house-hunting expeditions in their new American Studebaker. Borys was, by his own admission, a reckless driver, but Conrad loved being driven fast, and would rebuke their usual passenger, Hugh Walpole, for being so "damnably timid." When he needed to get to London in ninety minutes to sign some papers at the American Embassy for a £3000 deal for the film rights of his books, Conrad encouraged Borys to beat his own record, and did not mind when his hat was knocked off by the nose of a cart horse as they cut a corner; Walpole had to be carried out of the car (BC pp. 141–142). Most of Conrad's contracts were now being measured in thousands of pounds, but his "needs" inevitably expanded in proportion, and as he put it to Curle, "I am spending more than I ought to—and I am constitutionally unable to put the brake on unless in such a manner as to smash everything" (Curle, p. 156).

After some months of searching, the Conrads settled on a handsome Georgian house called Oswalds, in the village of Bishopsbourne, about four miles southeast of Canterbury. It had fine gardens, but was in a dip of the downs, and Conrad would complain of the lack of a view. By this time, John had started at Tonbridge School, but he had had a very free life, and never seems to have been very happy there. Conrad wrote to Galsworthy, "It was sad to behold the dear little pagan in the Eton jacket and horrible round collar. Those people are full of kindness and tact (I can see it plainly), but they have not the slightest conception of what he is. They will understand him presently when he has become like one of themselves. But I shall always remember the original—the only genuine John—as long as I live" (LL 2, p. 220). There are echoes here of the ambivalence of *Lord Jim*, but however much he may be tempted by the eloquence of Stein, Conrad will always opt for the "round collar." He wore one himself that, according to Epstein, "enclosed his neck like an Iron Maiden" (see Ch. 31).

In November 1919, Sir Robert Jones had Jessie in a nursing home at Liverpool for about three weeks, and the family stayed nearby at 85 Kingsley Road. At this time, as well as Curle, G. Jean-Aubry was in attendance (CC p. 217). This young French journalist with an interest in Polish affairs had worked with Retinger in Paris, and Conrad seems to have found his company increasingly congenial. By listening so long to Conrad's own versions of his past, Aubry felt himself uniquely qualified to be his biographer, and would later persuade Curle, who became Conrad's executor, to give him official status. This was, of course, from the point of view of getting at the facts, a fatal handicap, and although Aubry spent twenty years in travel and research before producing his biography, it still contains a fair proportion of pure Conradian fiction.

29. *The Emperor's Island*

Early in 1920, when he had finished revising *The Rescue*, Conrad worked on a dramatization of *The Secret Agent*, and followed it with *Laughing Anne*, a play based on "Because of the Dollars." No one wanted it as a play, but the collector Thomas J. Wise, who was now competing with John Quinn, gave Conrad £100 for the typescript, Conrad having assured him that it was well scribbled over in genuine pen and ink (Karl, p. 853).

For the rest of 1920, Conrad was preparing for his great novel on the Napoleonic era. He had first expressed his intention of writing it eighteen years before, in a letter to Blackwood (BM p. 158) : fifteen years ago he had been borrowing books on the subject in Capri, and twelve years ago, in Montpellier, he had told Pinker that he was visiting the town library and "reading up all I can discover there about Napoleon on Elba," though when Aubry subsequently investigated the resources of this library, he found that they had one book on the subject (LL 2, p. 41). This did not discourage Conrad from writing at the same time to Gide to tell him that "I am going to set to work to deal with Napoleon's influence on the Western Mediterranean : two volumes with notes, appendices, and statistical tables. And this to be a novel. I have an idea I shall never finish it" (SD p. 227). In the summer of 1920 he was visiting the British Museum, and the catalogue of his own books, compiled for their sale in

1925, shows that he had more on this subject than on any other (JB p. 343).

From what he left of *Suspense*, it would appear that if his letter to Gide was anything more than a joke, he had considerably reduced his ambitions. He did not have the temperament to organize great quantities of factual information, and as with earlier books, he chose to borrow heavily from one or two fruitful sources, and to keep in touch with his own experience. Most of the detail comes from a translation of the *Memoirs* of the Comtesse de Boigne, published in London in 1907, while the action is centered on a voyage to Elba in a *Tremolino*-type vessel with a Dominic Cervoni-like sailor called Attilio, accompanied by a thoughtful young English nobleman who admires the "genius" of Napoleon.

To help with the atmosphere, Conrad wanted to visit both Corsica and Elba. Jessie says it was a "cherished dream of many years, an obsession since childhood. He always declared that he was no admirer of Napoleon, but the fact remains that this tragic personality exercised a spell over the Author." Napoleon has, of course, exercised a spell over most romantically-minded writers from the time of Stendhal onwards, and it is unfortunate that Conrad's fragment does not reach the point at which the emperor was to make his entry. He left no outline of the plot, and Jessie says, "He told me once that he had quite half a dozen ways to bring it to an end" (AK p. 160).

Thus, at the end of 1920, as soon as Jessie was able to move, Conrad was organizing a trip to Corsica. They left London on January 23, 1921, taking Borys with them so that he could show them the battlefields in France. He had obtained for them a man whom he believed would be an excellent chauffeur, as his previous employer had been Count Louis Zobrowski, racing driver and owner of the original "Chitty-Chitty Bang-Bang," but Jessie was to find the chauffer "a raw yokel and unused to travel," while their nurse, also unhappy in foreign parts, was "not very helpful" (BC pp. 152–153).

The party spent two days visiting the battle area around Armentières. When Borys, still unsettled, became overexcited in recounting his experiences, Conrad would say, "Enough, boy, it is past and over, let us forget that part of it. Have a cigarette." From here, Borys returned to England, as he was working in a new radio equipment company into which his father had put some money. This was soon to collapse, but later he found a good job with the Daimler Company at Coventry (BC p. 153).

At Rouen the Conrads were joined, as far as Lyons, by Jean-Aubry, and with one breakdown, reached Marseilles on January 30. At one hotel on the way, Conrad decided to sleep on a small bed in the dressing room, which was almost filled with a large bath: "I can have my bath and keep the lights burning as long as I like without disturbing you, my dear." During the night Jessie was woken by cries of "Damn!" "Why, it's raining hard!" and finally a thud and cries for help. The bath had overflowed (CC p. 226).

They spent three days in Marseilles, Conrad showing Jessie the "haunts of his youth," and then embarked on a "desperately uncomfortable passage" for Corsica. They had booked rooms at the Grand Hotel in Ajaccio, having been assured that it had a lift, but when they arrived the owner confessed that this was a "mistake." He made up for it by giving them the best suite on the ground floor. Conrad did not feel at home in this "beastly hotel," mostly occupied by the British—"an atmosphere of intense good form pervades the place. Low tones—polite smiles—kind enquiries—small groups" (LL 2, p. 254).

Pinker and his wife and daughter came out to join them, as guests, together with Conrad's secretary, Lilian Hallowes. He had hoped to do some work, but apart from borrowing books from the local library, not much was done. He liked wandering round the harbor, and spent some time in conversation with the skipper of a small boat such as Attilio would use. They made some tours, and Conrad wrote to Aubry, "The Corsicians are charming (I mean the ordinary people) but the mountains get on my nerves with their roads which wind and wind endlessly over precipices. It makes one want to howl" (SD p. 280).

They had a glimpse of Corsica's most famous bandit, Romanetti, and writing later to the young daughter of a friend who was visiting Corsica, Conrad said, "Did Cook's people show you a vendetta? I haven't seen one but I saw a bandit. He was quite tame. He took a cigarette from my

237

hand most delicately" (LL 2, p. 300). They made a pilgrimage to the house in which Napoleon was born, where Conrad "spent several long hours." At the end of March they moved to Bastia, in the northeast of the island, with the intention of returning via Elba, but finally came straight back through Marseilles, and were met by a railway strike in England (CC pp. 230–232).

During the remainder of 1921, Conrad kept on with his preparations for the novel, but age and ill health continually unsettled him. Towards the end of the year he put the project aside to start a longish short-story that would, with other recent tales, make up another volume. This grew beyond its intended hundred pages to make his last completed novel, *The Rover*. It is very much a by-product of his meditations for *Suspense*, and "originated in the reading of Napoleon's dispatch to the admiral commanding Toulon in 1804." Once again it features a Cervoni-like seaman, Peyrol, with a *Tremolino*-type tartane, during the British blockade of the French coast. It has exciting adventures, superficial characters, and fine descriptions of the French countryside. The mood of the book, and doubtless of the author, is reflected in the epigraph from Spenser:

> Sleep after toyle, port after stormie seas,
> Ease after warre, death after life, does greatly please.

At the end of 1921 Conrad had reached the age of sixty-four, and poor health and his prodigal output of nervous energy had used up his strength. As Jessie said after his death, "I marvel that he lived so long. . . . He was never still, never in repose, even when resting. It is perfectly true that he wore himself out" (AK p. ix).

Conrad was visited at Oswalds by the American critic Elbridge Adams, who urged him to come to America; his publisher, Doubleday, was also keen for him to come. At the beginning of 1922, Pinker was due to go to New York, but he was not in good health either. He spent a few days at Oswalds before he sailed, and Jessie says that he was "very quiet and sad," and as he was leaving he said, "Well, I will confess that I am going on this trip with a heart as heavy as lead. I feel somehow that I shall never come back." His intuition was correct: he died in New York on February 8, 1922, and it was a deep shock to Conrad—"He always promised to see me off, and do his best for you" (CC p. 239).

In the autumn Doubleday came to England again, and said,

"Mr. Conrad, we have made you many visits, but you have never made us one. Don't you think you should return our calls?"

"When would you like me to call?" he asked.

"I said, 'The first of May,' and the first of May he came." (Doubleday, p. 124)

Conrad insisted that it should be simply a personal visit, and not a lecture tour, such as it was common for British authors to make.

Pinker's elder son, Eric, now in charge of the agency, had been negotiating a production of Conrad's dramatization of *The Secret Agent* at the Ambassador's Theatre. Conrad attended rehearsals where, according to Curle, "he was driven almost to distraction by the inability of the actors to catch, or to interpret his meaning" (p. 125). Something of this is conveyed by his letters to J. Harry Benrimo, the producer: speaking of the Professor, Conrad says that "not a single one of my directions as to tone and expression has been, I won't say carried out, but even so much as indicated," while "Inspector Head is very young and physically too tall and not heavy enough. His voice is young. For goodness' sake put a heavy moustache on him or something, and make him bear himself like a man of forty-five at least" (LL 2, p. 277).

Benrimo seemed unable to appreciate, as Conrad put it, that "you are not presenting a Guignol horror but something with a larger meaning." When talking with the producer, Conrad felt that "An air of unreality, weird unreality, envelops the words, the ideas and the arguments we exchange, the familiar words of the play, the figures of the people; clings to the walls, permeates the darkness of the fantastic cavern which I can by no means imagine will ever contain anything so real as an audience of men and women—" (Karl, p. 876n).

On the first night of the play, November 2, 1922, Conrad went up to London, but could not bring himself to watch it, and spent the evening in the lounge of his hotel. Arnold Bennett saw the play, and thought it "the best I have seen for a very, very long time, and by a long way the best," but as Bennett wrote to Pinker, "Twenty years will pass before such a play can possibly hope to have a success in London. London is fed on pap, and dishonest pap at that" (Hepburn 1, p. 317). The play was "put to death by the press," and had to be withdrawn after nine days (LL 2, p. 282).

30. *America*

Conrad may have intended his visit to America to be private, but there was no attempt to keep it secret, and his welcome there would be quite overwhelming. As well as enthusiastic readers, there was a considerable Polish population, and beyond that, an attitude towards the man of letters rather different from that which prevailed in England. In Henry James's "An International Episode," Bessie Alden, visiting London, is disappointed to find none of her favorite authors around, and asks Lord Lambeth where are "the eminent people—the authors and artists?" He says, "Oh, there are other eminent people besides those."

Soon after Conrad's death, Richard Curle visited the United States and he wrote:

> The position which Conrad's name holds in America is a really remarkable one and touched with the true quality of romance. His is not only the fame of a writer, but the fame of a personality, and it is not alone fame, it is glamour, as though his genius and career had really stirred a responsive chord in the generous heart of the great Republic. His individuality has, I believe, impressed itself more firmly upon the imagination of America than that of any other contemporary author. (Curle, p. 202).

This is not surprising : Conrad's life can be seen very much as a paradigm of the American immigrant experience. Like the American artist, he had had to absorb Anglo-Saxon culture and then adapt and extend it. Critics have found signs of his influence in writers as diverse as Faulkner and Scott Fitzgerald, so that he can be seen as part of a tradition, whereas in Britain he had neither forebears nor followers. The day-to-day incidents of his time in America would be seemingly trivial, but as the last great event of his life, and coming in his penultimate year, the voyage has a symbolic significance of which he himself seems to have been aware : it was a kind of homecoming.

He made extensive preparations, and bought what even Jessie regarded as "an excessive trousseau," including the first new dress suit since his marriage, six other suits, and "a dozen of everything." His fingers were now nearly useless, and Jessie fitted all his shirts with studs and links before he left. He felt that perhaps a fate like that of Pinker awaited him, giving him "a curious air of determination that disturbed me somewhat." A few days before he was due to leave, his oldest friend, G. W. F. Hope, suffered a stroke that deprived him of speech, and Conrad insisted on going to Essex to see him (CC pp. 240–241; LL 2, p. 309).

At the Curzon Hotel, on his last night in London, just before Conrad went to bed, a page boy brought him a registered express letter. He declined to open it and gave it to Jessie to look after. This "fateful piece of paper" stated that eight months previously Borys had married. It came from his mother-in-law, who being of a perfectly respectable family, was beginning to wonder when she would be allowed to meet them. Jessie says, "I glanced at the paper and as quickly crushed it in my fingers, and blindly made for the door." She went to her room, trembling violently, sent for brandy, and locked the door. Evidently imagining that Conrad's reaction would be as violent as her own, she decided not to tell him until after his return, a decision that would cause some agony to all three of them.

Accompanied only by Curle, Conrad reached Glasgow the following evening, where he gave at his hotel a small dinner party, which included the artist Muirhead Bone and the

Scottish writer Neil Munro, whom he had met in Glasgow in 1898. Curle says that on that evening Conrad "was yet as full of vitality as a man in the prime of life" (p. 180). He sailed the next day, April 21, 1923, on the *Tuscania*. Bone's son David was the captain of the ship, and the father was a fellow passenger, with a cabin that connected with Conrad's. During the voyage he made an excellent etching of Conrad, who found the ship "an unpleasantly unsteady imitation of the Ritz Hotel." He contrasted it unfavorably with the *Torrens*, where the passengers had a share in the life of the ship, "that sort of life which is not sustained on bread (and *suprême au volaille*) alone, but depends for its interest on enlarged sympathies and awakened perceptions" (LE p. 38).

From New York he wrote to Jessie, "I will not attempt to describe to you my landing, because it is indescribable. To be aimed at by forty cameras held by forty men is a nerve shattering experience. Even Doubleday looked exhausted after we had escaped from that mob of journalists." There was also a Polish deputation that included "a swarm of little girls dressed in national costume" who "rushed me on the wharf and thrust enormous nosegays into my hands" (LL 2, 301). According to Doubleday, "of all the foreign visitors who came to New York, I think Conrad was perhaps the most successful. This came about through his perfectly simple and open manner." When asked if he was going to lecture, he replied "that the people of the United States had always been very kind to him and he saw no reason why he should lecture them—as a matter of fact, he had come only to visit a friend, not for business. This seemed very striking, and started the Conrad publicity ball going in a way which I thought remarkable and certainly unusual" (Doubleday, p. 125).

It is fairly plain from this remark, as from what followed, that Doubleday had set himself the double task of keeping "the publicity ball going," and protecting Conrad from its effects, setting in train an impressive series of non-events and brief interviews, while his young associate, Christopher Morley, wrote "innumerable" articles about it. No doubt some protection was necessary, for according to Aubry, who heard a first-hand account on Conrad's return:

He was assailed by journalists wanting interviews, authors desiring advice about their books, sending him theatre tickets, and demanding to know his opinion of their plays. He was urged to preside at a poetry contest for a sonnet on the sea. Young girls wrote to him hysterically from California; Harvard students and West Point cadets wanted to see him, a stenographer offered his services for the duration of the visit. Of course there were thousands of requests for autographs too, not to mention a few cranks, among them a man apparently quite sane, who claimed, in beautifully fine handwriting, to have discovered "planetary breathing." (SD p. 283)

The high point of the visit, socially, was a gathering at the house of Arthur Curtiss James on May 10, where the cream of New York society were to hear Conrad give a talk on his work, and readings from *Victory*. Conrad's acute nervousness apparently communicated itself to Doubleday, who says:

> It was given to me to introduce him to the audience. He was in a state of nervous collapse, and I was not far behind. I remember that I was almost in a trance when I got up to make the introduction, and I was surprised to hear myself say, "This is the first time that Mr. Conrad has ever spoken in public, and please God, if I have anything to do with it, it will be the last."
> It was the last. It nearly killed him, because of his extraordinary nervousness. (pp. 125–126)

Although Conrad began with an accent that few could comprehend—one or two businessmen went out for a smoke—those who persevered became acclimatized to it, and when he had concluded, an hour and a half later, by reading the chapter of *Victory* in which Lena dies, many had been moved to tears. In a letter to Jessie, he told her that "it was a most brilliant affair, and I would have given anything for you to be there, seen all that crowd and all that splendour. . . . There was a most attentive silence, some laughs and at the end, when I read the chapter of Lena's death, audible snuffling. Then handshaking with 200 people. It was a great experience" (LL 2, pp. 309–310).

He spent about six weeks in America, most of the time at Doubleday's comfortable house on Long Island. He met the most influential of the publisher's friends, Edward Mandell House, once chief advisor to President Wilson, who told him "a great many interesting stories." He also had a long meeting with that other great Polish expatriate, the pianist and composer Paderewski. Three years younger than Conrad, Paderewski's background was very similar. His father, like Conrad's had managed an estate in Podolia. His mother had died when he was six months old, and his father had been imprisoned by the Russians after the uprising of 1863. More of an extrovert than Conrad, and accustomed to public appearances, he had combined his artistic vocation with a whole-hearted participation in national affairs. He had won President Wilson to the Polish cause, and for a few months in 1919 he had been the first prime minister of the new Poland.

Staying with Doubleday, Conrad was not far from the cottage at Great Neck where the recently married Scott and Zelda Fitzgerald were living, with Ring Lardner as neighbor. They knew that Conrad was there, spiritually so near, but socially so far, and one night, after getting drunk, Lardner and Fitzgerald danced round the Doubleday mansion in the hope of attracting his attention. The caretaker threw them out, and that was the nearest that Conrad ever came to meeting the man who would be regarded as his greatest disciple. (Milford, p. 95). In August of the following year, Fitzgerald would be found by a friend one morning gazing out to sea from the balcony of his rented villa at Hyères. When at last he became aware of the visitor, Fitzgerald said quietly, "Conrad is dead."

From May 15 to 24, Doubleday took Conrad on a motor tour of New England. Conrad had told him that he would not accept any honorary degrees, adding that he had already declined offers from the universities of Oxford, Edinburgh, Liverpool and Durham (LL 2, p. 297), but Yale was apparently preparing to bestow one upon him. Doubleday says that Conrad promised he "would go the next morning to see the secretary of the university, thank him for the honour, and decline it in a way which would not give offense. When we got fifty miles beyond New Haven on our way east, I asked Conrad how he had gotten along with the secretary of the university. He said he was sorry to say he had forgotten all about it" (p. 127) .

If Conrad ever had a serious conversation with anyone in America, it has not been recorded, but we do have the account of a frustrated attempt at one by a Jewish writer, Louis Weitzenkorn, who wrote about it for the New York *World:* "In the role of a duenna guarding a Spanish virgin, Frank Doubleday personally conducted an 'interview' for me Wednesday with Joseph Conrad. I write still in the shadowy edge of indignation over what will probably be the first and last time that I shall ever have talked with the man I think the greatest writer upon the face of the earth." As he entered, Doubleday told him in a dramatic whisper that Conrad was not feeling well, and "I saw a man older than I had hoped to see. There was a great width to his shoulders, the broadness of a once powerful frame, but the hunching stoop made Conrad seem short." While Weitzenkorn searched for words, Doubleday told him how Conrad had been impressed with the intelligence of American journalists, and with this kind of assistance, the conversation did not get very far, but it had for Weitzenkorn some "impressive silences."

He then had to make way for a young man who under the pen name of "Boswell" specialized in interviewing the great. Weitzenkorn asked if he could stay, and has preserved it on ice :

"You visited some of our colleges," he began. "Did you like them?"

"He only saw the outside," said Doubleday.

"I saw many faces—interesting American faces," Conrad replied for himself. "You know, I get many hints from a passing face. I saw Lord Jim that way."

Young Boswell wrote steadily for a minute. Then :

"Did you like the appearance of the college buildings at Yale? I'm fond of New Haven myself. I want to go back there often."

Conrad complimented the buildings at Yale. Boswell, reminded of youth, spoke of Conrad's book of that name.

"The spirit of youth," said Boswell. "That's it. But how did you get it?" He poised his pencil.

Conrad did not answer at once. Doubleday stood up,

walked down the room and back. He drew out his watch
and spoke—in the air—of a luncheon appointment.
Conrad was hunched again in his chair. The hollows of
his cheeks seemed deeper. (N.Y. *World*, June 23, 1923)

Conrad's own view of himself in America seems to accord
very closely with this. To Bruno Winawer, a Polish writer
with whom he had corresponded since 1921, he wrote, after
his return:

> I prefer not to talk about my voyage. *Entre nous*, I
> felt all the time like a man *dans un avion*, in a mist, in a
> cloud, in a vapour of idealistic phraseology; I was lost,
> bewildered, amused—but frightened as well. It was
> something that could not be caught either by eye or by
> hand! Obviously some power is hidden behind it—great
> power undoubtedly—and certainly talkative. (NP p.
> 292)

He sailed for England on the liner *Majestic* on June 2, and
with typical generosity, the Doubledays delivered him all the
way home, and obtained from Jessie a formal receipt, on
which she wrote across a twopenny stamp, "Received with
thanks, from Mr. and Mrs. Doubleday, one rejuvenated husband. Jessie Conrad" (CC p. 245).

31. *The End*

Jessie had refused to meet Borys's wife before Conrad returned, and had forbidden Borys either to go to Glasgow to say goodbye to his father, or to meet him on his return, as she wanted to break the news herself. On arrival, Conrad looked so tired that she put it off again until their tea arrived the next morning. Conrad interrupted her explanations by saying, "I don't want to know anything more about it. It is done, and I have been treated like a blamed fool, dam'!" It would seem that Borys's reluctance to tell his father had not been from any fear that he would object to his choice, but because of his father's strong insistence that he should not marry until his finances were secure.

Conrad decided to make Borys and his wife an allowance of £200, and told Jessie, "They will come here to lunch on Sunday week—I don't care how, but mind they are not late." Borys says that his father "greeted my wife with his usual elaborate courtesy, putting her at ease immediately," but his mother was "far more reserved and it was several years after J. C.'s death before our relationship again became normal" (BC p. 158).

John, now sixteen, was still not very happy at Tonbridge, and at the suggestion of Aubry, it was decided to let him spend a year in France. In September 1923, with John and Jessie, Conrad went to Le Havre to introduce him to a Protestant pastor of Aubry's acquaintance, the crossing being Conrad's last encounter with the sea. He carried on with dictating *Suspense* to Miss Hallowes, and complained in his letters of bad health and poor progress with his work—the same complaints that he had been making in his forties, then somewhat poetic, but now, alas, just literally true. A medical examination at the end of 1923 showed that Conrad had a "flabby heart," which "missed about every fourth beat" (Karl, p. 899).

The American collector John Quinn had now decided to sell off most of his great accumulation of pictures and manuscripts, auctioning the items, so many a month, in alphabetical order. Conrad was the main attraction in Section "A–C," which was offered in November 1923. The script of the well-promoted *Victory* fetched $8100; *Under Western Eyes*, $6900; *Chance*, $6600; *Almayer's Folly*, $5200; and altogether Quinn received about $110,000. He never paid a penny more to Conrad, though he might well have done if he had not been so deeply offended by Conrad selling a few items to his rival Thomas J. Wise.

The sale, as well as bringing in perhaps more money than Conrad had ever earned by writing, also brought him, even in England, far more publicity than he had ever had before, and he wrote to Doubleday that "the reverbration in the press here was very great indeed; and the result is that lots of people, who had never heard of me before, now know my name, and thousands of others, who could not have read a page of mine without falling into convulsions, are proclaiming me a very great author. And there are a good many also whom nothing will persuade that the whole thing was not a put up job, and that I haven't got my share of the plunder" (LL 2, p. 324).

One of those who perhaps "could not have read through a page of mine" but now knew of his fame was engineer John Nieven, recently retired. Unaware that he had featured in several stories, and even by name in *The Shadow Line*, he wrote to ask Conrad if he remembered once serving in a ship called the *Vidar*. Conrad replied that he often recalled it, "since there is nothing to remember but what is good and pleasant in my temporary association with three men for whom, I assure you, I have preserved to this day a warm regard and sincere esteem" (LL 1, p. 99).

Ford, who was in Paris where he had launched the *Transatlantic Review*, with the assistance of Pound and Hemingway, came to London in January 1924, where he saw Conrad for the last time. Conrad was cautious: "We met as if we had seen each other every day for the last ten years. . . . As we talked pleasantly of old times I was asking myself, in my cynical way, when would the kink come." In another note to Eric Pinker a couple of days later he says that Ford wanted to be friendly, "in fact, *entre nous*, too friendly" (JB p. 433).

Borys, now doing well in the marketing of Daimler cars, had moved to London. His son Philip was born on January 11, 1924, and Conrad and Jessie went to see them. Borys says that Conrad was "in a great state of excitement and even Mrs C's placidity was showing one or two cracks—they were both obviously delighted with their grandson" (BC p. 160). Daimler supplied cars to the Royal family, who were currently replacing their 1910 models. After George V and Mary had rigorously inspected the new vehicles, they agreed to the sale of the old ones, provided that the purchaser's name was first approved by them, and Borys thought that one of these cars, with its specially wide doors, would be ideal for the use of his mother. He took it down to Oswalds, where Jessie found she could get in and out unaided, and the purchase was completed (BC p. 159).

In March the sculptor Jacob Epstein came to start work on a bust of Conrad. Born in New York of parents from Poland, he had admired Conrad's work since his days as a student, and had long wanted to work from him, but he had been at the center of repeated artistic controversies. Many of Conrad's friends, notably Curle and Cunninghame Graham, had strongly supported him, but Galsworthy, deeply disturbed by one of Epstein's early representations of Christ, had persistently taken the lead in protests against his work. Epstein's request to portray Conrad ten years before had been refused "owing to the intervention of a friend," but now, through Muirhead Bone, it had finally been arranged, and Epstein, with his wife and five-year-old daughter Peggy Jean, moved into an inn near Conrad's house. Of Conrad, Epstein wrote:

His manners were courtly and direct, but his neurasthenia forced him at times into outbursts of rage and irritability with his household which quickly subsided. I already had a fairly clear notion of how I should treat the bust. A sculptor had previously made a bust of him which represented him as an open-necked, romantic, out-of-door type of person. In appearance Conrad was the very opposite. His clothes were immaculately conventional, and his collar enclosed his neck like an Iron Maiden's vice or a garroter's grip. He was worried if his hair or beard were not trim or neat as became a sea captain. There was nothing shaggy or Bohemian about him. His glance was keen despite the drooping of one eyelid. (Epstein, pp. 90–91).

Though they slept at the inn, the Epsteins ate at Oswalds, and since they were well endowed with those Bohemian virtues that the Conrads lacked, there was an inevitable clash of temperaments. Epstein would stride fuming round the garden and up and down the stairs, an area that Conrad regarded as his own exclusive fuming ground, while Mrs. Epstein lay on the sofa in a black nightdress, confiding to Jessie that "black had the advantage of keeping clean all the summer."

The climax came when Epstein's gang of Italian plasterers moved in. The bust was now in a room over the kitchen, and Jessie tells us that "water poured between the floor planks so that the maids became tearful and preparing of lunch was almost impossible." Epstein "fumed" up the front staircase and down the back staircase, leaving white footprints everywhere. "Joseph Conrad locked the door between the two staircases, and the next moment, almost before he reached his study, Mr. Epstein was rattling and shaking the door in a fury." After this, "Epstein and his helpers occupied the room with the bust, my husband and his secretary locked themselves in the study, Madame Epstein went to sleep in the drawing room, and I was left to the tender mercies of Peggy Jean. What a Sunday!" (CC p. 237).

Nevertheless, Conrad was well pleased with the result, and wrote to Elbridge Adams, "It is really a magnificent piece of work. . . . I was reluctant to sit, but I must say that now I am glad the thing has come off. It is nice to be passed to posterity in this monumental and impressive rendering" (LL 2, p. 341). Now in the National Portrait Gallery, it is the head of an old man, but certainly of one who sees visions.

Joseph Retinger, back in London after some years in Mexico, went to see Conrad for the first time since their jealousy over Jane Anderson. In 1918, when Retinger was penniless in Spain after his expulsion from France, Conrad had been the only former friend who sent him any "material help" (Pomian, p. 42). He found life at Oswalds "totally different" from that at Capel House—"Conrad was earning good money and could afford all the comfort which his age began to demand from him." He added that though Conrad "certainly showed all the signs of the greatest friendship and cordiality," he still felt that "the shadow of a woman stood between us, a distance of six years of fulfilment on one side and disappointment on the other" (Retinger, p. 165).

Conrad's adopted country's approval now extended beyond the permission to purchase a cast-off royal car: the message of the sale of his manuscripts had evidently reached the highest circles, and in May 1924 he received a long official envelope. Burdened with guilt over his income-tax returns, he was convinced that he was now about to be sent to jail, and as with messages from France when Borys was there, he was reluctant to open it. When he did, he found it contained the offer of a knighthood (Doubleday, p. 128), which he courteously declined. One can only guess at the reasons, but it came rather long after it had been bestowed on his neighbor who had made his fortune from diamonds, or after it had been declined by Galsworthy, while Ford had always treated such things with derision, as not appropriate to the artist. He would not have refused the Order of Merit, for which he had been unsuccessfully measured against Kipling in 1919, nor the Nobel Prize, of which he had hopes in 1919, when *The Rescue* was published, and again in 1924, when *The Rover* came out (Karl, p. 3).

Conrad had never been happy with the lack of view and fresh air at Oswalds—it was "living in a hole"—and he spent a lot of time with Pinker, Walpole or Curle motoring around to look for a better place. In an open car, with Conrad's fingers almost useless, elaborate preparations had to be made for him to light his cigarettes, the car being slowed down at the appropriate moment. Borys writes of an occasion when he neglected to do this, "and looked back over my shoulder just in time to see J. C. hurl overboard his matches, the packet of cigarettes and the unlighted cigarette from his mouth, in the order named. Pinker assumed an expression of alarm and held on to his hat with both hands" (BC p. 149). Conrad was attracted by "a little house on the bleakest part of the North Foreland, in the teeth of every wind that blew," but Jessie vetoed that (CC p. 266).

Somewhere about this time their driver and Jessie's maid asked if they could marry, and Conrad decided to give them the furniture from Jessie's bedroom, saying that she could have the double bed on which he slept, and he would use an old single bed:

> The single bed proved very unsuitable for Joseph Conrad, because, apart from its legitimate purpose as a resting place, his bed had to be hospitable to a heap of books, all open and face downwards, maps, bed-rest, and more than once a Spratt's dog-biscuit box he had ordered his man to place at the foot of his bed to brace his feet against. I seem to see him now looking desperately uncomfortable. He had not trimmed his beard for several days, being gouty. He crouched between the erect bed-rest and the Spratt's biscuit box. Numerous books lay around him, and he was restlessly pulling the silk threads out of an old Italian bedspread. Two or three small tables stood around within reach, and from the many ash trays on them spiral columns of cigarette smoke rose. Sitting in that crumpled condition in the haze of smoke he had the appearance of a pathetically thin and angular idol. (CC p. 268)

On June 11, Conrad made his last trip to London, for a luncheon in his honor at the Polish legation (SD p. 285), and Jessie took this opportunity to put in a new bed. He was very angry, and "retired without kissing me goodnight for the first time in his married life, and that night I spent in tears—foolish I have no doubt" (CC p. 272). The next day Jessie had to go into the Nursing Home at Canterbury, and would stay there for about six weeks. Conrad was suffering badly from gout, and could not be cheerful. When he visited her he usually fell asleep in his chair, and would repeat insistently, "I want you back home again, Jess, quickly." She came home in an ambulance late in July. She had to stay in her room, but typed the last things that he wrote, and in the evenings they played bezique.

Curle came each weekend, and arrived on the night of Friday, August 1, at about 11:00 P.M. After a supper that was always ready for him, he went to Conrad's bedside. He found Conrad cheerful over his wife's return, and enthusiastic about taking him to see a house they had found. They talked about the recent death of John Quinn, but this "did not come home to him with a reminder of his own mortality. 'They get such strange diseases,' he said speaking at large." The next morning, after breakfast, they went to his study and talked about *Suspense*. The last few pages contain a rather strange, and strangely symbolic account of an old boatman, about to die, who is given the tiller of Attilio's boat, and a star to steer by, and has just enough strength to keep his hand in place. He slips off his seat just as the boat comes to the shore, and the fragment concludes:

> "Where is his star now?" said Cosmo, after looking down in silence for a time.
> "Signore, it should be out," said Attilio with studied intonation. "But who will miss it out of the sky?"

Conrad told Curle that morning, "My mind seems clearer than it has been for months and I shall soon get hold of my work again." He then continued with what was to be a new book of memoirs, and at eleven they went out to see the house. About a mile and a half before reaching it, Conrad put his hand to his chest, saying, "I feel that pain I had a few days ago." Curle insisted, against Conrad's wishes, on turning back, and Conrad went to bed. He was having occasional paroxysms of breathlessness, but his pulse was good, and the doctor saw no cause for alarm.

John was home, and at eight o'clock that evening Borys and his family arrived, not because they had been summoned, but to spend the August Bank Holiday with their parents. Conrad had a difficult night, but seemed to improve in the early morning, and got out of bed to doze in a chair. Jessie was in bed in the room next door, and he called out to her, "I'm better this morning. I can always get a rise out of you." Then at 8:30 A.M., she heard a cry, and he slipped out of his chair (Curle pp. 219ff.). His hand had left the tiller, but his star has not gone out.

Although his attitude had been what one might call "imaginative atheism," and he had once or twice, in letters to Garnett, expressed a dislike of Christian doctrines, Conrad was not hostile to the Church, nor had he ever uttered anything in public unbecoming to a "Pole, Catholic and gentleman": he was buried with the rites of the Church, on August 7, at St. Thomas', Canterbury. In an otherwise too sentimental account of the occasion, Cunninghame Graham produced one image that echoes the close of Conrad's "beloved *Nigger*": "A gleam of sun lit up the red brick houses of the town. It fell upon the towers of the cathedral, turning it into a glowing beacon pointing to the sky." He refers also to the "wild voices" of the circling gulls. As children of the sea, with their sunlit grace and their harsh and unintelligible cries, they can represent, perhaps as well as any creature, Conrad's vision of the world.

Abbreviations

For works frequently referred to in the text, the following abbreviations are used:

JOSEPH CONRAD *(Collected Edition)*

HD *Youth and Two Other Stories*
("Youth," *Heart of Darkness* and
The End of the Tether)
LE *Last Essays*
LJ *Lord Jim*
MS *The Mirror of the Sea*
NLL *Notes on Life and Letters*
PR *A Personal Record*
SL *The Shadow Line*

AK *Joseph Conrad as I Knew Him* by Jessie Conrad
BC *My Father, Joseph Conrad* by Borys Conrad
BM *Joseph Conrad: Letters to William Blackwood and David S. Meldrum*, ed. by William Blackburn
CC *Joseph Conrad and His Circle* by Jessie Conrad
CD *Congo Diary and Other Uncollected Pieces* by Joseph Conrad, ed. by Z. Najder
CH *Conrad: The Critical Heritage*, ed. by Norman Sherry
EG *Letters from Conrad, 1895 to 1924*, ed. by Edward Garnett
ES *Conrad's Eastern World* by Norman Sherry
GS *Letters from Joseph Conrad to Marguerite Poradowska*, ed. by John A. Gee and Paul J. Sturm
JB *Joseph Conrad: A Critical Biography* by Jocelyn Baines
LL *Joseph Conrad: Life and Letters* by G. Jean-Aubry
NP *Conrad's Polish Background*, ed. by Z. Najder
SD *The Sea Dreamer* by G. Jean-Aubry
SY *The Sea Years of Joseph Conrad* by Jerry Allen
WS *Conrad's Western World* by Norman Sherry

Conrad's Works

Conrad's *Works*

The above made up Dent's Uniform Edition (1923–1928), and have
been kept in print as the Collected Edition since 1946. The pagination
is identical with the Canterbury Edition issued by Doubleday in New
York.

Also, in collaboration with Ford Madox Ford (Hueffer):
The Inheritors: An Extravagant Story 1901
The Nature of a Crime 1924

Plays
One Day More, a Play in One Act (from "Tomorrow") 1913
The Secret Agent: Drama in Four Acts 1921
Laughing Anne, A Play (from "Because of the Dollars") 1923

Congo Diary and Other Uncollected Pieces, edited by Zdzislaw Najder,
(Doubleday, 1978), contains the *Congo Diary* (1890), the unfinished
fragment of *The Sisters* (1895–96), *The Nature of a Crime*, and
some shorter pieces.

Bibliography

(Limited to works quoted in the text)

Allen, Jerry. *The Sea Years of Joseph Conrad.* New York: Doubleday, 1965.

Aubry—see Jean-Aubry

Baines, Jocelyn. *Joseph Conrad: A Critical Biography.* New York: McGraw-Hill, 1960.

Barker, Dudley. *The Man of Principle: A View of John Galsworthy.* London: Heinemann, 1963.

Berryman, John. *Stephen Crane.* New York: William Sloane, 1950.

Blackburn, William (ed.). *Joseph Conrad: Letters to William Blackwood and David J. Meldrum.* Durham, N.C.: Duke University Press, 1958.

Conrad, Borys. *My Father, Joseph Conrad.* London: Calder & Boyars, 1970.

Conrad, Jessie. *Joseph Conrad as I Knew Him.* New York: Doubleday, 1926.

————. *Joseph Conrad and His Circle.* New York: Dutton, 1935.

Curle, Richard. *Joseph Conrad: A Study.* London: Kegan, Paul, 1914.

————. *Conrad to a Friend: 150 Selected Letters from Joseph Conrad to Richard Curle.* New York: Doubleday, 1928.

————. *The Last Twelve Years of Joseph Conrad.* New York: Doubleday, 1928. (Unless otherwise stated, references in the text are to this book.)

Doubleday, F. N. *Memoirs of a Publisher.* New York: Doubleday, 1972.

Edel, Leon. *Henry James: The Master, 1901–1916.* Philadelphia: Lippincott, 1972.

Epstein, Jacob. *Let There Be Sculpture.* London: Michael Joseph, 1940.

Fleishman, Avron. *Conrad's Politics.* Baltimore: Johns Hopkins Press, 1967.

Flower, Newman (ed.). *The Journals of Arnold Bennett.* London: Cassell, 1932.

Ford, Ford Madox. *Joseph Conrad: A Personal Remembrance.* Boston: Little Brown, 1924.

————. *Return to Yesterday.* New York: Liveright, 1932.

————. *The March of Literature.* London: Allen & Unwin, 1938.

Galsworthy, John. *Castles in Spain and Other Screeds.* London: Heinemann, 1927.

Garnett, David. *The Golden Echo.* London: Chatto & Windus, 1953.

Garnett, Edward (ed.). *Letters from Conrad, 1895 to 1924.* Indianapolis: Bobbs-Merrill, 1928.

Gathorne-Hardy, Robert. *Ottoline: The Early Memoirs of Lady Ottoline Morrell.* London: Faber, 1963.

Gee, John A., and Paul J. Sturm (eds.). *Letters of Joseph Conrad to Marguerite Poradowska, 1890–1920.* New Haven: Yale University Press, 1940.

Gordan, John Dozier. *Joseph Conrad: The Making of a Novelist.* Cambridge, Mass.: Harvard University Press, 1940.

Guerard, Albert J. *Conrad the Novelist.* Cambridge, Mass.: Harvard University Press, 1958.

Harris, Frank. *My Life and Loves.* London: W. H. Allen, 1966.

Hart-Davis, Rupert. *Hugh Walpole: A Biography.* London: Macmillan, 1952.

Hepburn, James (ed.). *Letters of Arnold Bennett.* London: Oxford University Press, 1966–1968.

Hervouet, Yves. "French Linguistic and Literary Influences on Joseph Conrad." Unpublished thesis, University of Leeds, 1971.

Jean-Aubry, G. *Joseph Conrad: Life and Letters.* New York: Doubleday, 1927.

————— (ed.). *Joseph Conrad: Lettres Françaises.* Paris: Gallimard, 1930.

—————. *The Sea Dreamer: A Definitive Biography of Joseph Conrad.* New York: Doubleday, 1957.

Karl, Frederick R. *Joseph Conrad: The Three Lives.* New York: Farrar, Straus & Giroux, 1979.

Kirschener, Paul. *Conrad: The Psychologist as Artist.* Edinburgh: Oliver & Boyd, 1968.

Kuehn, Robert E. (ed.) *Twentieth Century Interpretations of Lord Jim.* Englewood Cliffs, N.J.: Prentice-Hall, 1969.

Leavis, F. R. *The Great Tradition: George Eliot, Henry James, Joseph Conrad.* London: Chatto & Windus, 1948.

—————. *Anna Karenina and Other Essays.* London: Chatto & Windus, 1967.

Mann, Thomas. *Past Masters and Other Papers.* London: Martin, Secker & Warburg, 1933.

Mégroz, R. L. *Joseph Conrad's Mind and Method: A Study of Personality and Art.* London: Faber, 1931.

Meyer, Bernard C. *Joseph Conrad: A Psychoanalytic Biography.* Princeton: Princeton University Press, 1967.

Milford, Nancy. *Zelda Fitzgerald: A Biography.* New York: Doubleday, 1970.

Mizener, Arthur. *The Saddest Story: A Biography of Ford Madox Ford.* New York: World, 1971.

Morf, Gustav. *The Polish Heritage of Joseph Conrad.* London: Sampson, Low & Marston, 1930.

Moser, Thomas. *Joseph Conrad: Achievement and Decline.* Cambridge, Mass.: Harvard University Press, 1957.

Najder, Zdzislaw (ed.). *Congo Diary and Other Uncollected Pieces by Joseph Conrad.* New York: Doubleday, 1978.

———— (ed.). *Conrad's Polish Background: Letters to and from Polish Friends.* London: Oxford University Press, 1964.

Pomian, John (ed.). *Joseph Retinger: Memoirs of an Eminence Grise.* Brighton: Sussex University Press, 1972.

Randall, Dale B. J. (ed.). *Joseph Conrad and Warrington Dawson: The Record of a Friendship.* Durham, N.C.: Duke University Press, 1968.

Retinger, J. H. *Conrad and His Contemporaries: Souvenirs.* London: Minerva, 1941.

Russell, Bertrand. *Portraits From Memory.* London: Allen & Unwin, 1956.

Sherry, Norman. *Conrad's Eastern World.* Cambridge: Cambridge University Press, 1966.

———— *Conrad's Western World.* Cambridge: Cambridge University Press, 1971.

————. *Conrad and His World.* London: Thames & Hudson, 1972.

———— (ed.). *Conrad: The Critical Heritage.* London: Routledge & Kegan Paul, 1973.

Watt, Ian (ed.). *Conrad: The Secret Agent. A Case Book.* London: Macmillan, 1973.

————. *Conrad in the Nineteenth Century.* London: Chatto & Windus, 1980.

Watts, C. T. (ed.). *Joseph Conrad's Letters to R. B. Cunninghame Graham.* Cambridge: Cambridge University Press, 1969.

Wells, H. G. *Experiment in Autobiography.* London: Macmillan, 1934.

Index

Index